EYEWITNESS TRAVEL
THE ITALIAN RIVIERA

DK

EYEWITNESS TRAVEL

THE
ITALIAN
RIVIERA

LONDON, NEW YORK,
MELBOURNE, MUNICH AND DELHI
www.dk.com

PRODUCED BY Fabio Ratti Editoria Srl, Milan, Italy
PROJECT EDITOR Emanuela Damiani
EDITORS Emanuela Damiani, Giovanna Morselli
DESIGNERS Silvana Ghioni, Alberto Ipsilanti, Modi Artistici
CONTRIBUTORS
Fabrizio Ardito, Sonia Cavicchioli,
Maurizia De Martin, Gianluigi Lanza
PHOTOGRAPHER
Lucio Rossi
ILLUSTRATORS
Andrea Barison, Gianluca Fiorani
CARTOGRAPHY
Roberto Capra, Luca Signorelli
Dorling Kindersley Limited
PUBLISHING MANAGERS Fay Franklin, Kate Poole
SENIOR ART EDITOR Marisa Renzullo
TRANSLATOR Fiona Wild
EDITOR Emily Hatchwell
CONSULTANT Leonie Loudon
PRODUCTION Linda Dare

Reproduced by Colourscan (Singapore)
Printed and bound by South China Printing Co. Ltd., China
First American Edition, 2005
11 12 13 14 10 9 8 7 6 5 4 3 2 1
Published in the United States by DK Publishing, Inc.,
375 Hudson Street, New York, New York 10014.

Reprinted with revisions 2008, 2011

Copyright © Mondadori Electra SpA 2003.
Published under exclusive licence by Dorling Kindersley Limited.
English text copyright © Dorling Kindersley Limited 2004, 2011.
A Penguin Company.

A CATALOG RECORD FOR THIS BOOK IS AVAILABLE FROM THE LIBRARY OF CONGRESS.

ISSN 1542-1554

ISBN 978-0-75666-959-1

FLOORS ARE REFERRED TO THROUGHOUT IN ACCORDANCE WITH EUROPEAN
USAGE; IE THE "FIRST FLOOR" IS THE FLOOR ABOVE GROUND LEVEL

Front cover main image: Vernazza, Cinque Terre

MIX
Paper from
responsible sources
FSC™ C018179

**The information in this
DK Eyewitness Travel Guide is checked regularly.**
Every effort has been made to ensure that this book is as up-to-date
as possible at the time of going to press. Some details, however, such
as telephone numbers, opening hours, prices, gallery hanging
arrangements and travel information are liable to change. The
publishers cannot accept responsibility for any consequences arising
from the use of this book, nor for any material on third party
websites, and cannot guarantee that any website address in this book
will be a suitable source of travel information. We value the views
and suggestions of our readers very highly. Please write to: Publisher,
DK Eyewitness Travel Guides, Dorling Kindersley, 80 Strand,
London, WC2R 0RL, Great Britain, or email: travelguides@dk.com.

CONTENTS

Ecce Homo by Antonello da
Messina, Palazzo Spinola, Genoa

INTRODUCING
THE ITALIAN
RIVIERA

Sant'Andrea in Levanto

The delightful scene at Paraggi, near Portofino

The port of San Remo

Prized Ligurian olive oil

Genoa's revamped Porto Antico

HOW TO USE THIS GUIDE

The detailed information and tips given in this guide will help you to get the most out of your visit to the Italian Riviera. *Introducing the Italian Riviera* maps the region of Liguria and sets it in its historical and cultural context. The section *Genoa Area by Area* describes the main sights in the regional capital. *The Italian Riviera Area by Area* describes the sights and resorts east

and west of Genoa along the Riviera di Levante and the Riviera di Ponente respectively, using maps, photographs and illustrations. Restaurant and hotel recommendations can be found in the section *Travellers' Needs*, together with information about shopping, out-door activities and entertainment. The *Survival Guide* has tips on everything from transport to making a phone call.

GENOA AREA BY AREA

The centre of Genoa has been divided into two sightseeing areas, each with its own chapter. *Further Afield* describes areas outside the city centre. All the sights are numbered and plotted on an *Area Map*. Detailed information for each sight is presented in numerical order, making it easy to locate.

Sights at a Glance lists the chapter's sights by category: Churches, Museums and Galleries, Historic Buildings, Streets and Piazzas.

All pages relating to Genoa have red thumb tabs.

A locator map shows where you are in relation to other areas of the city centre.

1 Area Map
All the sights are numbered and located on a map.

2 Street-by-Street Map
This gives a bird's eye view of the heart of each sightseeing area.

Stars indicate the sights that no visitor should miss.

A suggested route for a walk covers the more interesting streets in the area.

3 Detailed information
All the sights in Genoa are described individually. Addresses, telephone numbers, opening hours and admission charges are also provided.

1 Introduction
The landscape, history and character of each region is described here, showing how the area has developed over the centuries and what it offers to the visitor today.

THE ITALIAN RIVIERA AREA BY AREA

The Italian Riviera has been divided into two areas, each of which has a separate chapter. The most interesting sights to visit are highlighted on a *Regional Map*.

Each area can be quickly identified by its colour coding.

2 Regional Map
This shows the road network and gives an illustrated overview of the whole region. All the sights are numbered and there are also useful tips on getting around the area.

For all the top sights, a Visitors' Checklist provides the practical information that you will need.

3 The top sights *are given two or more pages. Historic buildings are dissected to reveal their interiors; museums and galleries have colour-coded floorplans to help you locate the most interesting exhibits.*

4 Detailed information
All the important towns and other places to visit are described individually. They are listed in order, following the numbering on the Regional Map. Within each town or city, you will find detailed information on important buildings and other sights.

INTRODUCING
THE ITALIAN
RIVIERA

FOUR GREAT DAYS IN THE ITALIAN RIVIERA

The Italian Riviera is best known for its glitzy resorts, sandy beaches and azure seas, but the region has much more to offer. These four tours will help you truly discover this delightful part of Italy – from picturesque fishing villages and historic cities, to prehistoric treasures and Roman remains. There are

museums and galleries to visit, ancient churches to admire and unspoilt countryside to explore. Each tour is themed but can easily be adapted to suit individual needs. The family day in Genoa can be done on foot, but a car is needed for the other itineraries. The price guides include the cost of food and admission fees.

Butterfly on a flower

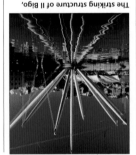

The striking structure of Il Bigo, inspired by the masts of a ship

FAMILY FUN IN GENOA

- **The port and lighthouse**
- **Fish life at the Aquarium**
- **The historic centre**
- **Strolling on Via Garibaldi**

Family of 4 allow at least €185

Morning

For stunning views take a ride on the panoramic lift, **Il Bigo** ("the crane"), at the ancient port (see pp60–61). Children might like to see if they can spot **La Lanterna**, the 12th-century lighthouse that is the symbol of Genoa. The **Aquarium** (see pp62–3), built within a ship anchored in the port, is another great choice for kids. The tanks exhibit all forms of ocean life, including seals, sharks and stingrays. Wander back through the **Biosfera**, a futuristic dome full of tropical plants, or go to the **Città dei Bambini**, a high-tech entertainment centre. Stop for lunch in one of the restaurants around the port.

Colourful Riomaggiore, one of the pretty villages of the Cinque Terre

Afternoon

Head for the historic centre, where you can see the supposed boyhood home of Christopher Columbus (see pp56–7). Stroll though the atmospheric alleyways that snake out around **Piazza De Ferrari** (see p54), or visit the **Palazzo Ducale** (see p54) and the **Duomo di San Lorenzo** (see pp52–3). End the day with a slow walk along **Via Garibaldi**, lined with elegant palazzi, and an ice cream at one of the city's pasticcerie.

SECRETS OF THE CINQUE TERRE

- **Pretty Levanto**
- **Monterosso's churches**
- **The Path of Love**
- **Ice cream in Manarola**

Two adults allow at least €55

Morning

Start at **Levanto** (see p117), exploring the zebra-striped church of Sant'Andrea, famed for its medieval artworks.

Stunning coastal views from the Ligurian hills

Drive on to **Monterosso al Mare**, the first of the lovely villages known as the **Cinque Terre** (see pp118–19). Monterosso is split in to two parts. In the newer section is the church of San Francesco, with a painting of the Crucifixion by Van Dyck. Above the old town is the Sanctuary of Soviore, built over the remains of an 8th-century church. Continue to the picturesque **Vernazza** for lunch.

Afternoon

The **Via dell'Amore** ("Path of Love") is a 20-minute scenic walk that leads from **Manarola** to **Riomaggiore**, the liveliest of the Cinque Terre. For glorious sea views take the lift from the railway tunnel entrance to the top of the town. Dinner is best enjoyed in any of the excellent fish restaurants.

The bridge into the medieval village of Dolceacqua

PREHISTORIC SITES AND ARTISTIC TREASURES

- **Roman ruins in Ventimiglia**
- **Plant life at Hanbury Botanical Gardens**
- **Palaeolithic remains**
- **Monet's inspiration**

TWO ADULTS allow at least €115

Morning

The lively town of **Ventimiglia** (see pp168–9) should be visited during the morning, when it is possible to see the remains of the original Roman town, built in the 3rd century BC, at Albintimilium. A short drive along the coast will take you to **Hanbury Botanical Gardens** (see pp170–71), where exotic plants grow in the grounds of a beautiful 14th-century palazzo. Nearby are the **Balzi Rossi** ("Red Caves") (see p169), where Palaeolithic remains and elaborate tombs dating back around 240,000 years have been found.

Afternoon

A 25-minute drive inland is **Dolceacqua** (see pp166–7), famous for its red wine and architecture. The medieval castle and arched bridge of this pretty village were painted by the French artist Claude Monet. Further along the coastal road is **San Remo** (see pp164–5), where you can visit the medieval old town, which contains many finds from local Palaeolithic caves. End the day with dinner at a seafront restaurant.

SECLUDED ABBEYS AND EXCLUSIVE HIDEAWAYS

- **Camogli's seafaring history**
- **San Fruttuoso's abbey**
- **Exclusive Portofino**
- **Villa Durazzo's gardens**

TWO ADULTS allow at least €110

Morning

Camogli (see p108) is the starting point for this tour. A pretty medieval village, it has a charming harbour crowded with brightly painted houses. Nearby is the Basilica di Santa Maria Assunta, lavishly decorated with gold, frescoes and sculptures. From the harbour you can take a boat trip to the hamlet of **San Fruttuoso** (see p110), with its Benedictine abbey. The little church there has a cloister containing tombs of the Doria family. From Camogli it is around a half-hour drive to the exclusive resort of **Portofino** (see pp110–13), where you can stop for lunch.

Afternoon

A walk around Portofino's lovely *piazzetta*, and then on to the view point at Fortezza di San Giorgio, is the perfect way to start the afternoon. A 10-minute drive up the coast is **Santa Margherita Ligure** (see p109), home to the Parco di Villa Durazzo, a 16th-century villa set in lovely gardens above the town. End the day at a local restaurant.

Boat trip to San Fruttuoso and its Benedictine abbey

Putting the Italian Riviera on the Map

Liguria covers 5,418 sq km (2,090 sq miles) and is the
second smallest region in Italy. Administratively, it is
divided into four provinces: from west to east, these
are Imperia, Savona, Genoa and La Spezia. Squeezed
between the Mediterranean and the peaks of the
Maritime Alps and the Apennines, Liguria's
population is concentrated largely along the
stunning coastal strip of the Riviera di Levante
and the Riviera di Ponente, known collectively
as the Italian Riviera – a
term commonly used to
describe the region of
Liguria as a whole.

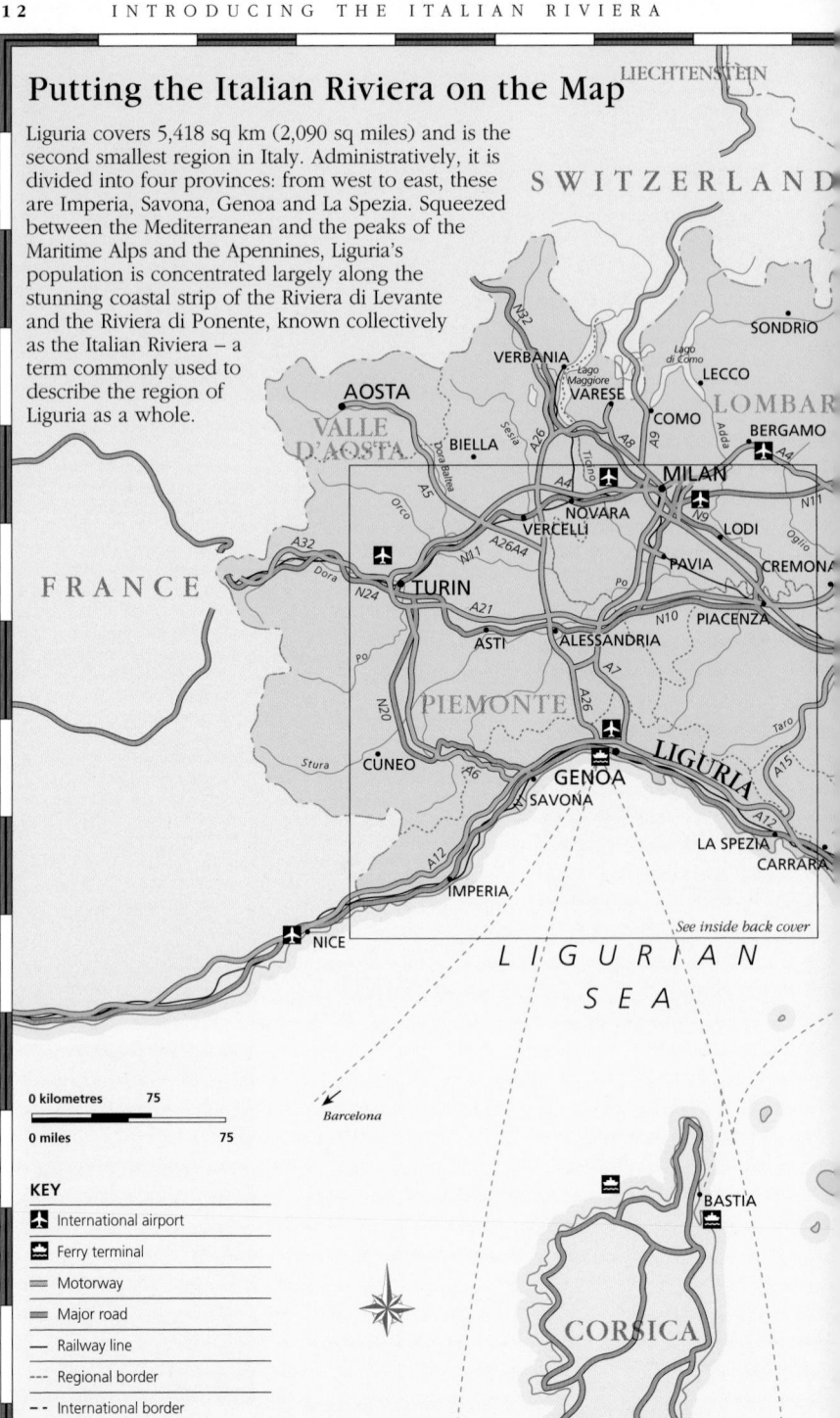

See inside back cover

KEY

✈ International airport

⛴ Ferry terminal

━━ Motorway

━━ Major road

━━ Railway line

--- Regional border

-- International border

---- Ferry route

◁ **Detail of the beautiful Byzantine mosaic in the Baptistry in Albenga**

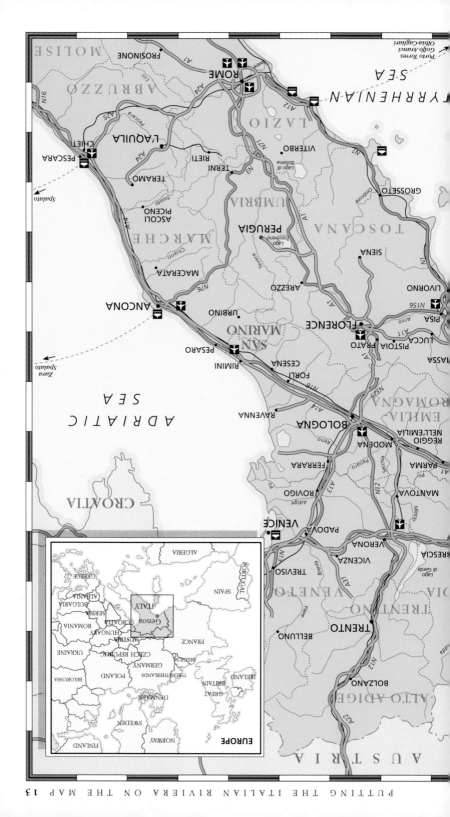

A PORTRAIT OF THE
ITALIAN RIVIERA

*T*he blue water of one of the loveliest stretches of sea in Italy laps the coast, with its rocks, maquis and pastel-coloured villages proud of their maritime tradition. Just behind, hills that are often silver with olive trees rise steeply to the Apennines, which separate Liguria from the other regions of northern Italy.

Bound to the north by alpine Piedmont, to the south by rolling Tuscany and to the east by the plains of the Po Valley, Liguria is a world apart: no other Italian region has such a generous climate or mountainous landscape, nor one where the sea and the mountains are in such close proximity (in Liguria you are never more than 35 km/22 miles from the Mediterranean). This is a region that was always more easily reached by sea than by land.

The characteristics of Liguria derive from the geology that has shaped it. The margins of the region are clear: the mass of the Alps, partly handed over to France after World War II, lead as far as the threshold of the Colle di Cadibona, which marks the point where the long chain of the Apennines begins, running first east- and then southwards. To the south of these mountains is the narrow strip of land where, over the course of millennia, the Ligurian civilization developed: the people were naturally more inclined to turn to the sea and the large islands of the Mediterranean than towards the peaks behind.

It would be wrong, however, to assume, when pausing to admire the waters of Portofino, Genoa or Camogli, that a Liguria of the hinterland does not exist. Reached along

Monument to sailors

The spectacular rocky coast of the Cinque Terre, plunging into the sea

▷ A staircase decorated with plants in one of Liguria's typical *carrugi* (narrow alleys)

There is also a third Liguria, that of the mountainous region behind the coast. Traditionally, the people of the mountains mistrusted not just the coastal folk but the people living in the valleys. And the inhabitants of one valley would almost certainly be suspicious of the inhabitants of a neighbouring one. Such complex relationships are still part of everyday life in Liguria. To further complicate matters, there has been a steady exodus of people from the mountains towards the coast. While agriculture in the interior is in decline, tourism on the coast is booming.

Demographically, Liguria is in deep water. It has the lowest birth rate in Italy, making it the lowest in Europe, and an unusually aged population: 25 per cent of Ligurians are over 65 years old; one reason for this is the influx of retirees, attracted by Liguria's warm climate.

Retirees playing bocce, the local version of boules

TOURISM

The tourism industry started in the Italian Riviera in the 19th century, and it is now the dominant industry. The main attraction is, of course, the coast, with its 300 km (186 miles) of sandy or pebbly beaches, cliffs and small islands. Many of the towns and even the old fishing villages, from San Remo to Portovenere, are now devoted to tourism. While in the most

THE PEOPLE

The temperament of the Ligurian people can be said to vary according to the character of the coast, being generally more open and sunny on the beach-rich Riviera di Ponente and more terse and taciturn along the rockier Riviera di Levante. The writer Guido Piovene noted in his *Viaggio in Italia*, published in *the 1960s, that* "The greatest diversity can be observed going from Genoa to the west. Here, the air of Provence breathes on a Liguria that is closed, laconic... and lacking imagination, creating a loquacious, colourful Liguria of storytellers, a halfway link between the Genoese and the Marseillais".

A typical gozzo, fishing dinghy

The seaside resort of Camogli

steep roads, en route to the mountain passes that were once crucial staging posts on any journey northwards, are fascinating towns such as Dolceacqua, beloved of Monet; Triora, known as the village of witches; or the villages of the Val di Vara. These places are just as Ligurian as the gentrified ports of the jet set.

Fishermen, here on the beach at Spotorno, pulling nets in at dawn

Apricale, in the hinterland behind Imperia

famous seaside resorts you will find grand hotels built for the visiting aristocrats of the 19th century, many of the old fishing villages have a harbour rather than a beach and are riddled with the characteristic car- *ruggi* (the narrow alleys found in every medieval *centro storico* in Liguria), which rise and fall between tall, pastel-coloured houses.

Genoa, the Ligurian capital regally positioned at the centre of the region, is not easy to get to know. There is an abrupt change between the open spaces of the port and the narrow alleys of the town. The former has been the subject of a major but gra- dual regeneration, which has seen the creation of, among other things, the futuristic Aquarium, considered one of the finest in Europe. However, a Mediterranean soul can still be found in the streets of Genoa's historic cen- tre, still redolent of those distant cen-

turies when the galleys of "Genoa The Proud" were familiar in all the ports of the Levante.

When you have had your fill of the wealth, ostentation or over-deve- lopment of the coast, then you should head into Liguria's interior, which is attracting growing numbers of visitors. They come looking for an unspoilt land of woods, rivers, lakes and peaks, where towns show another aspect of the history and people of Liguria.

Ligurian olives, used for some of Italy's finest oils

THE CUISINE

Getting to know the Italian Riviera also involves trying the local food and wine, which is offered in most local restaurants. Liguria's olive oil can compete with Italy's best, the fish and seafood are superb, and there are all sorts of other traditional foods, including delicious snacks, known as *stuzzichini*.

The food is just one facet of a region which, even to the most ardent fans of the sea, should not be regarded as merely a seaside resort.

The Landscape of Liguria

For most visitors to Liguria, the region means only one thing – the beaches, luxuriant vegetation and rocky slopes of the Riviera. Behind the coast, on the fertile plains and in the valleys, agriculture takes over – in particular, the age-old cultivation of olives and a burgeoning modern horticultural industry. Step further back and you're in the mountains, with their isolated villages and silent forests (Liguria is the most forested region in Italy). In winter, snow whitens the peaks just a short distance from the Mediterranean.

The rocky coast of Portovenere

THE COASTAL PLAINS

Although the plains occupy just one per cent of the region, they have always performed an important function. The climate is temperate and favourable for agriculture, and the soil very fertile. As a result, the plains are crammed with cultivated fields, as well as industries that cannot be located in rockier areas. This is the most densely populated part of Liguria: despite large areas of natural landscape, the plains have an average population of more than 300 inhabitants per square kilometre.

Mimosa, originally from southwestern Australia, brightens up many parks and gardens with its bright yellow flowers in spring.

Glasshouses are a common feature of the plains. The cultivation of vegetables, fruit and flowers is one of Liguria's prime economic resources.

THE COAST

Liguria's coastline would measure 440 km (274 miles) if a line were traced following the shore into every inlet and cove. To the west, the beaches are wider and the coastline gentler, while to the east, the landscape is characterized by cliffs and mountains reaching down to the shore, making beaches a rarity. The Ligurian Sea is the richest area for cetaceans (whales and dolphins) in the Mediterranean.

Dolphins can be seen in the Ligurian Sea, especially in the sea off the coast of the Cinque Terre, as well as sperm whales and the occasional marine turtle. It is not unusual to see groups of these friendly creatures following the wash behind ferry boats, emerging from the water and performing somersaults.

The palm tree ("la palma" in Italian) was imported from North Africa and is now so common on the Riviera that it has given its name to a stretch of the Riviera di Ponente.

WILDLIFE IN LIGURIA

The natural habitats of Liguria are very varied and the animal species that live there are equally diverse. In addition to the rich marine life, including whales in the waters extending southwards towards Corsica, there are many species of seabird (cormorants, shearwaters, gannets and terns). The hills are home to small mammals such as the fox, marten, badger and wild boar. In some areas roe deer and fallow deer have been reintroduced. At higher altitudes, in a gradual recolonization of the Apennine mountains, wolves have returned.

Roe deer, found in the hills

Seagulls, never far away

THE HILLS

Thirty per cent of Liguria consists of hill slopes, where the economy is based on the cultivation of olives (producing high-quality olive oil), ornamental plants, flowers and vines. In places where nothing is grown, the natural shrubby vegetation of the Mediterranean (known as maquis or *macchia*) dominates, followed, at higher altitudes, by pine woods and woods of chestnut and oak.

Olives *are cultivated on hill terraces, often overlooking the sea, as in the area of the Cinque Terre. The best-quality olive variety is the taggiasca, which yields a fine extra virgin olive oil.*

The fox, *like other small mammals, is a constant presence in hillside woods. They can also be seen in inhabited areas, searching for food.*

THE MOUNTAINS

The Maritime Alps, to the west, and the Apennines, to the east, account for the largest chunk of Ligurian territory: as much as 69 per cent of the region is over 1,000m (3,281 ft) high. The proximity of the mountains to the Mediterranean has resulted in some botanically fascinating close juxtapositions of alpine and coastal plant and flower species. At the highest altitudes are Scotch pine, silver fir, Norway spruce and larch predominate.

Edelweiss, *a lovely alpine flower, is found at higher altitudes. Look out for it during the flowering period, from July to August.*

The wolf *has been gradually moving up through the Apennines and has recently appeared in the Parco Naturale Regionale dell'Aveto, close to the border with Emilia-Romagna.*

Parks and Nature Reserves

The wildest and most unspoilt natural areas of Liguria are found, not surprisingly, in the hinterland. Here, a crisis in upland agriculture has seen the abandonment of mountain villages, with many vineyards and olive groves left to lie fallow; plants and wildlife are the main beneficiaries of such depopulation. Liguria's protected areas make up around 12 per cent of the region's land area and include six national parks, as well as nature reserves, mostly in the mountains. Each has a different character, from the Alpine valleys on the border with Piedmont, to the hills close to Tuscany. On the coast, after decades of tourist development, a series of marine and coastal reserves aims to conserve the last remaining unspoilt fragments of the Ligurian coast.

The Parco del Finalese (p144), *above Finale Ligure, has fascinating karst formations.*

THE ALTA VIA DEI MONTI LIGURI

Created around a series of mule tracks which criss-cross the region and traverse more than one regional park, the Alta Via dei Monti Liguri is a protected trail which extends the length of Liguria (see p201). It can be explored either on foot or, for the more energetic, by bike.

The Alta Via dei Monti Liguri, *offering stunning walks and views*

Isola Gallinara (see p151) and Isola Bergeggi (see pp140–41), already regional nature reserves, are set to become marine reserves.

The Parco del Monte Beigua (see pp134–5) *is a park of high mountains. Its territory includes Monte Beigua and a series of other peaks which are only 6 km (4 miles) from the coast and yet exceed 1,000 m (3,280 ft) in height. Towards the border with Piedmont, the vegetation is typically alpine, while lower down, pines and larches give way to chestnut forest and then to Mediterranean maquis.*

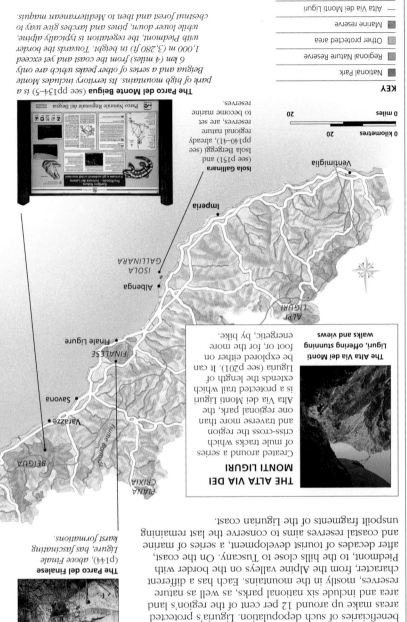

KEY

■	National Park
■	Regional Nature Reserve
■	Other protected area
▨	Marine reserve
—	Alta Via dei Monti Liguri

0 kilometres 20
0 miles 20

Ventimiglia

Imperia

Albenga

ISOLA GALLINARA

ALPI LIGURI

FINALESE

Finale Ligure

Savona

Varazze

BEIGUA

Fiume Bormida

PIANA CRIXIA

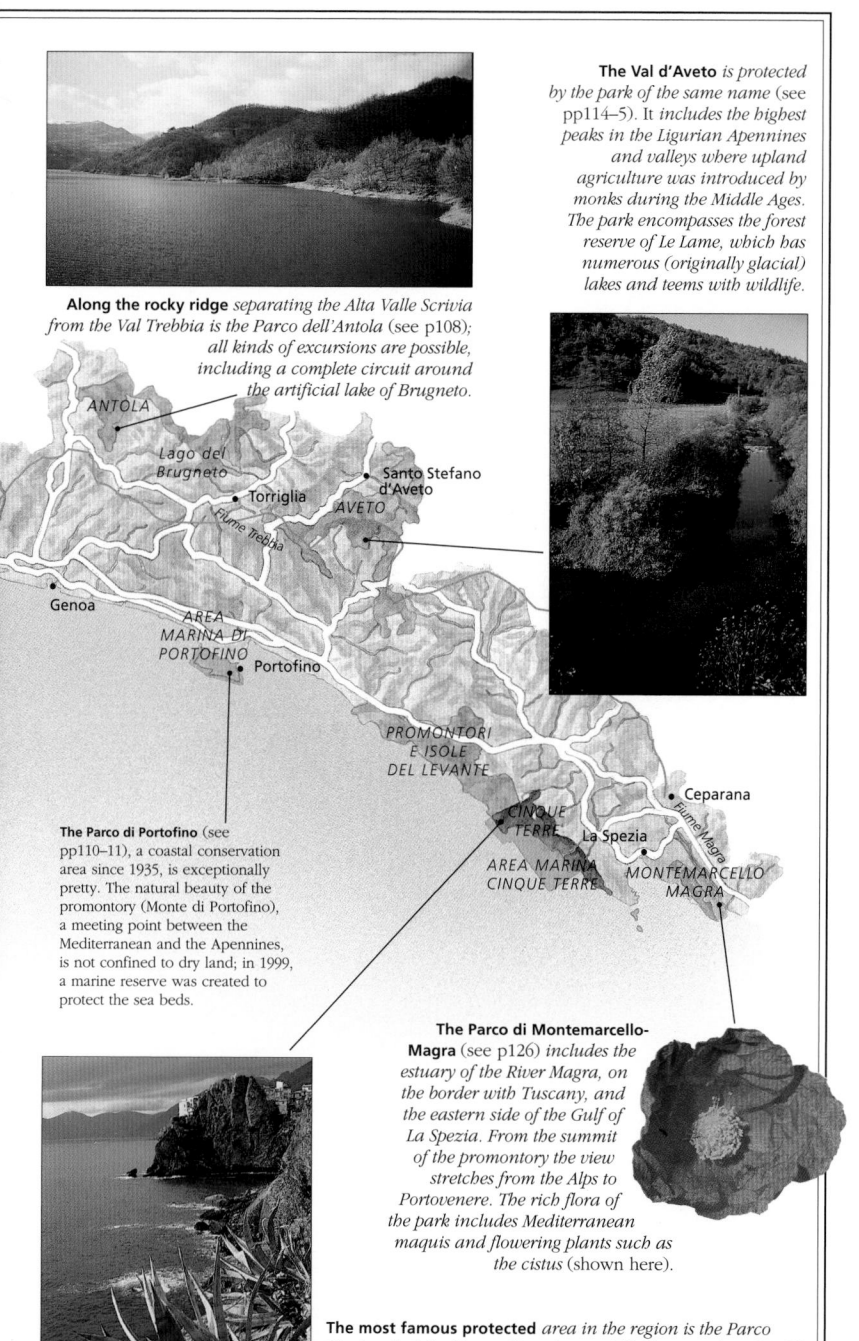

The Val d'Aveto *is protected by the park of the same name (see pp114–5). It includes the highest peaks in the Ligurian Apennines and valleys where upland agriculture was introduced by monks during the Middle Ages. The park encompasses the forest reserve of Le Lame, which has numerous (originally glacial) lakes and teems with wildlife.*

Along the rocky ridge *separating the Alta Valle Scrivia from the Val Trebbia is the Parco dell'Antola (see p108); all kinds of excursions are possible, including a complete circuit around the artificial lake of Brugneto.*

The Parco di Portofino (see pp110–11), a coastal conservation area since 1935, is exceptionally pretty. The natural beauty of the promontory (Monte di Portofino), a meeting point between the Mediterranean and the Apennines, is not confined to dry land; in 1999, a marine reserve was created to protect the sea beds.

The Parco di Montemarcello-Magra (see p126) *includes the estuary of the River Magra, on the border with Tuscany, and the eastern side of the Gulf of La Spezia. From the summit of the promontory the view stretches from the Alps to Portovenere. The rich flora of the park includes Mediterranean maquis and flowering plants such as the cistus (shown here).*

The most famous protected *area in the region is the Parco Nazionale delle Cinque Terre (see pp118–9), now also a World Heritage site. Crammed into narrow inlets between cliffs that plunge into the sea, the five villages of the Cinque Terre are an eloquent expression of the ancient relationship between humans and their environment. The villages look up to sculpted terraces carved into the steep slopes between the sea and the mountains.*

The Italian Riviera Coastline

The density of the population along the Italian Riviera's coast is due largely to the fact that, unlike the marshy shores of Tuscany, Liguria's often rocky shores are eminently habitable and, historically, easy to defend. The beaches are more often pebbly than sandy, with pebbles at San Remo and Rapallo, for example, but sugar-fine sand at Alassio and Lerici. Many beaches show a Blue Flag and have gorgeous, limpid waters.

The shores around Savona are generally low-lying. From Albissola, Celle Ligure and Varazze, pebbly and sandy beaches alternate as far as Arenzano, at the western edge of the sprawling city of Genoa.

KEY

▬	Motorway
▬	Major road
▬	Minor road
▬	River

The coast is *flattish around Bordighera (vast fields of cultivated flowers lie nearby). Beyond lies Capo Nero and the huge sheltered bay of the Golfo di San Remo.*

Close to the French border the first stretch of coast is steep and rocky, and includes the remarkable Balzi Rossi. These famous cliffs face the sea as far as Ventimiglia, where the rivers Roia and Nervia have carved out valleys.

Varazze

Savona

Varigotti

Pietra Ligure

Loano

Albenga

Alassio

RIVIERA DI PONENTE

Imperia

A 10

Ventimiglia

San Remo

Bordighera

Before reaching the *sandy beaches of Alassio, the coastal landscape alternates between rocky stretches and shallow bays, while inland lies the plain washed by the River Centa. Coastal resorts follow in succession – Albenga, Loano, Pietra Ligure and Borgio Verezzi – as far as the cliffs of Finale and Capo Noli.*

Within the province of La Spezia, *the coastline is rocky and dramatic, with the road forced through numerous tunnels. The drama culminates in a vertiginous 20-km (12-mile) stretch of coast in the famous Cinque Terre.*

East of Greater Genoa, where steep cliffs predominate, every scrap of level ground has been terraced and cultivated for centuries. Along here, you will find the lovely fishing village of Bogliasco and stunning Camogli, with a rich seafaring tradition.

0 kilometres 20

0 miles 20

At Rapallo the cliffs dip, only to rise again near Zoagli, overlooking the Golfo del Tigullio. The mouth of the Entella torrent has created a narrow plain around Chiavari.

LAGO DEL BRUGNETO

A7

Genoa

Nervi
Recco
Camogli

Rapallo

Portofino

Santa Margherita Ligure

Chiavari

Sestri Levante

Moneglia

A10

Fiume Magra

Levanto
Monterosso
Vernazza
Manarola

Corniglia

La Spezia
San Terenzo

Riomaggiore

Lerici

Portovenere

Isola Palmaria

RIVIERA DI LEVANTE

The Monte di Portofino *is best explored by foot or by boat from Portofino or Santa Margherita Ligure, the two most exclusive and romantic towns on this stunning promontory.*

Portovenere *is the gateway to the Golfo della Spezia, with its indented and rocky shores on the west side and gentler coastline, with the beaches of Lerici and Tellaro, to the east. The long headland of Punta Bianca faces the plain formed by the River Magra, beyond which lies the border with Tuscany.*

Art in Liguria

Since the time of the Romans, Liguria has always been an important region, even a rich one from time to time, but it has never really been at the centre of events, whether political, cultural or artistic. Of crucial significance artistically, however, was Liguria's role as a major crossroads between the European mainland and the Mediterranean (and, beyond, the rest of the world). This meant not only that works of art from foreign parts passed through Liguria, but that foreign artists (including from other Italian states) visited and even stayed on to work.

ANTIQUITY

The earliest evidence of artistic expression in Liguria include Palaeolithic carvings linked to famous sites such as Balzi Rossi (see p169). Surprisingly few traces of the Romans survive in Liguria. Much of their energy was spent gaining control of the area (only Genoa gave in willingly). The city of Luni (see p127), founded in 177 BC, has some examples of Roman sculpture, but these are best described as well-made crafts rather than works of great artistic merit.

MIDDLE AGES

Liguria in the Middle Ages, which consisted of walled towns linked to one another by sea rather than by land, was of greater interest architecturally than artistically.

The first important examples of figurative art from this era emerged from the Lunigiana (the area around Luni, an important port until the 12th century), which was culturally close to Tuscany. One such example is the *Crucifixion* (1138) now in the cathedral of Sarzana (see p128). The work of a Tuscan called Maestro Guglielmo, this is

Crucifixion (1138), in Sarzana cathedral

probably the only work of significance from the 12th century in Liguria. In fact, in the 13th and 15th centuries, it was generally easier to find Tuscan artists rather than local ones working in Liguria. In terms of sculpture, one of the period's most significant works was the funerary monument (1313–14) of Margaret of Brabant, now in Genoa's Museo di Sant'Agostino (see p57). It was commissioned by the Tuscan Giovanni Pisano. The same museum has the remains of a 14th-century statue of Simone Boccanegra, the first doge of Genoa.

Political and territorial upheavals increasingly opened up Ligurian cities to the influence (and presence) of artists from Lombardy and Flanders: the

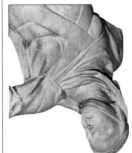

Funerary monument of Margaret of Brabant

Santuario della Madonna delle Grazie, not far from Chiavari (see p114).

In the 17th century Genoa was a rich city, in terms of both commercial banking and art, and several of the city's fine private art collections were begun in this period: the city's newly wealthy families needed a large number of paintings to fill their vast palaces. The work available in the city attracted artists from all over

THE RENAISSANCE AND BAROQUE PERIODS

In the 16th century, an era in which Genoa's top families became rich through their dealings in international finance, new artistic genres reached Liguria, including the art of fresco-painting. Among Liguria's best-known fresco painters was Luca Cambiaso, born in Moneglia in 1527 and active mainly in Genoa. His works can be seen in the Cappella Lercari in Genoa's San Lorenzo cathedral (see pp52–3), and also in the

Equestrian portrait of Gio Carlo Doria by Rubens

works to find favour. Trade with Flanders and Burgundy brought a series of painters (David, Provost, Van Cleve) to Genoa, their religious works are now found throughout the region.

Crucifixion (15th century) by the Pavia artist Donato de' Bardi, now in Savona's Pinacoteca Civica (see p136), was one of the first "Nordic"

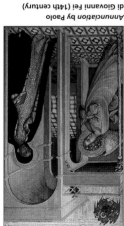

Annunciation by Paolo di Giovanni Fei (14th century)

and fell in love with the city. He became a major influence in the development of Genoese Baroque. Another influence at this time was Antony Van Dyck, some of whose works are on display in Genoa's Palazzo Rosso gallery (*see pp72–5*). Among other fine Renaissance works on show in the same gallery are *Judith and Holofernes* (c.1550–80) by Veronese, *San Sebastiano* (1615) by Guido Reni and *The Cook* (c.1620s) by Bernardo Strozzi. There are also some fine portraits by Dürer, Pisanello and Paris Bordone. The Pinacoteca Civica in Savona (*see p136*) has interesting works of art from the same era, including works by Donato De' Bardi and Taddeo di Bartolo. La Spezia's Museo Amedeo Lia (*see p124*), affectionately known as the "Louvre of Liguria", houses various Renaissance works of considerable value. Among these are the *Portrait of a Gentleman* (1510) by Titian and an *Annunciation by Paolo di Giovanni Fei* (14th century), as well as works by some of the great artists of the 16th century – including Raphael and Veronese. Liguria's greatest fresco painters, both active in the 17th century, were Gregorio De Ferrari and Domenico Piola, rivals whose work can be seen side by side in Genoa's Palazzo Rosso.

Italy, as well as from abroad. In general, most of the works commissioned or bought by Genoa's noble patrons were not by Liguria's home-grown artists. It was around this time that works by Flemish artists started to reach Liguria, evidence of the cultural and commercial influence that the Low Countries had on Ligurian merchants. The Palazzo Spinola di Pellicceria gallery in Genoa (*see p64*) houses several international masterpieces dating from this period, such as the *Ecce Homo* by Antonello da Messina and *Equestrian Portrait of Gio Carlo Doria* (1606) by Peter Paul Rubens. The latter arrived in Genoa in the early 17th century.

NINETEENTH CENTURY TO PRESENT DAY

The 19th and 20th centuries in Liguria have been more remarkable for the developments in architecture than in art. Modern art in Liguria lacks a strong regional identity. Among the most significant collections of modern art in Liguria are the Villa Croce in Genoa (*see p57*) and two collections in Nervi (*see p89*). These are the Raccolta Frugoni in Villa Grimaldi, and the Raccolta d'Arte Moderna. The latter's vast collection of drawings, sculptures, paintings and engravings dates from the 19th and 20th centuries. The core of the collection consists of the art owned by Prince Oddone di Savoia, which was donated to the community in 1866. The museum's collection is largely regional with some works by national and international artists. The Sandro Pertini Collection, in the Pinacoteca Civica in Savona (*see p136*), is devoted to modern art. There are mostly Italian paintings by Morandi, De Chirico, Rosai, Guttuso and Birolli, and sculptures by Henry Moore and Joan Miró.

Portrait of the Contessa de Byland by Boldini (1901)

Anton Maria Maragliano (1664–1739), from Genoa was a pupil of Domenico Piola, but made his name as a sculptor of wood. His fine crucifixes can be found in churches all over Liguria.

Fresco by Cambiaso, Santuario della Madonna delle Grazie, Chiavari

Architecture in Liguria

The truly creative expressions in Liguria's past lie less with art, or sculpture, than in the people's exceptional capacity to adapt their buildings to the contours of an often harsh and difficult landscape. Perched above the sea and hemmed in by the Apennines, the cities of the Italian Riviera developed in a totally individual way. In Genoa, in particular, the defining characteristic of the city was as a meeting point between the port – the hub of commercial traffic – and the city streets.

Coloured marble on the façade of
San Lorenzo, Genoa

ANCIENT ARCHITECTURE

The first examples of individual buildings were Bronze Age settlements which, although they bore similarities to other megalithic structures of the same period, introduced a new element: a fortification capable of defending people and their work. In the Roman era various cities were built or expanded, among them Luni, Genua (Genoa) and Albingaunum (Albenga), which were all given typical Roman features, such as bridges, aqueducts, amphitheatres, and trading quays in the ports. The most impressive amphitheatre in Liguria can be seen among the ruins of ancient Luni, at the foot of the Apuan Alps (a source of white marble much in demand in ancient Rome). The remnants of a Roman road also survive between Albenga and Alassio.

Settlements called "castellari" were
fortifications on high ground made
up of concentric circles of
dry-stone walls designed
to protect villages
and pasture.

The houses were
usually cabins.

**Defensive
wall**

THE MIDDLE AGES

Medieval architecture in Liguria shows similarities with the building styles that developed in other areas along the Tyrrhenian coast. In Genoa, the main development in architecture involved the construction of mansions for rich families or merchants, grouped together in small districts and headed by families linked by business connections. Genoese churches constructed in the Romanesque and Gothic styles were typically built with black and white stripes, and laden with materials from earlier (including Roman) eras. Elsewhere in Liguria this was a period of local rivalries and disputes characterized by the construction of numerous castles and tower houses. Liguria's pretty hilltop villages are another symbol of the Middle Ages, many of which still preserve their medieval structure. Of particular note are the region's famous *carrugi*, the narrow and usually steep lanes that penetrate into the heart of these often labyrinthine settlements.

The church of San
Lorenzo in Genoa
(see pp52–5), begun in
1118, is the most famous
example of Ligurian
Gothic.

The doors are flanked by rich
decoration in marble.

RENAISSANCE PALAZZI

In Genoa, the 16th and 17th centuries were a boom period – referred to as the "Genoese Century" – during which a handful of powerful families financed the construction of numerous grand palaces. A figure of particular importance in Genoese Renaissance history was Andrea Doria (1468–1560), admiral and patron of the arts, who built the magnificent Palazzzo Doria Pamphilj *(see p78–9)*. The laying of Via Garibaldi, or "La Strada Nuova", in the mid 16th century, was a great example of civic town planning. The palazzi along this monumental street, including Palazzo Doria Tursi, symbolized the power of the great Genoese families. Other impressive schemes included the construction of the Molo Nuovo (new quay) and of the famous Lanterna (lighthouse), both in the port. Such was the reputation of Genoa's architects that they exported their palazzo designs and materials to Spain, France and northern Europe.

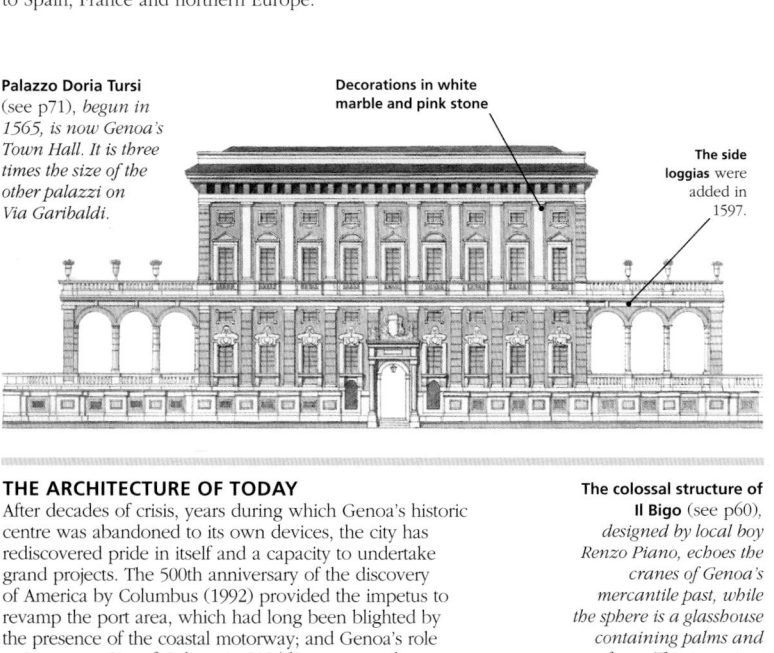

Palazzo Doria Tursi (see p71), *begun in 1565, is now Genoa's Town Hall. It is three times the size of the other palazzi on Via Garibaldi.*

Decorations in white marble and pink stone

The side loggias were added in 1597.

THE ARCHITECTURE OF TODAY

After decades of crisis, years during which Genoa's historic centre was abandoned to its own devices, the city has rediscovered pride in itself and a capacity to undertake grand projects. The 500th anniversary of the discovery of America by Columbus (1992) provided the impetus to revamp the port area, which had long been blighted by the presence of the coastal motorway; and Genoa's role as European City of Culture in 2004 has prompted renovation and building work elsewhere. One of the aims of the restoration of the port area was to link it, finally, to the narrow alleys of old Genoa.

The colossal structure of Il Bigo (see p60), *designed by local boy Renzo Piano, echoes the cranes of Genoa's mercantile past, while the sphere is a glasshouse containing palms and vast ferns. The Aquarium was built in 1992 for the Columbus celebrations.*

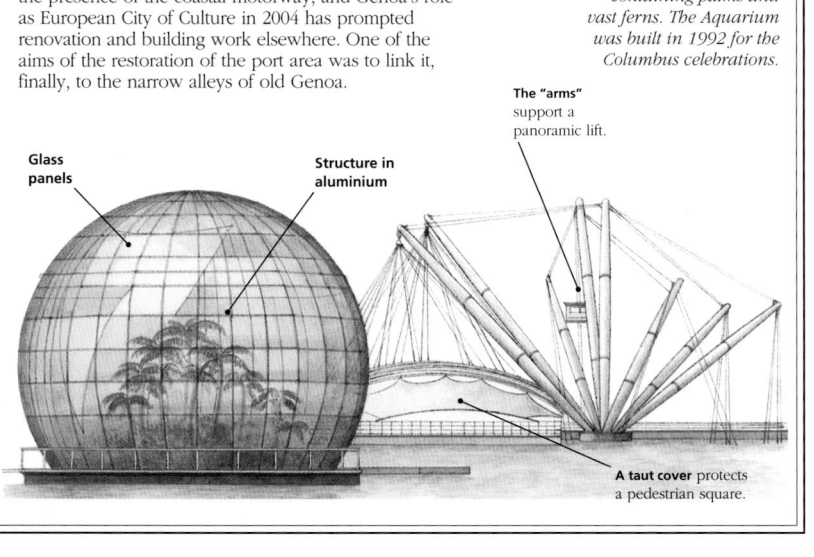

Glass panels

Structure in aluminium

The **"arms"** support a panoramic lift.

A taut cover protects a pedestrian square.

THE ITALIAN RIVIERA THROUGH THE YEAR

The pleasant and mild typically Mediterranean climate, the intense contrasts of light and colour, the romantic coastline and the equally fascinating interior have made Liguria a desirable destination for tourists since the mid-19th century. The clear blue sea, the beaches and the stunning and lush coastal scenery are

consistent attractions all year round, but there are also numerous special events which can add extra local colour to any trip. These events include many religious and gastronomic festivals and also historical re-enactments and regattas, the latter a colourful reminder of the importance of the seafaring tradition to this part of Italy.

The mid-May fish festival at Camogli

SPRING

Mild temperatures and pure air characterize spring in Liguria, which welcomes visitors with colour and unforgettable scents. The profusion of colourful flowers contrasts with the blue of the sea and the snow-capped peaks of the Ligurian Alps.

MARCH

Rassegna dell'Olio d'Oliva, Balestrino. This village north of Albenga is proud of its 17 different types of olive. During the festival the public can taste different types of oil and olives as well as other traditional foods.

Fiera di San Giuseppe, La Spezia *(19 Mar)*. This immensely popular festival

APRIL

Riviera dei Fiori, to celebrate the advent of spring.

Good Friday processions. Good Friday (Venerdì Santo) has a fervent following, especially on the Riviera di Ponente. It is celebrated with processions in which local confraternities file past, with *casse* (carved wooden sculptures) portraying scenes from the Passion. The processions in Savona and Genoa are particularly popular, but similar events take place in the Ligurian hinterland, too.

Settimana Santa. Cerиana. Processions of confraternities and representations of the Descent from the Cross (*Calata della Croce*), with religious songs.

MAY

Sagra del Pesce (Fish festival), Camogli *(second Sun in May)*. A gigantic frying pan is used to fry a huge quantity of fish, which both locals and visitors are then invited to eat: a lovely gesture done in the hope that the seas will be equally generous to the fishermen.

Festa della Focaccia con il Formaggio, Recco *(fourth Sun)*. A bustling festival held to celebrate the famous cheese focaccia of Recco, a small but gastronomic town just north of Camogli. Abundant tastings on offer.

is held in honour of the town's patron saint. It offers more than 800 street stalls and vendors and abundant entertainment for all the family.

Milano–San Remo *(1st Sat after 19 Mar)*. A classic, long-distance cycle race.

Festa di Primavera *(all month)*. Music, art and flower shows along the

A cyclist celebrating his victory in the Milano–San Remo race

Advert for the Battaglia di Fiori

Sunshine
In both spring and summer the long days of sunshine, which are never excessively hot, are perfect for swimming and sailing. The light and colours of autumn, meanwhile, are delightful, while a clear winter's day means that the white peaks of the Alps are visible in the distance.

AVERAGE DAILY HOURS OF SUNSHINE

Hours

10 8 6 4 2 0

Jan Feb Mar Apr May Jun Jul Aug Sep Oct Nov Dec

SUMMER

The high season for tourists, summer is hot and sunny along the coast and fresher and wetter in the hilly interior.

JUNE

Infiorata *(first week of Jun).* To celebrate Corpus Domini (Corpus Christi), many towns strew carpets of flowers along processional routes; the best take place in Sassello, Imperia, Diano Marina and Pietra Ligure. There is also a *Battaglia di Fiori* (battle of flowers) in Ventimiglia.

Regata delle Antiche Repubbliche Marinare. Genoa *(early Jun, every four years).* A regatta in which teams from the cities of the four ancient maritime republics (Genoa, Pisa, Amalfi and Venice) compete in old sailing ships; there are processions, too. Genoa is the host every four years (the next regatta will be in 2012).

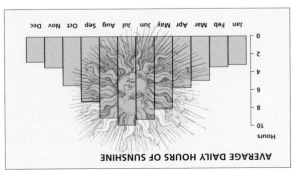

An enormous carpet of flowers, part of an Infiorata

Festa di San Giovanni, Genoa *(24 Jun).* Celebrations in honour of St John. Also in Laigueglia, where 5,000 lit candles are placed on the water, and Triora.

Festa e Palio di San Pietro, Genoa *(29 Jun).* A race with traditional boats, as well as illuminations.

Palio marinaro del Tigullio *(Jun/Jul).* Regattas in resorts along the Tigullio coast, including Chiavari, Rapallo and Lavagna.

JULY

Raduno delle Fiat 500, Garlenda *(early Jul).* Participants come in their Fiat 500s from all over Europe.

Girl in historical costume

Cristo degli Abissi, San Fruttuoso di Camogli *(end Jul).* Nocturnal mass and torchlit procession of divers to the massive statue of Christ on the sea bed.

Sagra delle Rose and Sagra delle Pesche, Pogli d'Ortovero *(end Jul).* A celebration of the roses and peaches grown in this area near Albenga. A chance to try local specialities.

AUGUST

Stella Maris, Camogli *(first Sun).* A festival of the sea, with a procession of boats to the Punta della Chiappa, with thousands of little wax candles bobbing on the waves.

Torta dei Fieschi, Lavagna *(14 Aug).* The re-enactment of the lavish 13th-century wedding between Opizzo Fieschi and Bianca de' Bianchi, with a historical procession and the cutting of an enormous cake.

Castelli di Sabbia, Alassio *(mid-Aug).* National competition for the best sandcastle on the beach.

Processione dell'Assunta, Nervi *(15 Aug).* Evening procession, with a blessing of the sea and a firework display.

Festa della Madonna Bianca, Portovenere *(17 Aug).* At 9pm torchlights are lit during a procession to the headland of San Pietro.

Miss Muretto, Alassio *(end Aug/early Sep).* The prettiest girl is elected and given the title dedicated to the town's famous "Muretto" (wall) of celebrities.

The Muretto of Alassio, during a beauty competition

AVERAGE MONTHLY RAINFALL

MM / Inches

	Jan	Feb	Mar	Apr	May	Jun	Jul	Aug	Sep	Oct	Nov	Dec

Rainfall
Liguria's weather is characterized by a fair amount of rainfall, especially during the autumn, when violent storms may occur and sometimes rivers may flood. The Riviera di Ponente is generally drier and sunnier than the Riviera di Levante.

Yachts at their moorings in Imperia

AUTUMN

Autumn, with its warm colours and still balmy and sunny days, is the ideal season for visiting Liguria. Towns and villages are less crowded, and it is easier to find accommodation; in short, you can get to know the area's sights, towns, culture and gastronomy in greater peace.

SEPTEMBER

Regata Storica dei Rioni, Noli *(first or second Sun)*. The four districts of the town challenge each other to a rowing race; processions in historical costume, too.
Sagra del Fuoco, Recco (7–8 Sep). Festival in honour of the patron saint, Nostra Signora del Suffragio.
Anchovy Festival, Monterosso Al Mare *(second week)*. People come from all over

Bottle of Pigato white wine

Italy to celebrate the village's specialty. There are tastings, music and fireworks.
Sagra del Pigato, Salea di Albenga *(early Sep)*. A festival in honour of Pigato wine, with exhibitions, food pavilions, dancing and sporting events.
Festa della Madonna della Villa, Ceriana *(early Sep)*. Solemn candle-lit processions and a music festival of folk music in the village square, with choirs singing traditional songs.
Commemorazione della Battaglia Napoleonica, Loano. Exhibitions, ceremonies and parades in historical costume are staged in order to commemorate the Battle of Loano, in 1795, in which the French revolutionary army succeeded in routing the Austrian army.
Sagra dell'Uva, Varazze. A traditional festival with tastings and the sale of local

wines. A similar festival is held at Vezzano Ligure *(see below)*.
Sagra dell'Uva, Vezzano Ligure *(mid-Sep)*. A festival in honour of the grape *(uva)*, including a costumed procession, a challenge in dialect and a series of contests between grape harvesters.
Sagra della Lumaca, Molini di Triora *(last week)*. Enormous frying pans full of snails *(lumache)* are cooked following an ancient recipe once used by the village's noble families, who would present them as the pièce de resistance at sumptuous banquets, because of their supposed magical powers.

OCTOBER

Salone Internazionale della Nautica, Genoa *(first and second week)*. This is the largest nautical fair to be held anywhere in the Mediterranean, with yachts, motorboats, inflatables and associated nautical paraphernalia.
Sagra della Farinata, Voltri *(late Oct)*. Tastings of local, mostly Genoese, gastronomic specialities, including

A motor launch on display at Genoa's nautical fair

JANUARY

Festa di Capodanno (New Year), Genoa. The city's *carrugi* and the Porto Antico are thronged with people.

FEBRUARY

Festa dei Furgari, Taggia *(early Feb)*. Dedicated to San Benedetto. *Furgari* (bamboo canes filled with gunpowder) are set alight, while banquets go on all through the night.

Fiera di Sant'Agata, Genoa *(5 Feb)*. Stalls sell knick-knacks and sweetmeats, on the Sunday closest to 5 Feb. (Also in San Fruttuoso.)

Carnevale, Loano. Allegorical carriages and people in fancy dress parade through the town.

Sagra della Mimosa, Pieve Ligure. Floral carriages and costumed processions.

Festival della Canzone Italiana, San Remo *(last week Feb)*. Annual pop-music festival with international guests.

Mimosa in flower, brightening the gardens of the hinterland

WINTER

Although it can be windy, winter in the Italian Riviera often provides days with full sun, which make it a good time to explore the region's medieval towns and villages.

DECEMBER

Natale Subacqueo, Tellaro *(24 Dec)*. The village is illuminated with 1,000 torchlights, and at midnight divers emerge with the statue of Baby Jesus, which is welcomed with fireworks.

"U Confögu" (Confuoco), Pietra Ligure and Savona *(Sun before Christmas)*. Traditional ceremony with a costumed procession and the lighting of a propitiatory bundle of laurel: auspices for the coming year are divined from the resulting flames.

NOVEMBER

Olioliva, Imperia *(late Nov)*. Held in the area where *taggiasca* olives are grown. Visits to olive presses *(frantoi)* are arranged, and a produce market is held at Oneglia. Restaurants offer special menus.

Festa dei furgari at Taggia

Liguria's famous baked chick-pea snack *(farinata).*

PUBLIC HOLIDAYS

New Year's Day (1 Jan)
Epiphany (6 Jan)
Easter Sunday
Easter Monday
Anniversario della Liberazione (25 Apr)
Labour Day (1 May)
Festa della Repubblica (2 Jun)
Ferragosto (15 Aug)
All Saints (1 Nov)
Immaculate Conception (8 Dec)
Christmas (25 Dec)
Boxing Day (26 Dec)

Temperature
The coastal strip, exposed to the south, experiences sea breezes which refresh the hottest and boltest summer temperatures and temper the winter temperatures; the latter are never too severe, even in the interior. Autumn and spring offer warm and clear days.

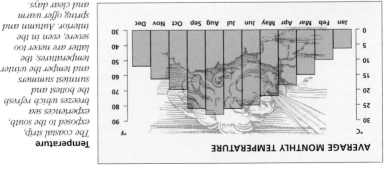

AVERAGE MONTHLY TEMPERATURE

THE HISTORY OF THE ITALIAN RIVIERA

The history of Liguria is linked inextricably with the sea. The coastal climate encouraged early settlement and the Romans built the first ports. Most importantly, from the start of the second millennium, the Republic of Genoa became a major seapower whose tentacles reached all over the Mediterranean and beyond.

The climate and geography of Liguria were highly favourable to humans in the far distant past. The coast was suitable for settlements and navigation on the open sea, while travel to what is now the Côte d'Azur and France was made easy by the low coastal hills. As a result, the population of this part of the Mediterranean was very scattered. Proof of this comes from the numerous traces of tombs and hearths found in the caves and on the hills of the region, forming an almost uninterrupted line from Liguria to Provence.

The first Ligurians appeared during the Bronze Age. In an era of migration and battles to occupy the best positions, the Ligurians fortified their settlements with walls to defend villages, pasture and access to the sea. They were mentioned for the first time (under the name of Ligyes) in the 7th century BC by Greek sources, who described how the land controlled by the ancient Ligurians extended far beyond the current boundaries of the region, as far as the limits of Catalonia and the

Roman amphora in Albenga

Cévennes. While clashes and power struggles were taking place both in the lowlands and in the mountains to the north, new arrivals turned up on the Ligurian coast: the Greeks and the Etruscans who were, at the time, in total control of the Mediterranean and its markets. The Greeks were by then firmly installed in Marseille, and sought space to settle in the Ligurian valleys. The Etruscans had founded ports and trading cities along the Tuscan coast.

A series of settlements was established during this period, including proper villages at Genoa, Chiavari and Ameglia. Traces of necropoli in which the ashes of the deceased were buried have been discovered.

The onset of the Roman era was marked by the arrival of Roman legions in around 218 BC; this represented a much more significant change for the region than the disruptions caused by previous populations of travellers and merchants. For Rome, Liguria represented a fundamental transit point for expansion into nearby Gaul.

TIMELINE

300,000 BC	100,000 BC	50,000 BC	10,000 BC	1,000 BC	100 BC
	240,000 BC First burial in the cave at Balzi Rossi	**80,000–60,000 BC** Presence of Neanderthal man in Ligurian sites	**12,340 BC** Date of hand and foot prints found in the Grotta di Toirano	**218 BC** The Romans establish their first base in Liguria	

Finds in the Balzi Rossi museum

36,000–10,000 BC Era of *Homo sapiens sapiens*

Footprints in the Grotta di Toirano

First millennium BC Golden age of the Ligurians and contact with the Greeks and Phoenicians

◁ **Detail from the frescoes by Perin del Vaga in the Loggia degli Eroi, Palazzo Doria Pamphilj, Genoa**

Prehistoric Liguria

The long rocky coast, with steep, vertical cliffs facing the sea, made Liguria a particularly attractive destination for our ancient ancestors. The rise and fall of the sea level, over the course of millennia, has brought about the emergence and disappearance of hundreds of caves which have been inhabited by man since the prehistoric era. As well as offering coastal shelter, food and fishing possibilities, Liguria also provided a series of staging posts between the coast and the hinterland and the plains of the Po valley. At the end of the prehistoric era, man regularly made use of the remote Monte Bego and the Vallée des Merveilles, just across the border into France. In the western Riviera, in the meantime, a new urban and military set-up had emerged: the settlements known as *castellari*, which protected villages and pastures from invasion by peoples approaching from the sea, intent on expanding their dominion in the hinterland.

Stone finds from the Balzi Rossi

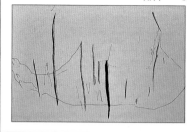

Monte Bego
In the area around Monte Bego, a sacred mountain, and in the Vallée des Merveilles, prehistoric man has left over 100,000 rock carvings of religious significance on rocks smoothed and etched by the passing of ancient glaciers.

The Triplice Sepoltura (Triple Grave)
Found in the Barma Grande at Balzi Rossi, this provides important evidence of human presence in the area. Accompanying the skeletons of one adult, a boy and a girl was a rich collection of funerary objects.

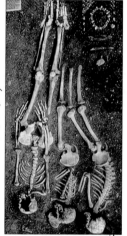

The caves of the Balzi Rossi form part of a reddish, calcareous wall jutting out over the sea. There are 12 caves in all.

Ventimiglia
San Remo
Taggia
Imperia
Triora
Pieve di Teco

CRAFTMANSHIP IN LIGURIA

The first crafts to be discovered in the region date back 35,000 years, to the late Paleolithic period. Treasures from the Balzi Rossi caves (now in the museum) include a unique Przewalskii Horse incised on a wall of the Grotta del Cavigliione 20,000 years ago, and 15 soapstone Venus figurines, symbols of fertility, found in the Barma Grande.

Venus figure Barma Grande.

Przewalskii horse

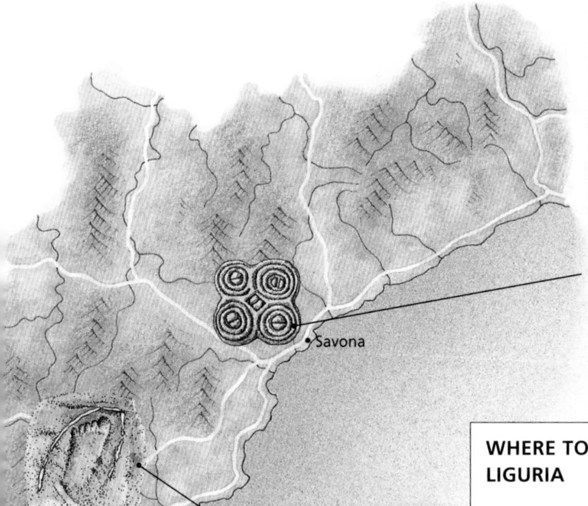

WHERE TO SEE PREHISTORIC LIGURIA

Some of Liguria's most significant prehistoric sites are also fascinating places to visit, in particular the site of the Balzi Rossi and the Grotte di Toirano *(see p169)*, with its museum formations of stalactites and stalagmites. Breathtaking hikes can also be taken along the Alpine paths of the Vallée des Merveilles and Monte Bego, which lie just across the border in France.

Hikers in the Vallée des Merveilles

The interior of the Balzi Rossi museum

Arene Candide
The "white sands" cave (a sand dune once covered it) is closed to the public. Finds from it are in the archeological museum at Pegli near Genoa.

Grotte di Toirano
In the Grotta della Basura are hand-, knee- and footprints of Cro-magnon men, women and children.

THE CAVES OF LIGURIA

The women of Liguria's most ancient ancestor died in the Grotta del Principe around 240,000 years ago. The great cave complex of Balzi Rossi, however, continued to be used by Neanderthal man even after that. Groups of hunter-gatherers lived in many other Ligurian caves, too: at Arma di Taggia near San Remo, and in the Grotta delle Fate at Toirano near Finale Ligure. With the passing of millennia, our closest ancestor *(Homo sapiens sapiens)* settled in Liguria, where traces of his presence have been found at Balzi Rossi, at Toirano and in the grotto of Arene Candide in Savona province, where archaeologists found 20 graves, including the famous tomb of the Giovane Principe (Young Prince).

Savona

Finale Ligure

Albenga

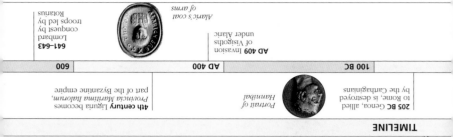

205 BC Genoa, allied to Rome, is destroyed by the Carthaginians

Portrait of Hannibal

4th century Liguria becomes *Provincia Maritima Italorum*, part of the Byzantine empire

Alaric's coat of arms

AD 409 Invasion of Visigoths under Alaric

641–643 Lombard conquest by troops led by Rotarius

100 BC   AD 400   600

ROMAN LIGURIA

The focus of the Romans was to establish landing stages for merchants and ships, but they did not have an easy time establishing their presence in Liguria. Genoa was one of the few places that fell to the Romans without conflict; it was incorporated into the Roman empire in the 2nd century BC. The toughness of the Ligurians attracted the Carthaginians (under the command of Hannibal and his brothers Hasdrubal and Mago), who co-opted as allies the tribes of the Intimeli and Ingauni. In 205 BC, the Carthaginians besieged and destroyed Genoa. The Romans prevailed, however and, once the Carthaginians had been driven back, they continued their expansion, attacking Gallic tribes and extending the road network, which became a vital means of communication within the empire. The Via Postumia reached Roman Genua (Genoa) from Mediolanum (Milan) in 148 BC, although the road of greatest significance was the Via Julia Augusta, which was laid along the coast; the modern Via Aurelia follows its route.

As they conquered territory, the Romans also colonized it, gradually establishing a whole series of towns, along the coast. The most important of these Roman settlements were: Portus Lunae (Luni), Ingaunum (Albenga), Alba Docilia (Albisola), Genua (Genoa), Portus Delphini (Portofino) and Segesta Tigulliorum (Sestri Levante). Roman Liguria, however, was never more than a backwater: the result of its distance from the main routes of communication through Italy, and the fact that the Romans' most important ports were elsewhere.

BARBARIAN INVASIONS

The armies of the Visigoths under Alaric reached Liguria from North Africa in AD 409, and after that the region was raided by the Goths and their allies, the Heruli. Armies came and went, while both the political and military situation in the whole Italian peninsula was in a constant state of flux. In AD 536 Italy was invaded by the forces of the Eastern Empire, under the leadership of Justinian I. They eventually overcame the Goths, and a fairly peaceful period under Byzantine rule followed. Bishoprics had already started to emerge in the 5th century, and continued to be created under the Byzantines, including that of Albenga. Liguria was given the name of *Provincia Maritima Italorum* by its new rulers.

The period of Byzantine rule came to a close with the arrival in 641 of the Lombards, led by King Rotarius. The towns of Liguria became part of a

Rotarius, king of the Longobards, who reached Liguria in 641

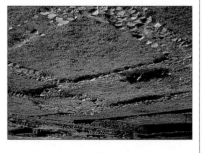

Ruined Roman villa at Alba Docilia, now Albisola

Frankish territory which included tracts of land which now form part of Tuscany. The Saracens made incursions in 901, often from bases in the south of France. Later in the 10th century, during the reign of Berengarius, northeast Italy was divided into three: *Obertenga*, to the east, included Genoa, *Aleramica*, in the centre included Albenga, and *Arduinica*, to the west, included Ventimiglia. The families that had control of these territories (such as the Del Carretto) found themselves in a powerful position that lasted for centuries.

THE RISE OF GENOA

Around the year 1000, the golden age of the free communes dawned. Their main activities revolved around maritime trade and the arming of commercial or military fleets. In this era of economic and political development, Genoese predominance became increasingly noticeable, though life was not entirely peaceful. In the mid-12th century, the city built a new wall to protect it against the ravages of Emperor Frederick I, known as Barbarossa. Nevertheless, after the independence of the Genoese commune was recognized, it began to compete with Pisa for control of the Mediterranean and islands of Corsica and

The port of Genoa as portrayed in a 16th-century painting

Sardinia. Genoese ships from the ports of Noli and Savona also took part in the Crusades.

GENOA EXPANDS ALONG THE COAST

Besides its growing power at sea, Genoa also sought to expand its sphere of influence, both commercially and militarily, on dry land; they gained control of cities, valleys and the mountain passes linking the coast to the Po valley, and even extended their dominion along the banks of that great river – a move crucial to a republic dependent on agricultural provisions.

Battle with the Saracens, a 14th-century miniature

After a century of clashes, battles and alliances, by 1232 virtually the entire Riviera di Levante coast was effectively under Genoese control. Among the cities which clashed most violently with Genoa were Ventimiglia (which fell in 1262) and Savona, which, following a long fight for independence, capitulated in 1528.

Cross of a knight who took part in the first Crusade

935 Sacking of Genoa by the Arabs

890 Beginning of raids by Saracens based in France

800

1097 Genoa contributes ten galleys to the first Crusade

1000

984 Benedictines rebuild the Abbey of San Fruttuoso

1162 The Holy Roman Emperor recognizes the autonomy of Genoa

1133 Genoa becomes the seat of a bishopric

1099 The "Compagna", a pact between the districts of Genoa, is set up

Genoa's Golden Age

The enterprising trading activities of Genoa's great shipowning families made the city into a Mediterranean power from the beginning of the 12th century. The exploits of aristocratic dynasties such as the Doria family took the Genoese to all corners of the known oceans. The growth in Genoa's power was consolidated with increasingly close links to other cities in Liguria, which were often in Genoese control, and to the area around Asti (in Piedmont) and Provence, indispensable suppliers of salt, grain and agricultural produce. Simone Boccanegra became Genoa's first lifetime Doge in 1339, although the most powerful institution during this period was the Banco di San Giorgio (Bank of St George). In a city riven by violent struggles between rival factions, the bank maintained a neutral position. At that time, thriving commercial houses from all over Europe were represented in Genoa, and the emissaries of the Banco di San Giorgio became familiar figures in treasuries all over Europe.

A genovino d'oro coin, minted in the 13th century

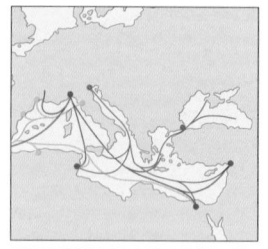

THE MEDITERRANEAN (1250)

— *Genoese trade routes*

— *Pisa trade routes*

— *Venetian trade routes*

Oberto Doria, founder of the illustrious Genoese dynasty, acquired the town of Dolceacqua in 1270.

The Pisan fleet consisted of 72 galleys. The defeat of Pisa was dramatic: 5,000 men died and 11,000 prisoners were taken in chains to Genoa.

Rivalry with Pisa and Venice
Genoa struggled against two rival powers, Pisa and Venice. Pisa was defeated at Meloria but, with the advance of the Turks, Genoa saw her possessions in the East increasingly under threat, and the republic's rivalry with Venice intensified.

Genoa expands its rule along the coast
Many cities along the Riviera di Ponente were in Genoa's orbit at the time, including Albenga, which was forced to sign increasingly restrictive pacts, until its final subjugation in 1251. Ventimiglia yielded in 1261, followed in 1276 by Porto Maurizio. Left is an engraving (1613) by Magini of ships off the western riviera.

GENOA AND THE CRUSADES

During the 250 years of the Crusades, the maritime republics vied for supremacy in the struggle over trade routes, colonies and beneficial alliances. The two Crusades that brought about the conquest of Jerusalem saw the Genoese take an active role in the naval front line, with their *condottiero* Guglielmo Embriaco. In the ports of Acre and Haifa (in modern Israel), Genoese merchants built homes and warehouses, as well as churches. At its peak, the city of Acre had 50,000 inhabitants and 38 churches; it was the last place in the Holy Land to be conquered by the Arabs, in 1291. When the Christian kingdoms present in the Holy Land found themselves in trouble, Genoa frequently allied itself to the Knights of St John, the Armenians and even the Tartars in the fight against Venice, Pisa, the Templars and the Mameluks of Egypt.

The taking of Jerusalem in the First Crusade (1096–99)

THE BATTLE OF MELORIA

One of the events that confirmed Genoese dominance in the Mediterranean was the Battle of Meloria, which saw Genoa fight and defeat her rival Pisa over possession of Corsica. In August 1284, a Genoese fleet under the command of Oberto Doria, took up position close to Porto Pisano. The battle was violent and the victor uncertain until the arrival of a second group of Genoese galleys, which took her adversary by surprise. Shown here is *Battle of Meloria* by Giovanni David, in Genoa's Palazzo Ducale.

Battles between the Guelphs and Ghibellines
During the long struggle between the Papacy and the Holy Roman Empire, the Guelphs supported the former, the Ghibellines the latter. Towns seldom had fixed loyalties but noble families did: the Doria were famously Ghibelline.

The Meloria rocks (after which the battle was named) lie off Livorno, some 7km (4 miles) offshore.

The Genoese fleet was made up of 93 galleys.

Meloria was also the setting for another battle, in 1241, in which the Pisans, allied to Holy Roman Emperor Frederick II, defeated the Genoese.

Banco di San Giorgio
Founded in the early 1400s, the Bank of St George not only ran the domestic treasury, but was also directly involved with Genoa's colonies, such as Famagusta, in Cyprus. Shown here, an "8 Reali" coin minted by the bank.

TIMELINE

	1250	1300	1350

1245–1252 Construction of the basilica dei Fieschi di San Salvatore

1251 Savona is attacked by Genoa

1252 The *genovino*, no is coined, Europe's first gold coin

1262 Ventimiglia, defeated, comes under Genoese influence

1284 Victory of Genoa over Pisa at Meloria

1298 Genoese victory over Venice at Curzola

1339 Simone Boccanegra becomes the first doge of Genoa

1361 San Remo becomes a free commune

Battle of Meloria

CLASHES WITH OTHER MARITIME REPUBLICS

Andrea Doria in a portrait by Sebastiano del Piombo

The centuries that witnessed the great geographical and commercial expansion around the Mediterranean of Italy's maritime republics, also saw Genoa extend its tentacles in all directions. With the Crusades – from the first, which brought about the capture of Jerusalem, to the ill-fated expedition of King Louis IX of France to North Africa – Genoa acquired ports and also *maone* (associations involved in the financing of commercial enterprises), in all corners of the Mediterranean. She then extended her sphere of influence towards the east and the ports of the Black Sea, important trading stations on the Silk Road.

It was a time of increasingly tough alliances and clashes: although Genoa succeeded in eliminating Pisan influence

from the Tyrrhenian Sea and from its major islands, taking decisive control of Corsica and defeating Pisa at the Battle of Meloria in 1284, the conflict with Venice was more protracted. The Genoese defeated the Venetian fleet in the Battle of Curzola in the Adriatic in 1298, but were unable to reap the fruits of this victory and turn the situation in the East to their advantage. Turkish pressure led to an alliance with Venice (1343) which was of brief duration. The last war between Genoa and Venice (a result of both cities setting their sights on Cyprus) was decisive. The battles of Pola (1379) and Chioggia (1380) led to the Pace di Torino (Peace of Turin), which heralded the final decline of Genoese hegemony.

THE REPUBLIC OF GENOA

The period of the great continental struggles between the papacy and the Holy Roman Empire by no means spared Genoa and other Ligurian cities. The international nature of the struggle meant that foreign princes – such as the Visconti of Milan, summoned by the Ghibellines of the Riviera di Ponente, or Robert of Anjou, who intervened in favour of the Guelphs – got involved in Liguria's local conflicts.

During this period, Genoa was governed for almost two centuries by life-appointed doges, a position inaugurated in the 14th century. In 1522, however, their relatively peaceful rule over Genoa was shattered by the arrival of Spanish troops. Andrea Doria later put the city under the protection of Charles V, King of Spain

Emperor Charles V, allied to Andrea Doria

1400	1450	1500
1407 Founding of the Banco di San Giorgio	**1451** Christopher Columbus is born in Genoa	**1522** Birth of the Republic of Genoa
	1458 Brief period of French rule over Genoa begins	**1528** Andrea Doria comes to power
	1492 Columbus discovers America	**1543** Construction of La Lanterna, which becomes the symbol of the city of Genoa

Caravel

and Holy Roman Emperor – a demonstration of how power in the city had shifted. Andrea Doria was a talented soldier and admiral, and a member of one of Genoa's great families (see p79); he was named lord of the city in 1528.

In 1553, for reasons connected to the wars between France and Spain, the French decided to land on Genoa-dominated Corsica, intending to establish a base in the Mediterranean Sea. Many Genoese fortresses fell, but a peace treaty eventually forced the French to withdraw.

This was not the end of trouble in Corsica, however. The defeat of the Ottoman fleet at the Battle of Lepanto in 1571 led to instability (and also pirate raids) in the Mediterranean. The 17th century saw numerous revolts by the Corsicans, as well as renewed attempts by the colonial power to impose its authority. But the decline of Genoa, along with widespread dissatisfaction among Corsicans, provoked yet more revolts in the early 18th century, eventually resulting in the annexation of Corsica to France.

OTHER LIGURIAN CITIES DEVELOP

Columbus, a native of Genoa

Alberga, which had long sought to resist the power of Genoa, finally came under Genoese control following a clash between Guelphs and Ghibellines. The town of San Remo was acquired by the Doria family but managed to liberate itself in 1361, becoming a free commune within the Genoese republic.

After years of autonomy, Savona was defeated by the Genoese in 1528 and the conquerors' first action was to rebuild the port. A great new fortress, Il Priamàr, was built, but the local population went into decline. La Spezia, subject to Genoa and, from 1371, seat of the Vicariate of the Riviera di Levante, was fortified at the end of the 14th century and remained under the control of the Genoese until the early 19th century.

Smaller towns also managed to find a role for themselves in a region dominated by the Genoese. Camogli, Portofino and Chiavari all lived off the sea, and their shipyards prospered.

A 16th-century view of the Battle of Lepanto

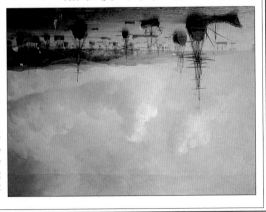

The bombardment of Genoa by the French fleet in 1684

THE DECLINE OF GENOA

Two important constitutions were established in Genoa in the 16th century: one by Andrea Doria, in 1528, and another in 1576, which created the hierarchical structures that were to rule the city. But, as time went by, Genoa became decidedly more important for the financial power wielded by its banks than for its political or military strength. A striking sign of the diminished political role of "Genoa La Superba" (Genoa the Proud) was the 1684 bombardment of Genoa by the French fleet under Louis XIV.

With the decline in Genoese power, a series of autonomous political entities arose in the region, such as the Magnifica Comunità degli Otto Luoghi ("magnificent community of eight towns"), set up in 1686 around Bordighera. However, in a Europe in which the role of nation states was increasing in importance, there was no longer much room for such auto-nomous powers. The rich families of Genoa increasingly moved away from commerce in order to concentrate more on financial investments. The 17th and 18th centuries passed with no great incident, though Corsica was finally sold to the French in 1768. Liguria also found itself in conflict with the expansionist policies of Piedmont. Occupied in 1746 by the Austrians and the Piedmontese, Genoa responded with a revolt provoked by the gesture of a young boy named Balilla, who sparked off an insurrection by hurling a stone at an Austrian cannon.

PIEMONTESE LIGURIA

The arrival of Napoleon Bonaparte's French troops in Italy completely upset the political equilibrium of Liguria. In 1794 the troops of Massena and Bonaparte conquered the mountain passes which gave access to Italy. Three years later the Republic of Liguria was established, becoming part of the Napoleonic empire in 1805. Napoleon's defeat at Waterloo and the Congress of Vienna in 1815 finally put an end to the independence of Genoa and Liguria: the region was assigned to Piedmont and became part of the Kingdom of Sardinia, governed by the House of Savoy.

The only port of any size in the Kingdom of Savoy, Genoa was linked to Piedmont and to France by new

Giuseppe Mazzini, Genoese-born

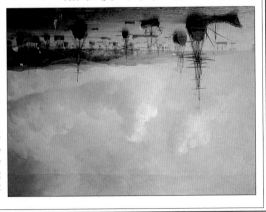

1550	1600	1650	1700	1750

1576 Second constitution of Genoa

Louis XIV, king of France

1684 The French fleet bombards Genoa, causing considerable damage

1686 The Magnifica Comunità degli Otto Luoghi is set up around Bordighera

1746 Balilla sparks off a popular revolt against the Austro-Piemontese

1768 Permanent loss of Corsica

1800		1850		1900	1950	2000
1797 The Republic of Liguria is established	**1815** Liguria becomes part of the Kingdom of Sardinia	**1860** The expedition of the Thousand departs from Quarto			**1992** Columbiadi (Columbus) celebrations held in Genoa	
1782 Niccolò Paganini is born in Genoa	**1805** Giuseppe Mazzini is born in Genoa	**1828** Carlo Barabino designs Teatro Carlo Felice in Genoa	**1874** Construction of a new port at Genoa begins	**1940–45** Genoa is badly damaged by bombing in World War II	**2004** Genoa is City of Culture	**2007** The 10th Annual Genoa Film Festival is held in July

Garibaldi departing from Quarto

Logo of the Colombiadi

communication routes. The city was also greatly altered by House of Savoy architects. In 1828 Carlo Barabino built the Teatro Carlo Felice and, in 1874, construction of the new port of Genoa began. (It was greatly enlarged again in 1919 and in 1945.)

Perhaps due to Liguria's traditional resentment of Piedmont, the Risorgimento movement, which sought a united Italy, was particularly strong and heartfelt in Liguria. Giuseppe Mazzini, one of the key leaders, was born in Genoa, and it was from Quarto (now a Genoese suburb) that Garibaldi's "Thousand" set sail for the south in 1860. Eventually, a united Kingdom of Italy, which Liguria joined in 1861, was formed.

TOURISM AND LIGURIA TODAY

The building of the railway line along the coast, following the line of the Via Aurelia, represented a crucial stage in the future development of the region. The smaller towns, such as Bordighera, San Remo, Alassio, Santa Margherita and Lerici, became popular destinations with a growing number of visitors, largely the wealthy and the aristocratic of Europe. In the 1930s Genoa was reshaped by Mussolini-era demolition in the heart of the historic centre. Further modifications were carried out in the 1960s and 1970s.

The ports and harbours of Liguria were badly damaged during World War II and, in the valleys and the mountains of the Apennines, the Resistance fought hard against German occupation. Postwar Liguria has seen attempts to develop the

The architect Renzo Piano

region's industry, and to adapt its ports to the needs of tourism. Many industries have faced crisis, however, and Liguria has had more success in the field of agriculture, in particular the cut-flower industry. Tourism is also, of course, of prime importance economically. The building of the motorway in the 1960s has increased the speed of development on both sides of the Riviera, which are crowded with visitors for most of the year. As the coast has become more prosperous and, in some cases, very rich (as in Portofino), so the neglected villages of the interior have met a rather different fate: many people have moved away, while there has also been a historic lack of investment in the interior.

Genoa, on the other hand, has been the focus of attention for more than a decade. The port was revamped (with the help of local architect Renzo Piano) in the run-up to the celebrations in honour of Columbus's "discovery" of America, and more money poured in prior to Genoa's year as Europe's City of Culture (2004).

Good motorways, important for tourism

GENOA
AREA BY AREA

Genoa at a Glance

The capital of Liguria, "Genova la Superba" (Genoa the Proud) has enjoyed a dominant role in the region, both commercial and political, for centuries. It is a fascinating city in a spectacular site and with many important monuments. First built by the sea, around the basin of the Porto Antico (the old port), the city could only then expand upwards. A labyrinth of medieval *carruggi*, Liguria's distinctive narrow alleys, was created up the steep hills behind the port, followed by new streets laid out in the 16th and 17th centuries, lined with grand palazzi built for Genoa's merchant families. The 19th-century and modern quarters of the city climb steeply again, adapting to the rising terrain. This scenic but inflexible landscape has created the need for various funiculars and lifts, some of which provide fantastic views. The current dynamism evident in Genoa is thanks largely to the Columbus celebrations of 1992 and the city's status, in 2004, as European City of Culture.

Palazzo Reale (see p77), *built in the 17th century, belonged to the Balbi family, to the Durazzos and finally to the Savoys, and is now the seat of the Galleria Nazionale.*

Fontana del Nettuno

Palazzo Reale

Palazzo Doria Pamphilj (see pp78–9) *was the private residence of the great 16th-century admiral and politician Andrea Doria. It still has apartments decorated for him and paintings he commissioned from artists such as Perin del Vaga and Sebastiano del Piombo.*

The Aquarium

IL CENTRO STORICO
(see pp48–65)

The Aquarium (see pp62–3), *first opened in 1992 in the attractive setting of the Porto Antico, has become one of the most popular tourist destinations in Italy. It is extremely well laid-out, and features a rich variety of animal and plant life.*

 The Porto Antico, with Renzo Piano's Il Bigo in the foreground

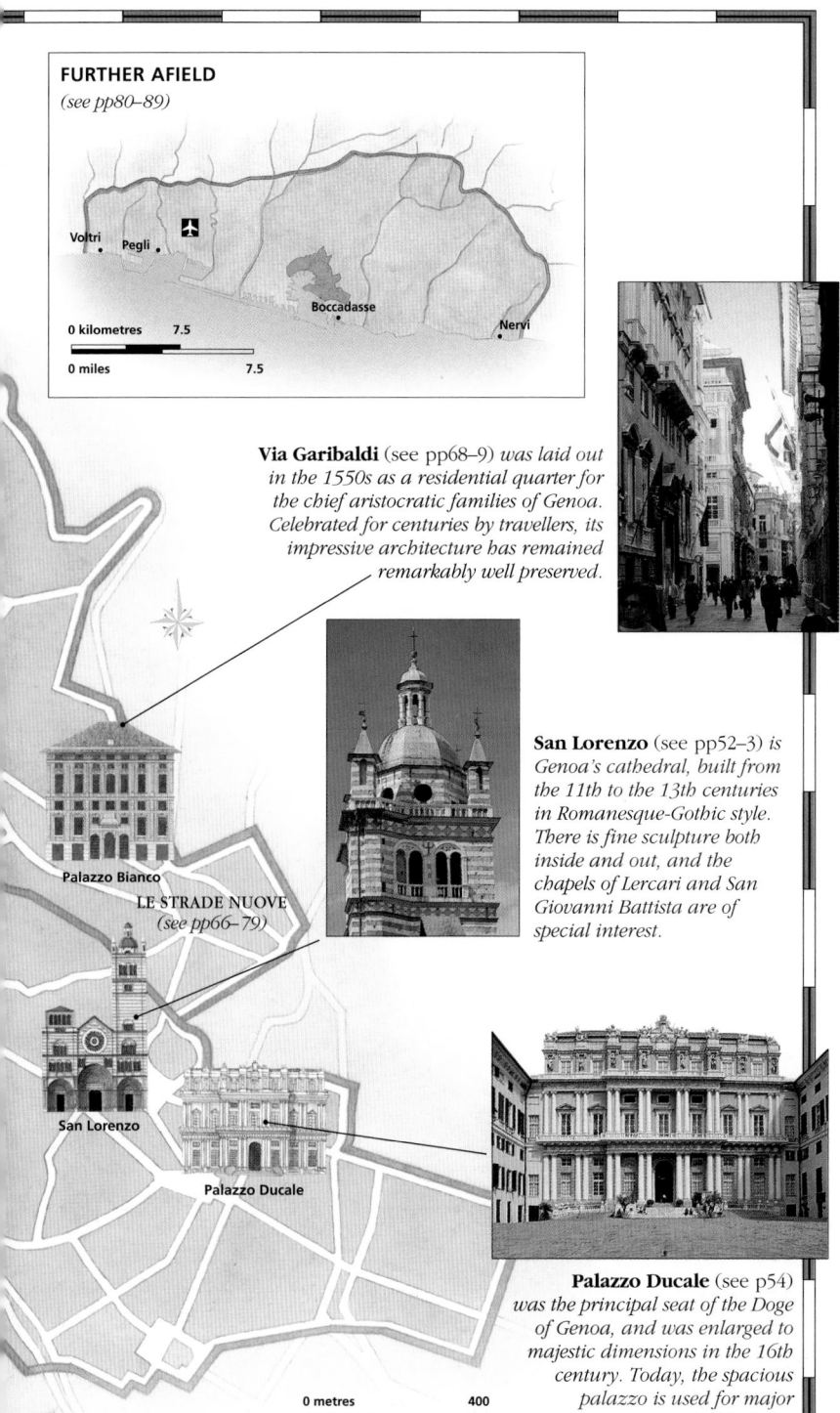

FURTHER AFIELD
(see pp80–89)

Voltri
Pegli
Boccadasse
Nervi

0 kilometres 7.5

0 miles 7.5

Via Garibaldi (see pp68–9) *was laid out in the 1550s as a residential quarter for the chief aristocratic families of Genoa. Celebrated for centuries by travellers, its impressive architecture has remained remarkably well preserved.*

San Lorenzo (see pp52–3) *is Genoa's cathedral, built from the 11th to the 13th centuries in Romanesque-Gothic style. There is fine sculpture both inside and out, and the chapels of Lercari and San Giovanni Battista are of special interest.*

Palazzo Bianco

LE STRADE NUOVE
(see pp66–79)

San Lorenzo

Palazzo Ducale

Palazzo Ducale (see p54) *was the principal seat of the Doge of Genoa, and was enlarged to majestic dimensions in the 16th century. Today, the spacious palazzo is used for major exhibitions.*

0 metres 400

0 yards 400

IL CENTRO STORICO

The old heart of the city is grouped around the Porto Antico and is made up of a hilly network of small piazzas, alleys and staircases. It is the largest medieval centre in Europe and is exceptionally well preserved, despite persistent neglect in some parts. The area is home to the cathedral of San Lorenzo and the Palazzo Ducale, the seat of power for centuries. Both public and private wealth has left its mark in the old town: Palazzo San Giorgio and the Loggia dei Mercanti on the one hand, the Doria family

Decoration at Palazzo San Giorgio

mansions in Piazza San Matteo and Palazzo Spinola on the other. The relationship between the old town and the port has been a centuries-old problem, largely due to the lack of integration between the two, which was further complicated in the 20th century by the building of a flyover. A chance to redeem the area and re-establish links with the seafront came in the 1990s: old buildings, such as the Teatro Carlo Felice, were restored, and new projects, including Renzo Piano's port buildings, were launched.

SIGHTS AT A GLANCE

Historic Buildings
Casa di Colombo ⑪
Loggia dei Mercanti ⑲
Porta Soprana
(or di Sant'Andrea) ⑩

Historic Streets and Piazzas
Piazza Banchi ⑱
Piazza De Ferrari ④
Piazza San Matteo ㉒
Porto Antico pp60–61 ⑮

Museums and Galleries
Accademia Ligustica
di Belle Arti ⑤

Aquarium pp62–3 ⑯
Museo Civico di Storia Naturale
Giacomo Doria ⑧
Museo di Sant'Agostino ⑫
Palazzo Spinola di Pellicceria ⑳

Theatres
Teatro Carlo Felice ⑥

Churches
Basilica di Santa Maria Assunta
in Carignano ⑨
Il Gesù (or Sant'Ambrogio) ③
San Donato ⑬
San Lorenzo pp52–3 ①
Santa Maria delle Vigne ㉑
Santa Maria di Castello ⑭
Santo Stefano ⑦

Palazzi
Palazzo Ducale ②
Palazzo San Giorgio ⑰

0 metres   400
0 yards   400

KEY
Street-by-Street pp50–51
Tourist information
M Metro station

Street-by-Street: around Piazza Matteotti

Within the dense warren of the Centro Storico, the square overlooked by the cathedral, Piazza San Lorenzo, and Piazza Matteotti, in front of the Palazzo Ducale, create welcome open spaces. Nearby is Piazza De Ferrari, a 19th-century project developed to link the old city with the western, modern and industrial part of Genoa. Within this maze of streets there is almost no sense of the nearby sea, except when you get a sudden glimpse of a blue horizon. There are numerous places and monuments of interest in this area: churches of ancient origin such as Santa Maria di Castello, Santa Maria delle Vigne and Sant'Agostino; a variety of public spaces (Piazza Banchi, Piazza San Matteo, Via di Sottoripa); as well as public and private buildings, including the supposed birthplace of Christopher Columbus, the aristocratic Palazzo Spinola di Pellicceria, and Palazzo San Giorgio, from whose frescoed façade there are beautiful views of the sea.

Palazzo Spinola

Piazza Campetto

★ Piazza San Matteo
At the heart of the district that was home for centuries of the Doria family, this medieval piazza preserves its original appearance. The beautiful church of San Matteo is also medieval. **3**

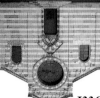

Salita S...

Piazza San Matteo

Via di Scurreria

★ San Lorenzo
The cathedral was surrounded by the medieval city until the building of Via San Lorenzo along the church's right-hand side and the addition of a flight of steps up to the façade, both dating from the mid-19th century **1**

The port, Piazza Banchi and Palazzo San Giorgio

Via San Lorenzo

Piazza Matteotti

Salita Pollaiuoli

Arcivescovado

★ Palazzo Ducale
The seat of the Doge of Genoa, this building was begun in the Middle Ages, but was much altered in the 16th and 18th centuries. The Palazzo has two large courtyards and contains valuable works of art **2**

Museo di Sant'Agostino
The cloisters of the ruined church of Sant'Agostino house a collection of sculpture and architectural relics from around the city, including this 17th-century Madonna with Child by Pierre Puget **12**

Vico Tre Re Magi

For hotels and restaurants in this region see pp176–8 and pp188–91

Chiesa del Gesù

Reconstructed by the Jesuits in the late 16th century on the site of the older church of Sant'Ambrogio, the Gesù has a sumptuous interior reflecting Genoa's golden age. Inlaid marble, stuccoes and frescoes create an ornate setting for two important works by Rubens, the Flemish artist who painted for various Genoese nobles **3**

LOCATOR MAP
See Street Finder, maps 2, 3, 5 & 6

Piazza De Ferrari

This square, home of the famous *Teatro Carlo Felice*, was radically redesigned and made into a pedestrian area in 2001. The fountain in the centre of the piazza was designed in 1936 by Giuseppe Crosa di Vergagni **4**

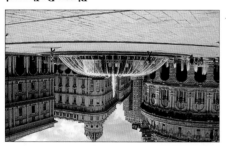

STAR SIGHTS

★ Palazzo Ducale

★ Piazza San Matteo

★ San Lorenzo

Porta Soprana

This striking landmark, part of the 12th-century city walls, today marks the boundary between the Centro Storico and the modern city. Nearby is the Casa di Colombo (see p56) **10**

Santa Maria Assunta in Carignano

VIA RAVECCA

SALITA DEL PRIONE

VIA PORTA SOPRANA

VIA DANTE

VIA XX SETTEMBRE

PIAZZA DE FERRARI

VIA XXV APRILE

0 metres 100

0 yards 100

KEY

- - - Recommended route

San Lorenzo ①

The church of San Lorenzo (St Lawrence) was founded in the ninth century and was chosen as the cathedral because of its secure position within the city walls. Romanesque-style reconstruction began in the 12th century but was never completed. The cathedral's present, primarily Gothic appearance, including the lower part of the cheerfully striped façade, dates from the 13th century. Important alterations followed later, however, mainly in the 15th to 17th centuries: these include the rose window in the upper part of the façade, the Renaissance cupola by Galeazzo Alessi and the beautifully frescoed Lercari chapel. The symbol of St Lawrence (Genoa's patron saint, along with St John the Baptist) is the purse, a fact that prompts much teasing of the Genoese, who are famous for being frugal with money.

The dome of the chapel of San Giovanni

The bell tower was created from the right-hand tower in the 16th century.

Black and white striped arches

The **rose window** was redone in 1869; of the original, from 1476, the symbols of the four Evangelists remain.

★ Sculptures at Main Entrance
Sculptures on medieval church doors introduced the faithful to important doctrinal subjects. Here, fine Romanesque bas-reliefs illustrate Stories from the life of Mary and the Tree of Jesse, on the jambs; and Christ blessing, the symbols of the Evangelists and the Marytdom of San Lorenzo, in the lunette.

Marble pillars

The Lions
Two 19th-century lion sculptures flank the main steps. A pair of Romanesque lions can also be seen on the edges of the façade.

For hotels and restaurants in this region see pp176–8 and pp188–91

STAR FEATURES

★ Cappella di San Giovanni Battista

★ Museo del Tesoro

★ Sculptures at Main Entrance

★ MUSEO DEL TESORO

Opened in the 1950s, this unusual museum was the work of Caterina Marcenaro and Franco Albini, and is one of the most elegant of its kind. Built underground near the chancel, the wonderfully atmospheric museum is covered in Promontorio stone, the dark construction material typical of medieval Genoa. Within this charming framework, picked out by spotlights, are displayed objects brought back during the Republic's forays into the Holy Land. Among the highlights are the Sacro Catino, a 9th-century Islamic glass vessel, once believed to be the Holy Grail, used by Christ at the Last Supper; the Croce degli Zaccaria, a 12th-century Byzantine reliquary made of gold and gemstones; the cope of Pope Gelasio, in brocade fabric with gold and silver thread (15th century); and the elaborately embossed silver chest (12th century), which contains the supposed ashes of St John the Baptist, and which is carried in procession through the streets of Genoa on 24 June.

La Croce degli Zaccaria

★ Cappella di San Giovanni Battista
This chapel, dedicated to St John the Baptist, was the work of Domenico and Elia Gagini (mid-1400s). It is richly decorated with marble and topped with flamboyant Gothic detailing. Reliefs on the front of the chapel illustrate the life of the Baptist. Inside, are six wall niches with statues and the stone reliquary that once held the supposed ashes of the saint (see below).

Romanesque blind arches

Dome by Galeazzo Alessi (1556)

In the right-hand apse, in the Senarega chapel, is a *Crucifix with Mary, John and St Sebastian* by Federico Barocci (1597).

The vault of the presbytery and the apse bears two frescoes by Lazzaro Tavarone (*San Lorenzo and the Church treasury*, *Martyrdom of the Saint*, 1622–4); in the apse is a lovely 16th-century wooden choir.

VISITORS' CHECKLIST

Piazza San Lorenzo.
Map 5 C3. *Tel* 010 247 18 31.
◯ **Church** 8am–noon, 3–7pm.
Museo del Tesoro 9am–noon, 3–6pm Mon–Sat.
🅿 🚻 ♿ ◻ by appt.

Palazzo Ducale ❷

Piazza Matteotti 9. **Map** 5 C3.
Tel 010 557 40 00. ☐ **Exhibitions**
9am–7pm Tue–Sun. **Shops** daily.
www.palazzoducale.genova.it

This palazzo, constructed during the course of the Middle Ages, was given its name (meaning Doge's Palace) in 1339, when the election of Genoa's first doge, Simon Boccanegra, took place here. It was enlarged to its current size in the late 1500s by Andrea Vannone, a Lombard architect. Further major changes, the work of Neo-Classical architect Simone Cantoni, were made in the late 18th century following a fire. These included the erection of the façade overlooking Piazza Matteotti (another lively, frescoed façade faces Piazza De Ferrari), which features pairs of columns and is topped by statues and trophies.

The palazzo is organized around Vannone's attractive atrium, with a large, elegant, porticoed courtyard at either end. The staircases up to the first floor are lined with frescoes by Lazzaro Tavarone and Domenico Fiasella. On the upper floor some of the public rooms are very fine: the doges' chapel was frescoed by Giovanni Battista Carlone (1655) with scenes celebrating the glorious history of the city of Genoa; this theme continues in the decoration of the **Sala del Maggior Consiglio** and the **Sala del Minor Consiglio**. The **Salone**, designed by Simone Cantoni, features paintings by Giovanni David (c.1780), among others.

Since extensive restoration in 1992, the palace has become a venue for major exhibitions. In addition, there are shops, bars and restaurants (including an expensive rooftop restaurant with panoramic views).

Door knocker in the shape of a triton, Palazzo Ducale

One of the spacious interior courtyards of Palazzo Ducale

Il Gesù (or Sant'Ambrogio) ❸

Via Francesco Petrarca 1. **Map** 5 C4.
Tel 010 251 41 22. ☐ 10:30am–noon, 4–7pm daily (9:30pm Sun).
⦿ with permission.

This church, overlooking Piazza Matteotti, was built by the Jesuits. It was begun in 1589, over the existing church of Sant'Ambrogio, and given the name of il Gesù. The façade, following the original design by Giuseppe Valeriani, was finished only at the end of the 19th century.

The sumptuous Baroque interior consists of a single room topped by a dome.

Multicoloured marble decorates the floor, the pilasters and the walls of the side chapels. The upper parts of the walls have been finished with gilded stucco and frescoes by the artist Giovanni Battista Carlone (17th century). The most valuable paintings in the church all date from the 17th century, including works by Guido Reni and a *Crucifixion* by Simon Vouet. There are also works that were commissioned by the Pallavicino family from Peter Paul Rubens: a *Circumcision* (1605) and *St Ignatius Exorcising the Devil* (1620), both acknowledged masterpieces and precursors of the Baroque style.

St Ignatius Exorcising the Devil, by Rubens, Il Gesù

Piazza De Ferrari ❹

Map 6 D4.

This piazza, with its large fountain, was created in the late 19th century with the aim of easing the flow of traffic between the Centro Storico and the western side of Genoa. Its design had to accommodate the existing buildings of the Accademia Ligustica di Belle Arti and the Teatro Carlo Felice, both built by Carlo Barabino in the 1820s. The new palazzi built around these two are eclectic in style. The building of the theatre in 1991, the restoration of the fountain and other alterations, including those of 2001, have given the Piazza De Ferrari a major facelift.

Accademia Ligustica di Belle Arti ⑤

Largo Pertini 4. **Map** 6 D3.
Tel 010 581 957. ◷ 2:30–6:30pm
Tue–Fri. ▣ by appt.
▣ ▣ with permission.
www.accademialigustica.it

Founded in 1751 by a group of aristocrats and scholars as a School of Fine Arts *(belle arti)*, the Accademia occupies a palazzo built for it in 1826–31 by Carlo Barabino. The museum on the first floor is home to paintings and drawings donated to the academy. Works of art from the 15th to 19th centuries are arranged chronologically: they include works by major Ligurian artists (Gregorio De Ferrari and Bernardo Strozzi among others) and artists who were active in Genoa (such as Perin del Vaga and Anton Raphael Mengs).

Polyptych of St Erasmus by Perin del Vaga

Teatro Carlo Felice ⑥

Passo Eugenio Montale 4. **Map**
6 D3. **Tel** 010 538 11, ticket office
010 589 329 or 010 591 697.
◷ for performances. ▣ Mon, by
appt. ▣ ▣ **www**.carlofelice.it

The Neo-Classical theatre designed in the 1820s by Carlo Barabino was virtually gutted by bombing in 1944, and only parts of the original façade survived. These give way to the modern part of the Teatro Carlo Felice, designed

The ultra-modern stage at the Teatro Carlo Felice

by Ignazio Gardella, Aldo Rossi and Fabio Reinhart in 1991. The theatre is dominated by a huge square tower pierced by small windows. Four sections of stage area are manoeuvred by a complex, state-of-the-art computerized system, making the theatre one of the most innovative in Europe.

Santo Stefano ⑦

Piazza Santo Stefano 2. **Map** 6 E4.
Tel 010 587 183. ◷ 3:30–6:30pm
Tue–Sun (Sun am only in Aug).

Built at the end of the 12th century, the Romanesque church of Santo Stefano stands on the site of a Benedictine abbey. The church underwent major restoration after being damaged in World War II.

The façade features bands of black and white striped marble, typical of Pisan and Ligurian Romanesque, with a main door surmounted by an oculus and a mullioned window. The brick-built apse is particularly lovely, ornamented by blind arches with arcading above. The bell tower and the 14th-century lantern are also constructed in decorative brick.

Inside, in the presbytery, are a *Martyrdom of St Stephen,* a fine work by Giulio Romano (1524), and paintings by various Genoese and Lombard artists, among them Valerio Castello, Gregorio De Ferrari and Giulio Cesare Procaccini.

Museo Civico di Storia Naturale Giacomo Doria ⑧

Via Brigata Liguria 9. **Map** 6 F5.
Tel 010 564 567. ◷ 9am–7pm Tue–
Fri, 10am–7pm Sat & Sun. ▣ ▣
▣ by appt. ▣ **www**.museodoria.it

Established in 1867 by Marchese Giacomo Doria, its director for more than 40 years, Genoa's Natural History Museum contains important zoological finds, many collected in the 19th century.

On the ground floor there are the rooms devoted to mammals and a series of reconstructed animal habitats. A definite must-see is the Palaeontology Room, with its skeleton of *Elephus antiquus italicus,* an ancient elephant found near Rome in 1941. On the first floor are displays of reptiles, amphibians, birds, butterflies and insects.

The museum does a lot of educational work and has a full calendar of conferences and exhibitions.

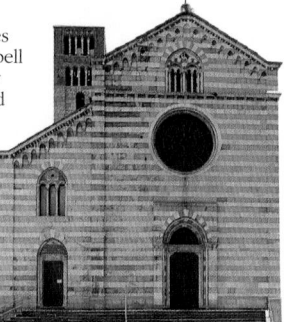

Santo Stefano, with its classic combination of black and white marble

Basilica di Santa Maria Assunta in Carignano ➒

Piazza di Carignano. **Map** 3 A4. **Tel** 010 540 650. ◯ 7:30–11:30am, 4–6:30pm daily.

This fine Renaissance church, one of the city's most prominent landmarks, was designed for the hill closest to the centre of the city by Galeazzo Alessi, the great Perugian architect. Begun in 1549, it took 50 years to complete.

A monumental flight of steps, designed by Alessi but built in the 19th century, leads up to the broad façade, flanked by two bell towers. Rising above is a high central cupola surrounded by four smaller domes. The elaborate sculptural decoration on the façade, the work of Claude David (18th century), includes a statue of the Virgin Mary over the door and statues of saints Peter and Paul in the side niches. A balcony runs along the roofs and around the central dome, making the most of the church's wonderfully panoramic position.

Inside, the harmonious exterior motif of pilasters with Corinthian capitals continues. As in St Peter's in Rome, the four vast pilasters that support the cupola have niches containing statues: these include *St Sebastian* by Pierre Puget (1620–94). On the second altar on the right is a *Martyrdom of St Blaise* by Carlo Maratta (1625–1713), and in the sixth on the left a famous *Pietà* (c.1571) by Luca Cambiaso. Other paintings, some of which have been adapted to fit the church's particular setting, are by Domenico Fiasella and Guercino. The organ, dating from 1656, is remarkable.

Statue of the Virgin Mary in Santa Maria in Carignano

The two majestic towers of Porta Soprana

Porta Soprana (or di Sant'Andrea) ➓

Via Di Ravecca 47 nero. **Map** 6 D4. **Tel** 010 246 53 46. ◯ 10am–6pm Sat, Sun & hols. 📷 weekdays only, groups only, by appt. 📷 with permission.

This gate corresponds to an opening made in the walls in the 9th century to connect Genoa to the east; the actual structure, however, was part of a ring of walls built in 1155 to defend Genoa from possible attack by Emperor Frederick I, known as Barbarossa *(see p87)*. It is similar to the Porta di Santa Fede, on the other side of the city. Restoration carried out in the 19th and 20th centuries has liberated the historic gate of the structures added to it over the centuries, and exposed the pointed arch flanked by a pair of imposing cylindrical battlemented towers. These are ornamented by delicate arcading and cornicing.

Casa di Colombo ⓫

Piazza Dante. **Map** 6 D4. **Tel** 010 246 53 46. ◯ 9am–5pm Tue–Sun. 📷

Tradition has it that this modest house near Porta Soprana was the childhood home of Christopher Columbus, the world-famous navigator who was born in Genoa in 1451.

The house that visitors can tour today is, in fact, an 18th-century reconstruction: the original house was destroyed by cannon fire during a French bombardment in 1684. Restoration carried out on the building

The supposed birthplace of Christopher Colombus

in preparation for the Columbus celebrations of 1992 extended to the adjacent 12th-century **Chiostro di Sant'Andrea** (cloister of St Andrew), all that is left of a Benedictine monastery that was demolished at the beginning of the 20th century, along with many of the other buildings in the area.

Museo di Sant'Agostino ⑫

Piazza Sarzano 35 rosso. **Map** 5 C5.
Tel *010 251 12 63*. ◯ *9am–7pm Tue–Fri, 10am–7pm Sat & Sun.*
www.museidigenova.it

This 13th-century monastic church was a lucky survivor of World War II bombing, which badly damaged Piazza Sarzano. The façade, with its black and white stripes, is typically Ligurian, while the elegant bell tower is coated with colourful majolica tiles.

Funeral monument of Margaret of Brabant

While the church functions now as an auditorium, the former Augustinian monastery buildings that are adjacent – including the two cloisters (a triangular one, dating from the 14th and 15th centuries, and a rectangular, 18th-century one) – have been skilfully adapted to house the **Museum**. The focus of the collection are the sculptures brought here from sites (including demolished churches) all over the city, but there are also detached frescoes, architectural fragments and examples of Genoese art from the Middle Ages to the 18th century.

There are two particularly important sculptures in the collection. One of these is the remains of the funerary monument of Margaret of Brabant, sculpted in honour of the wife of emperor Henry VII, who died in 1311 while visiting Genoa. The work was sculpted in Pisa in 1313–14 by Giovanni Pisano, one of

the most famous sculptors in Italy at that time. The other is a particularly moving *Penitent Madonna*, by Antonio Canova (1796).

San Donato ⑬

Piazzetta San Donato 10.
Map 5 C4. **Tel** *010 246 88 69.*
◯ *8am–noon, 3–7pm Mon–Sat, 9am–12:30pm, 3–7pm Sun.*
● *16–31 Aug.*

The church of San Donato, built during the 12th century, is one of the best examples of Romanesque architecture in Genoa.

The building's most striking and interesting feature, which is characteristic of early Romanesque architecture, is the splendid octagonal bell tower, erected over the church crossing; its three levels (the third is a 19th-century addition) are each pierced by windows. The tower was chosen as a model by the designers of the north tower of San Benigno, the so-called "Matitone" (great pencil) in the Porto Antico *(see p44)*.

The façade carries some noticeable features dating from late 19th-century alterations, when the rose

The bell tower of San Donato

window was added, but the main doorway is original and of particular beauty; it incorporates a Roman architrave in the moulding.

On the right-hand side of the church, look out for a shrine with a statue of the *Madonna and Child* (18th century); it is one of many erected in the Centro Storico.

The charming interior has a nave and two aisles, with Corinthian columns and a gallery of windows above; some of the columns are Roman. A *Madonna and Child* (1401) by Nicolò da Voltri is on the altar in the right-hand apse and, in the chapel of San Giuseppe in the left-hand aisle, there is a beautiful panelled triptych by the Flemish painter Joos van Cleve; this depicts an *Adoration of the Magi* (c.1515) in the central panel.

CONTEMPORARY ART AT VILLA CROCE

Villa Croce, surrounded by palms

Via Jacopo Ruffini 3. **Tel** *010 580 069.* ◯ *9am–1pm Tue–Fri, 10am–1pm Sat; temporary exhibitions: 9am–6:30pm Tue–Fri, 10am–6:30pm Sat & Sun.* (free on Sun).
www.museidigenova.it

The Museo d'Arte Contemporanea, in the residential district of Carignano, south of the city centre, is surrounded by a large park overlooking the sea. It occupies a lovely, late 19th-century classical-style villa, which was donated to the city by the Croce family in 1951. The museum currently possesses some 3,000 works, which document in particular Italian graphic arts and abstract art from 1930 to 1980 (including work by Fontana and Licini). There are also examples of work by young regional artists. The museum promotes young talent by collecting works, organizing exhibitions and assembling a digital archive of material related to local arts.

Santa Maria di Castello ⑭

Salita Santa Maria di Castello 15.
Map 5 B4. *Tel 010 254 95 11.*
⬜ **Church** *9am–noon, 3:30–6pm
daily.* **Museum** *varies during
religious ceremonies.*

This church rises on the
site of the Roman *castrum*,
or fort, around which the
earliest parts of the city were
constructed. Among the most
illustrious of old Genoese
churches, it was built in the
12th century on the site of an
earlier place of worship, at
a time when Romanesque
buildings were appearing
all over the city.

In the mid-15th century the
church was entrusted to the
Dominicans, who added
monastic buildings, including
three cloisters. The latters'
decoration was commissioned
by the Grimaldi family (in
line with the huge increase
in private patronage at that
time in Genoa) and turned
the complex into a point of
reference for artists in the
city. In the centuries to come,
other aristocratic families
commissioned the decoration
of the church's side chapels.

The stone façade is
crowned by a cornice of
blind arches. The central
doorway incorporates a
Roman architrave, and there
are other Roman elements
inside: several of the
Corinthian capitals which
adorn the red granite
columns in the nave came
from Roman buildings; and in

**The Loggia dell'Annunciazione,
Santa Maria di Castello**

the **Cappella del
Battistero** is a
sarcophagus of
Roman origin.

The apse, the
chapels and the
dome are the
result of changes
made from the
15th to the 18th
centuries. In the
chapel in the left
transept is a
*Virgin with the
saints Catherine
and Mary
Magdalen and
the effigies of
St Dominic* by
il Grechetto
(1616–70).
The high altar
has a splendid late 17th-
century marble sculpture of
the *Assumption*.

Among the monastic
buildings, the second cloister
is of special note. Here, the
lower of the two loggias, the
Loggia dell'Annunciazione,
features roundels with *Sibyls*
and *Prophets* (15th century)
in its vault, and a charming
fresco of the *Annunciation*
by Justus von Ravensburg,
signed and dated 1451.

There is a small **museum**,
with works such as *Paradise*
and *The Conversion of St Paul*
by Ludovico Brea
(1513); an
*Immaculate
Conception*,
a wooden
sculpture by
Maragliano (18th
century); and a
*Madonna and
Child* by Barnaba
da Modena (14th
century).

Next to the
church stands the
12th-century **Torre degli
Embriaci**, evidence of the
medieval power of the
aristocratic Embriaci family,
who lived in this quarter.

Porto Antico ⑮

See pp60–61.

Aquarium ⑯

See pp62–3.

The frescoed façade of Palazzo San Giorgio

Palazzo San Giorgio ⑰

Via della Mercanzia 2. **Map** 5 B3.
Tel 010 241 27 14. ⬜ *phone to
check opening hours of exhibitions,
or ask at the tourist office.* 📷

This palazzo is traditionally
identified as the place in
which Marco Polo was
imprisoned following the
Battle of Curzola (between
the Venetians and the
Genoese) in 1298. While
here, Polo met a writer from
Pisa called Rustichello,
with whom he
joined forces after
their release to
write *Il Milione*
("The Travels").

The palazzo is
made up of two
distinct parts: a
medieval part
turned towards
the city, which
was built in 1260
as the seat of the government
(the Capitani del Popolo) and
later became the Banco di
San Giorgio (1407); and a
second part, a huge 16th-
century extension built to
overlook the port. The fresco
decoration on the latter's
façade (1606–8), by Lazzaro
Tavarone, was discovered
only during restoration work
in the 1990s.

The expansion of the
palazzo, which involved
major restructuring of the
medieval section (later

**Detail of the façade of
Palazzo San Giorgio**

Piazza Banchi, overlooked by San Pietro in Banchi

heavily restored in the 1800s), was required because of the rise in power of the Banco di San Giorgio. The bank administered the proceeds from taxes collected by the Republic and also ran the Republic's colonies; it was, in effect, responsible for much of Genoa's prosperity in the 15th century. Today, the palace houses the offices of the harbour authorities. Inside, the **Salone delle Compere** is decorated with 16th-century statues of the Protettori del Banco (protectors of the bank) and the *Arms of Genoa with the symbols of justice and Strength* by Francesco De Ferrari (1490–91). The **Sala dei Protettori** features a monumental hearth by Gian Giacomo Della Porta (1554). You can also visit the **Manica Lunga**, a 128-m (420-ft) long corridor which once served as a dormitory for Benedictine monks, and the **Sala del Capitano del Popolo.**

Piazza Banchi 18

Map 5 B3.

Along harbourside Piazza Caricamento, flanked on one side by Palazzo San Giorgio, runs **Via Sottoripa.** Dating from the 12th century, this charming arcaded street was designed so that its shops could make the most of their proximity to the buzzing port area. Today, as it did in the past, the street houses various specialist foods shops, and there are snack bars, too. From here, Via al Ponte Reale leads to **Piazza Banchi,** the commercial core of the city up until the 18th century, and a crucial crossroads of major lines of communication between the city and the port. By the Middle Ages there was already a thriving grain market in the piazza, and money-changers also set up their stalls here, attracting merchants from all over the world; the piazza is named after the money-changers' tables. Later, money-changers and other traders did business in the 16th-century Loggia dei Mercanti.

The church of **San Pietro in Banchi,** founded in the 9th century, was destroyed by a fire which damaged the square in 1398, but rebuilding work didn't begin until the 16th century. The project was managed by Bernardino Cantone, who used a form of self-financing which involved the construction and the subsequent sale of several shops at ground level. As a result, the church is raised up on a terrace and is reached by means of a scenic flight of steps. It has a central plan with an octagonal dome with three pinnacles (four were originally planned). The façade bears frescoes by Giovanni Battista Baiardo (c.1650), which were restored in the 1990s.

Loggia dei Mercanti 19

Piazza Banchi. **Map 5 B3.**
◯ *for exhibitions, contact the tourist office for details.*

This elegant Renaissance loggia was built in Piazza Banchi in the late 16th century, to a design by Andrea Vannone, in order to accommodate the work of the city's money-changers. The loggia was a typical element of buildings intended for commerce during the Middle Ages, and there are many examples in the old city. The loggia in Piazza Banchi is built on a rectangular plan and has a single barrel vault supported by arches resting on paired columns; its openings were glassed in during the 19th century. The exterior features a sculptured frieze (16th century) by Taddeo Carlone, and the interior a fresco *of the Madonna and Child and saints John the Baptist and George* by Pietro Sorri (1556–1621).

In 1855, the loggia became the seat of the first trade Stock Exchange in Italy; it is now used as a site for exhibitions.

The Loggia dei Mercanti, with stalls in front, in Piazza Banchi

★ Il Bigo

Inspired by the masts of a ship and designed by Renzo Piano, the Bigo features a revolving panoramic lift. From a height of 40 m (130 ft), this offers great views over the port and city.

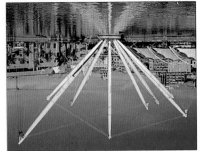

Boat trips are the only way to reach certain areas otherwise closed to visitors. From the quays of Porto Antico, boats offer guided tours lasting around 45 minutes. The bustle and activity of the port are fascinating and there is a breathtaking panorama of the city from the sea.

Museo Nazionale dell'Antartide Felice Ippolito is housed in the restored Millo building (1876). This museum features faithful re-creations of polar animal habitats and also scale models of the Italian base in Antarctica (Baia Terra Nova).

Porta del Molo

Also known as Porta Siberia, this gate was built in 1553 by Galeazzo Alessi. It was de-signed as a defensive bulwark for the port and as a place for the collection of taxes.

Porto Antico ⑮

The old port was the obvious venue for the staging of the Columbus celebrations of 1992, and these provided a perfect opportunity to restore the link between the port, for centuries detached from the rest of the city, with the Centro Storico. This project was undertaken by local architect Renzo Piano, who also transformed the district into an attraction in its own right, by restoring disused buildings such as the 19th-century cotton warehouses – now a multiplex cinema and exhibition centre – and by constructing landmarks such as Bigo and the Aquarium, the design of which includes maritime motifs, emphasizing the history of this district.

Biosfera by Renzo Piano

Built in 2001, the Biosphere is a futuristic glasshouse containing all sorts of tropical plants, from mangroves to rubber and cocoa trees, as well as numerous types of ferns, some of which are extremely rare. There are butterflies and chameleons, too.

VISITORS' CHECKLIST

Map 5 A2. **Tel** *010 248 57 11.*
www.portoantico.it **Museo**
Nazionale dell'Antartide
Tel *010 254 36 90.* ☐ *Oct–May:*
9:30am–5:30pm Tue–Fri, 10am–
6pm Sat, Sun & public hols; Jun–
Sep: 10:30am–6:30pm Tue–Sun.
🖾 **www**.mna.it **Boat trips**
Consorzio Liguria Via Mare.
Tel *010 256 775.* Golfo Paradiso.
Tel *0185 772 091.* **Biosfera**
☐ *10am–7pm daily.* 🖾 **Città**
dei Bambini Tel *010 234 56 35.*
☐ *10am–6pm Tue–Sun.* 🖾
www.cittadeibambini.net
La Lanterna Tel *010 910 001.*
☐ *10am–7pm Sat, Sun & hols*
(to 6pm Nov–Mar). **Il Bigo** ☐
2–6pm Mon, 10am–6pm Tue–
Sun & public hols. 🖾

La Città dei Bambini is the foremost educational/entertainment centre in Italy, aimed at children. The high-tech hands-on "play and learn" park includes two different routes, aimed at 3–5-year-olds and 6–14-year-olds.

★ Aquarium ⑯

Another work by Renzo Piano, the Aquarium is the largest of its kind in Europe and attracts over one million visitors a year (see pp62–3).

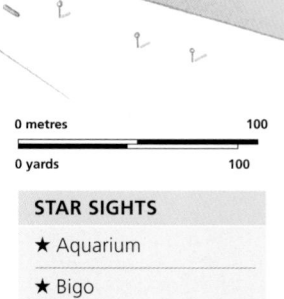

0 metres   100

0 yards   100

STAR SIGHTS

★ Aquarium

★ Bigo

LA LANTERNA

This is the symbol of Genoa, and the oldest working lighthouse in the world. The original lighthouse, dating from the 12th century, was destroyed by Louis XIII's French army. It was rebuilt in its current form, with two superimposed towers, in 1543, and its beam has a reach of 52 km (33 miles). There is a superb view from the top, if you can bear the 375 steps, and in 2006, the Museo della Lanterna opened in the adjacent fortifications.

Aquarium (Acquario) ⑯

The mascot Splaffy

The work of internationally renowned architect Renzo Piano (co-designer of the Pompidou Centre in Paris), with technical help from American architect Peter Chermayeff, the Aquarium is built within a ship anchored in the port. It is one of Europe's largest aquariums, with numerous tanks that are viewable from underwater level as well as from above. The aim is to help visitors to discover and marvel at different aspects of the sea and to promote understanding of the extent to which human life is linked to the oceans. There are spectacular reconstructions of diverse ecosystems on the planet, making it possible to observe animals, habitats and ocean floors at close quarters.

★ Hummingbird Forest
This area re-creates the luxuriant rainforest habitat of the smallest birds in the world. The hummingbird's signature features are its iridescent feathers, long bill and powerful wing-speed.

Level 2

A Coral Reef in Madagascar
This colourful zone is testimony to how coral reefs make a rich and desirable habitat for countless species of fish, from moray eels to angel fish (seen here).

The penguin tank houses both Magellanic and Gentoo penguins. Consisting of rocks, ice and water, the tank is visible from two levels, enabling the public to observe the penguins on the rocks as well as underwater.

La Grande Nave Blu (Great Blue Ship) is a real ship, acquired by the Aquarium in 1998. There are more than 20 tanks in around 2,500 sq m (27,000 sq ft) of exhibition space.

Red Sea Tank

★ Tactile Tank
One of the most popular attractions, this tank allows people to gently touch skate, gurnard and stingrays. The fish confidently approach the hands held out to stroke them.

The Forest of Madagascar reconstructs a tropical forest habitat of this island off the east coast of Africa. A paradise for naturalists, Madagascar teems with unusual plant and animal species. A terrarium nearby holds tortoises, turtles and iguanas native to the island.

★ Shark Tank
This large tank houses several species of shark, and also the sharklike ray, aptly known as a sawfish (shown here).

Reception

Entrance on Level 1

Auditorium (3D films)

Cloakroom

Seal Tank
In July 2001, Penelope (shown here) was born thanks to the first Caesarean section in the world to be performed on a common seal. After being cared for and fed by the Aquarium veterinarians and biologists, the baby seal was placed in the display tank with the other seals for company. Other seals were born naturally in 2003 and 2004.

Dolphin Tank
The resident dolphin Beta acquired two new companions in June 2006. Linda and Mateo are mother and son and used to live at the dolphinarium in Bruges, Belgium. These playful creatures are best admired during feeding time.

STAR SIGHTS

★ Hummingbird Forest

★ Shark Tank

★ Tactile Tank

One of the sumptuous rooms in Palazzo Spinola di Pellicceria

Palazzo Spinola di Pellicceria ⑳

Piazza Pellicceria 1. **Map** 5 B2.
Tel 010 270 53 00. ◯ 8:30am–
7:30pm Tue–Sat, 1:30–7:30pm Sun &
public hols. ● 1 Jan, 1 Aug, 25 Dec.
🎟 combined ticket for Palazzo
Spinola & Palazzo Reale. 📷 by appt.
♿ up to the 3rd floor. 📷 on request.
🖥 www.palazzospinola.it

With all the elegance and
fascination of an old aristocratic
mansion house, Palazzo
Spinola is richly frescoed and
has sumptuous furnishings and
paintings. Built in the 16th
century by the Grimaldi family,
the palazzo passed to the
Spinola family in the 18th
century, and they eventually
donated it to the state in 1958.

The first two floors house the
**Galleria Nazionale di Palazzo
Spinola**, in a manner that is
sensitive both to the building
and to the art collection. The
rooms have been restored to
their original style, with
paintings arranged as if this
were still a private home.
Two important fresco cycles
illustrate the two main phases
in the history of the palazzo.
One, by Lazzaro Tavarone,
illustrates in two rooms
*Exploits and Personalities in
the Grimaldi family* (1614–24),

while the other decorates
the Galleria degli Specchi
(hall of mirrors) and salons,
the work of Lorenzo De
Ferrari for the Spinola family
(1730–37). The Spinola donation includes works by Guido
Reni, Anthony van Dyck and
il Grechetto.

The **Galleria Nazionale
della Liguria**, on the third
floor, is reserved for works
which were not part of the
Spinola donation. These
include fine works such as
Antonello da Messina's *Ecce
Homo* (c.1474), *an Equestrian
Portrait of Gio Carlo Doria*
(1606) by Rubens, and *Justice*,
sculpted by Giovanni Pisano
for the funerary monument of
Margaret of Brabant *(see p57)*.

**Ecce Homo by Antonello da Messina,
Palazzo Spinola di Pellicceria**

Santa Maria delle Vigne ㉑

Vicolo del Campanile delle Vigne 5.
Map 5 C3. **Tel** 010 247 47 61. ◯
8am–noon, 3:30–6:30pm daily. ♿
📷 www.basilicadellevigne.it

The area now occupied by
the Piazza delle Vigne was
planted with vines *(vigne)* in
around the year 1000, but
was later engulfed by the
expanding city. The church of
Santa Maria was founded in
the same era, though the only
Romanesque element to have
survived is the bell tower.
The church was otherwise
completely rebuilt in Baroque
style in around 1640, after the
area around the apse had
already been reconstructed
in the 16th century at the
behest of the local Grillo
family. Further changes
have been made since.
The façade (1842) is the
work of Ippolito Cremona.

The interior, with a nave
and two aisles divided by
broad arcades, is bathed in
sumptuous gilding, stucco
and fresco decoration, dating
from different periods. The
presbytery was frescoed in
1612 by Lazzaro Tavarone,
with a *Glory of Mary*; the
aisles and the octagonal

DOOR CARVINGS

Slate ornamental panel showing St George and the Dragon

A recurrent sight in the Centro Storico are the doorways featuring carvings sculpted from marble or the characteristic black stone of Promontorio (from the Lavagna area). These panels were the product of economic necessity and the scarcity of building space: in the 15th century, noble families were obliged to extend the use of the ground floors of their palazzi in order to accommodate shops, and they therefore wanted to create handsome new doorways that would make their own residences stand out. Famous sculptors (in particular, members of the Gagini family) developed this craft, often producing work of great skill. Among the most common subjects were the triumphs of the commissioning family or holy scenes such as St George killing the dragon. There are some examples in the Museo di Sant'Agostino.

The Romanesque bell tower of Santa Maria delle Vigne

cupola were painted by various artists from the 18th century to the early 20th century. The church contains paintings by Gregorio De Ferrari, Bernardo Castello and Domenico Piola and a tablet depicting a *Madonna*, attributed to Taddeo di Bartolo (late 14th century).

Piazza San Matteo ㉒

Map 5 C3. Chiesa di San Matteo
Tel 010 247 43 61. 8am–noon, 4–5pm Mon–Fri, 9:30–10:30am, 4–5pm Sat & Sun. donations. outside only.

From the 12th to the 17th centuries this lovely square was the headquarters of the powerful Doria family, which, in common with the other powerful Genoese dynasties, gathered its political clique in a distinct area of the city. Despite changes to the palazzi facing the square, the piazza has kept its original compact form and a distinct charm, missing from other similar areas.

The buildings bear typical wall coverings of striped black and white marble, characteristic of Gothic civic buildings. Of particular note is **Palazzo di Lamba Doria**, at no. 15, named after the family member who defeated the Venetian fleet at Curzola in 1298; the typical structure of a medieval Genoese palazzo is still in evidence. Also noteworthy is **Palazzo**

One of the Doria palazzi in Piazza San Matteo

di Andrea Doria, at no. 17, which, according to the wishes of the civic senate, was given to the admiral in 1528.

The small church of **San Matteo**, the family place of worship of the Dorias, built in 1125, was rebuilt in the late 13th century in Gothic style. Pilasters divide the black-and-white striped façade into three, corresponding to the aisles. The interior was altered in the 16th century for Andrea Doria, who is buried in the crypt, as is his ancestor Lamba Doria. Giovan Battista Castello, known as il Bergamasco, modified the nave and aisles and painted the nave vault (1557–9), a collaboration with Luca Cambiaso. The statues in the apse niches and the decoration of the presbytery and the cupola (1543–7) are by Angelo Montorsoli.

To the left of the church is a pretty cloister (1308), with pointed arches resting on slim paired columns.

The 14th-century cloister attached to the church of San Matteo

LE STRADE NUOVE

Walking around the district known as Le Strade Nuove (or "new streets") – along Via Balbi and Via Garibaldi in particular – you are drawn back to the era of the 16th and 17th centuries, when Genoa dominated much of Europe in the field of finance. The "Genoese Century", or golden age, lasted from 1528 to 1630, when the power of several families was at its height. They poured their legendary wealth into new buildings and art commissions. The Centro Storico was not touched since they preferred to build anew –

Decorative frieze on the façade of Palazzo Doria Tursi

and magnificently – alongside, adapting Renaissance designs to the uneven terrain. The artist Rubens held the palazzi on Via Garibaldi in such high esteem that he made detailed drawings for a 1622 publication. The palazzi typically have loggias and hanging gardens, designed to disguise the steep slopes, and are the work of several architects; foremost among them Galeazzo Alessi. He found an ideal model in the Palazzo Doria Pamphilj (built in 1529 for Andrea Doria), which continued to inspire the palaces built for the Balbi family in the 17th century.

SIGHTS AT A GLANCE

Historic Buildings
Albergo dei Poveri **9**

Historic Streets and Squares
Piazza Fontane Marose **1**
Via Balbi **10**
Via Garibaldi **3**

Museums and Galleries
Galata Museo del Mare **14**
Galleria di Palazzo Bianco **6**
Museo di Arte Orientale Edoardo Chiossone **2**
Palazzo Rosso pp72–5 **5**

Palazzi
Palazzo dell'Università **11**
Palazzo Doria Pamphilj or del Principe **15**
Palazzo Doria Tursi **4**
Palazzo Reale **12**

Churches
San Giovanni di Pré and La Commenda **13**
San Siro **7**
Santissima Annunziata del Vastato **8**

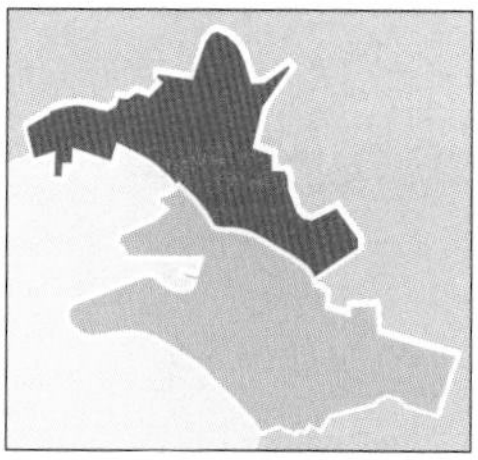

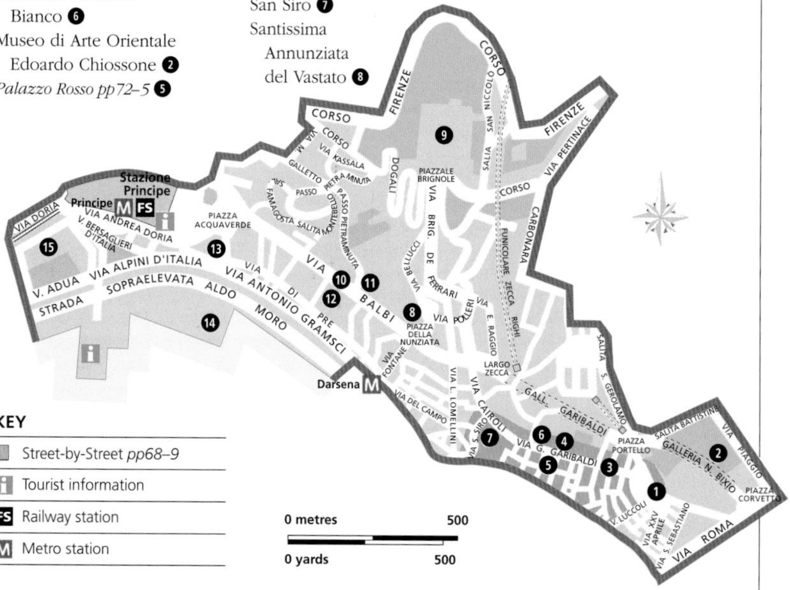

KEY

Street-by-Street *pp68–9*

Tourist information

FS Railway station

M Metro station

0 metres   500
0 yards   500

◁ **The opulent palazzi lining Via Garibaldi, evidence of the glorious "Genoese Century"**

Street-by-Street: Around Via Garibaldi

When Via Garibaldi was laid out in the mid-16th century, it was the first of the "new streets", and was known as La Strada Nuova. The mansions lining the street are wonderfully preserved, with sumptuous interiors, and often contain exceptional decoration or fine art collections, the fruits of shrewd collecting. Among the palazzi open to the public are Palazzo Doria Tursi (the largest in the street), which still serves as the town hall, and Palazzo Bianco and Palazzo Rosso, which house the Musei di Strada Nuova, the city's largest art gallery. Not far away is the church of San Siro, richly decorated in the 16th and 17th centuries and the first cathedral of Genoa. Beyond Piazza Fontane Marose, the attractive square at one end of Via Garibaldi, is the Edoardo Chiossone museum *(see p70)*, a rare collection of oriental art that was assembled in the 19th century.

Santissima Annunziata del Vastato, Palazzo Reale, Palazzo Doria Pamphilj

★ **Palazzo Rosso**
This gallery is home to treasures such as portraits by Van Dyck and Genoese works from the 16th to the 18th centuries ❺

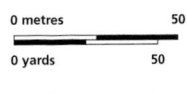

| 0 metres | 50 |
| 0 yards | 50 |

San Siro
Genoa's ancient cathedral probably dates from the 4th century. There are no traces of its origins, however, due to a fire that destroyed it in the late 16th century. The reconstruction was undertaken by the Theatine Order (see p76), which turned it into a temple resplendent with marble inlay and frescoes ❼

★ **Palazzo Bianco**
This gallery houses 13th–18th-century European paintings. The collection includes a large number of Genoese works, as well as some important Spanish, French and Flemish paintings, such as Venus and Mars *by Rubens, shown here* ❻

STAR SIGHTS

★ Palazzo Bianco

★ Palazzo Rosso

Palazzo Carrega Cataldi
now houses the Chamber
of Commerce.

Museo Chiossone

KEY

‑ ‑ ‑ Suggested route

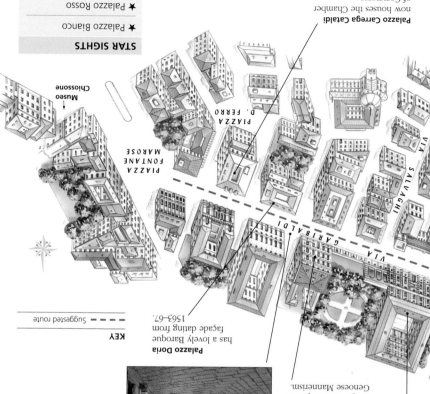

Palazzo Doria
has a lovely Baroque
façade dating from
1563–67.

Palazzo Podestà
was begun in 1563.
The façade is a
delightful example of
Genoese Mannerism.

④ arcaded loggia
staircase leading up to an
courtyard, with a double
palazzo has an exquisite
Garibaldi, this 16th-century
the other mansions in via
Three times the length of
Palazzo Doria Tursi

Via Garibaldi
Now pedestrianized,
this street transports
you back to the golden
age of the Genoese
aristocracy in the 16th
and 17th centuries.
The monumental
façades loom high
above you as you
walk beneath ③

LOCATOR MAP
See Street Finder, maps 2, 5 & 6

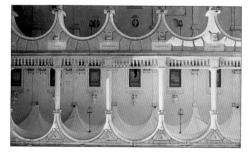

Piazza Fontane Marose ❶

Map 6 D2.

This square owes its name to an ancient fountain (fonte), which was recorded in a 13th-century document but destroyed in the 19th century. The piazza is attractive and free of traffic, but has an "assembled" look, the result of numerous changes in the layout and of the variations in street level.

Among the palazzi facing onto the square, the main one, at no. 6, is **Palazzo Spinola "dei Marmi"**, built in the mid-15th century and so-called because of its typically elegant covering of black and white striped marble (marmo). The palazzo's design had to adapt to the extremely uneven terrain and pre-dates the building of the palazzi in Via Garibaldi. The only building in the piazza contemporaneous with the buildings on Via Garibaldi is **Palazzo Interiano Pallavicini** (no. 2), which was constructed in 1565 by Francesco Casella.

Museo di Arte Orientale Edoardo Chiossone ❸

Villetta Di Negro, Piazzale Mazzini 4.
Map 6 D2. **Tel** 010 542 285.
🕐 *9am–7pm Tue–Fri, 10am–7pm Sat & Sun.* 🔵 *public hols.*
♿🔵 *ground floor.* **www**.museidigenova.it

Genoa's Museum of Oriental Art is set within the **Parco della Villetta Di Negro**, which was designed as a garden of acclimatization for exotic plants by the nobleman Ippolito Durazzo at the beginning of the 19th century. The gardens are still planted with the original mix of Mediterranean and exotic plants. The museum is housed in the villa at the top of the park

Sculpture at the Museo Edoardo Chiossone

that was built in 1971, as a replacement for an earlier villa, which was destroyed during World War II.

What is one of Europe's foremost collections of oriental art is named after Edoardo Chiossone (1833–98), a Genoese painter and engraver who, from 1875–98, ran the Printing Bureau of the Ministry of Finance in Tokyo, designing banknotes for the Japanese government. He also became a respected portrait painter at the Japanese court, as well as an avid collector of oriental art. Edoardo Chiossone bequeathed his collection of around 15,000 pieces to Genoa's Accademia Ligustica, where he had trained. These pieces, some of which are exceedingly rare, even in the Far East, include paintings, prints, lacquerware, enamels, sculptures, ceramics, textiles, and an exceptional collection of samurai armour. Specific works include a *Seated Buddha*, a lacquered wood Japanese sculpture, from the Kamakura period, and *Ukiyoe* paintings, a genre which flourished in Japan from the middle of the 17th century, including works by the masters Harunobu, Shunsho and Utamaro.

Colour woodblock print, early 19th century, Museo Chiossone

Via Garibaldi ❸

Map 5 C2.

The French writer Madame de Staël (1766–1817) was so struck by the magnificence of this street that she called it *Rue des Rois* (street of kings). For the Genoese it was simply "la Strada Nuova delli Palazzi" (the new street of mansions). Its construction resulted from the creation of an oligarchy by the Genoese admiral Andrea Doria, supported by a few wealthy families devoted to lucrative commercial and financial activity. In the mid-16th century, these families abandoned the old town, where space was severely restricted, and created this handsome residential street.

The entrance to Palazzo Lercari Parodi on Via Garibaldi

Designed by the treasury architect Bernardino Cantone, the palazzi were erected between 1558 and 1583. In the first section, you can see how the entrances to the palazzi run in parallel on both sides of the street, a sign of the planning involved in the layout. (The vast Palazzo Doria Tursi interrupts this symmetry.) Today, the palazzi are occupied mainly by offices, banks and museums. At no. 1 is **Palazzo Cambiaso**, which fronts onto both Via Garibaldi and Piazza della Fontana Marose, creating a clever continuity between the two spaces. Nearby, at no. 3, is Palazzo

Lercari Parodi (1571–8). Originally, this palazzo had loggias open to both the exterior and the interior, but today these are closed. The interior is unusual in that the rooms around the courtyard housed the servants' quarters while the public rooms were on the first floor, the opposite arrangement was more common. At no. 4 stands Palazzo Carrega Cataldi (1561), by Bernardo Cantone and G. Battista Castello; its façade is a delightful fusion of frescoes and stuccowork. At no. 7 stands lovely Palazzo Podestà, also built by Cantone and Castello. The façade has rich stucco decoration, echoed by an innovative interior with an oval atrium and a garden.

Palazzo Doria Tursi ④

Via Garibaldi 9. Map 5 C2. Tel 010 557 21 93. ◯ 9am–7pm Tue–Fri, 10am–7pm Sat & Sun.

Constructed for Nicolò Grimaldi (so rich that he was nicknamed "monarca" by his fellow citizens), this enormous palazzo breaks the coherence maintained up to this point of Via Garibaldi. Constructed from 1569–79 by Domenico and Giovanni Ponzello, with the help of sculptor Taddeo Carlone, the palazzo was acquired in 1596 by the Doria family, in whose hands it remained until 1848, when it was bought by Emperor Vittorio Emanuele I and became the seat of the town council. The façade, with its imposing entrance, is distinctive for the varied colours of the stone: a mixture of white marble, local pink Finale stone and slate tiles. A high plinth unites the central section with two airy side loggias; the latter were built in the late 16th century for the Doria but they blend in so nearly with the whole façade that they may have been part of the original design. Inside is one of the most magnificent courtyards in Genoa, with a grand staircase that splits elegantly into two after the first flight. The clock tower was added in 1820. Inside, the rooms flow harmoniously through the palazzo despite the uneven ground. Previously private rooms were opened up to the public as a museum in 2004. The highlights of the collection, which includes decorative and applied arts, coins and ceramics, are a 1742 violin owned by Nicolò Paganini, and various manuscripts relating to Christopher Columbus, including three signed letters.

Genoa's coat of arms on the façade of Palazzo Doria Tursi

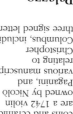

The grand interior courtyard of Palazzo Doria Tursi, with its lovely clock tower

Palazzo Rosso ⑤

See pp272–5.

Palazzo Bianco ⑥
Galleria di Palazzo Bianco

Via Garibaldi 11. Map 5 C2. Tel 010 557 21 93. ◯ 9am–7pm Tue–Fri, 10am–7pm Sat & Sun. www.museidigenova.it

Palazzo Bianco, found at the end of Via Garibaldi, was built in the mid-16th century for the Grimaldi family. It was altered in 1714 for Maria Durazzo Brignole-Sale, who introduced a new white façade, perhaps to distinguish it from the nearby Palazzo Rosso, the first home of the Brignole family.

In 1888 the palazzo and its art collection, including collections assembled by later occupants of the palazzo, were donated to Genoa by Maria de Ferrari, Duchess of Galliera, the last descendant of the Brignole family (who also donated the Palazzo Rosso to the city).

The gallery offers an exhaustive tour of Genoese painting as well as many great European paintings from the 13th to the 18th centuries. Genoese artists represented include Luca Cambiaso, Bernardo Strozzi, Giovanni Benedetto Castiglione, known as il Grechetto, and Alessandro Magnasco, whose famous *Trattenimento in un Giardino di Albaro* (1735) is here.

There is also an important core of Flemish paintings, with works by Gérard David, Van Dyck and Rubens, as well as paintings by Murillo, Filippino Lippi, Caravaggio and Veronese.

Ecce Homo (1605) by Caravaggio in Palazzo Bianco

Palazzo Rosso ⑤

This palazzo, which owes its name to the reddish colour of its exterior (*rosso* means red), is the last of the sumptuous mansions on Via Garibaldi, and one of the main noble residences in Genoa. It was built by Pierantonio Corradi for the Brignole-Sale family in the 1670s, then at the height of its power; the two main floors were intended for the art collector brothers Gio Francesco and Ridolfo, and their heirs. When the Duchess di Galliera, Maria Brignole-Sale De Ferrari, gave the palace to the city in 1874 she included its rich art collection. Palazzo Rosso was damaged during World War II, but Franco Albini's restoration in the 1950s successfully recaptured the majesty of the original building. Inside, the frescoes and gilt and stucco work are as much to be admired as the art. See pp74–5 for a detailed description of the exhibits.

Ceiling frescoes by Gregorio De Ferrari in Room 28 were destroyed by bombs that fell in 1942.

STAR FEATURES

★ **Allegory of Spring**

★ **Portraits by Van Dyck**

Entrance

★ Portraits by Van Dyck

Fine portraits of the Brignole-Sale family by Van Dyck in Room 29 include this picture of Anton Giulio, which pictures the 22-year-old frozen in a pose hitherto reserved for sovereigns, a superb affirmation of his social status.

★ Allegory of Spring by Gregorio De Ferrari

When Gregorio De Ferrari painted this allegory (1686–7) in the *Sale delle Stagioni*, he used the scene in which Venus seduces Mars. This masterpiece of Baroque "illusionism" was the fruit of the collaboration between De Ferrari and artists skilled in perspective and stuccowork.

Portrait of a Young Man by Albrecht Dürer

This work, dated 1506, can be found in Room 13. It was produced during Dürer's second trip to Italy. In abandoning the traditional sideways profile, the subject is brought into more direct contact with the onlooker.

Alcova

This enchanting 18th-century room is decorated with frescoes enclosed by lavish amounts of gilt and stuccowork. It is furnished with a large bridal bed (c.1780) and features pastel portraits of the Brignole-Sale family.

VISITORS' CHECKLIST

Via Garibaldi 18. **Map** 5 C2.
Tel *010 247 63 51.* **Fax** *010
247 55 57.* ☐ 9am–7pm
Tue–Fri, 10am–7pm Sat & Sun.
www.museidigenova.it

Rooms 38–43
Apartments of
Gio. Francesco II
Brignole-Sale

The Cook by **Bernardo Strozzi**
Local artist Strozzi (1581–1644) displays great virtuosity with his brushwork in this canvas, inspired by Flemish models and the naturalism of Caravaggio (Room 7).

GALLERY GUIDE

The main artworks are distributed between 33 rooms on the two main floors (an additional 19 rooms are on the mezzanine and third floor). On the first floor are works by Guido Reni and Guercino, as well as by Genoese artists such as Bernardo Strozzi. On the second floor, the magnificently decorated rooms are a big attraction, particularly the Sale delle Stagioni, along with the portraits of Brignole-Sale by Anthony Van Dyck. The gallery also has the finest library of art history in Liguria, as well as an education centre that organizes activities for children. The 2004 renovations restored the third-floor rooms to their former glory as the apartment of the director of the civic museums, Caterina Marcenaro (1906–76).

KEY

- ☐ Italian and European art, XV–XVII centuries
- ☐ Genoese art, XVI–XVIII centuries
- ☐ Roman art, XVII century
- ☐ Flemish art, XVI century
- ☐ Sale delle Stagioni
- ☐ Rooms with allegories of the human condition
- ☐ Non-exhibition space

Exploring Palazzo Rosso

The main museum takes up two floors, and occupies rooms which are still decorated with antique furniture, sculptures, mirrors and porcelain. On the upper floor (the only one to have been lived in) are rooms frescoed by the great painters of the 17th century in Liguria, magnificent examples of Baroque decoration. The paintings of the Brignole-Sale family, which form the core of the art collection, are primarily works by Italian and Flemish masters and the Genoese school, reflecting the taste prevalent in the centuries during which the collection was formed. Palazzo Rosso combines beautifully and seamlessly the role of a noble residence with that of a gallery of art assembled by a family of Genoese patricians.

Judith and Holofernes by Paolo Veronese, displaying great mastery of colour

ROOMS 1–6: ITALIAN AND EUROPEAN PAINTING, 15–17TH CENTURIES

The collection of paintings was assembled by the Brignole-Sale family, whose acquisitions lasted for more than two centuries. The marriage between Giovan Francesco Brignole-Sale and Maria Durazzo strengthened the collection further.

Room 1 has a fine *Portrait of Maria Brignole-Sale* (1856), one of many family portraits. In Room 2, in addition to the *Madonna with Child, St Joseph and St John as a Child* by an artist of the Penn del Vaga school, is a *Portrait of a Man* (15th century) thought to be by Michele Giambono or Gentile da Fabriano.

Room 3 is dedicated to the Venetian school from the 16th century, with works by Tinto-retto and Paolo Veronese, such as the latter's *Judith and Holofernes*. Other works here are by Paris Bordone and Alessandro Bonvicini (also known as il Moretto). The painting *Madonna and Child, St John the Baptist and Mary Magdalen* (1520–22) by Palma il Vecchio, is a beautiful work featuring a lovely use of colour.

Room 4 has 17th-century paintings of the Emilian school, among them an *Annunciation* by Ludovico Carracci, a key figure in the Bolognese school, along with his cousins Agostino and Annibale. Among Carracci's pupils was Guido Reni, whose *St Sebastian* (1615–16) reveals his ability to depict a range of emotions through measured classical painting. The works of Giulio Cesare Procaccini are also of interest.

The intense St Sebastian by Guido Reni, on display in Room 4

Room 5 contains works by Guercino (1591–1666), including the fine *Dying Cleopatra*, bought by one of the Durazzo family in 1648. By the same artist is *God the Father with Angel* (c.1620), once part of an altar painting entitled *Vestizione di San Guglielmo*, now in the Pinacoteca Nazionale di Bologna, and the *Suicide of Catone Uticense* (1641).

Room 6 is devoted to 17th century Neapolitan painting, including several works by Mattia Preti, such as *The Resurrection of Lazarus* (1630–40), which employs a dramatic use of light and shade.

ROOMS 7–10: GENOESE PAINTING FROM THE 16–18TH CENTURIES

These rooms document the richness and high quality of the works produced by the Genoa school during the city's so-called golden age, a period of great economic and cultural fervour that lasted from the 16th to the 18th centuries.

Room 7 is dedicated to local artist Bernardo Strozzi (1581–1644). His paintings range from the youthful *La Carità* to two devotional paintings depicting *St Francis* and magnificent works from his mature phase, such as a *Madonna with Child and San Giovannino*, showing the clear influence of Caravaggio, and *The Cook*, showing a Flemish influence.

In Room 9 are paintings by Sinibaldo Scorza (1589–1631) and Giovan Battista Castiglione, known as il Grechetto (1610–65). Scorza was primarily a painter of landscapes and animals, while il Grechetto, a draughtsman and engraver, dealt with pastoral themes. He was a brilliant interpreter of biblical scenes: his *Flight of the Family of Abraham* (1630s) is a good example. Room 10 is dedicated to Genoese artists of the 17th and 18th centuries, including Pellegro Piola, Giovanni Bernardo Carbone and Bernardo Castello, specialists in depictions of idyllic landscapes.

ROOMS 11-12: ROMAN PAINTING FROM THE 17TH CENTURY

Among the works in Room 11 is an exquisite *Madonna with Child in a Landscape* (1615–20), by Orazio Gentileschi, a friend and follower of Caravaggio. The painting is reminiscent of late-medieval works, especially in its portrayal of the Virgin Mary, who is sitting on the ground, a detail that underlines her humility. In Room 12 is Andrea Sacchi's *Dedalus and Icarus*. Despite the strong chiaroscuro effect, this painting represents Sacchi's successful break from Caravaggio-esque influences.

Ludovico Carracci's *Annunciation*, which can be admired in Room 4

ROOMS 14-16: DÜRER & FLEMISH PAINTING FROM THE 16TH CENTURY

The undisputed masterpiece of Room 14 is Albrecht Dürer's *Portrait of a Young Man* (1506). Part of the Vendramin Collection in Venice during the 16th century, the painting came to Genoa via Giuseppe Maria Durazzo, who acquired it in 1670 and passed it on to his daughter Maria, wife of Gio. Francesco II Brignole-Sale. The painting was subject to excessively vigorous cleaning in the 20th century, which has led to some damage. It remains, however, a great example of the Nuremberg artist's activity while in Italy. Also in Room 14 is Hendrick Avercamp's delightful *Winter Landscape with Ice Skaters*. One of the highlights in Room 16 is Jan Wildens's *July: Hay Gathering* (1614), part of the artist's series of 12 months (eight of which are held in Genoese museums). The large dimensions of the paintings suggest that they were probably commissioned and created with the aim to decorate the mansions of the Genoese nobility. Cornelis de Wael's *Fight Between Infantry and Cavalry* also hangs in Room 16.

ROOMS 27-33: ROOMS OF THE FOUR SEASONS AND LOGGIAS

Room 28 originally bore frescoes of the *Myth of Phaethon* by Gregorio De Ferrari. They were destroyed during World War II, although the preparatory drawings were fortunately saved. His work does survive, however, in the subsequent rooms. Frescoes on the ceiling in the next four rooms (29–32), completed in 1687–89, depict the Allegories of the Four Seasons: *Spring and Summer* are by Gregorio De Ferrari, and *Autumn* and *Winter* by Domenico Piola (assisted by perspective painters Enrico and Antonio Haffner). These superb works use complex iconography to exalt the glory

Loggia delle Rovine (or Loggia di Diana), frescoed by Piola

of the Brignole-Sale family, taking the form of illusionistic art that weaves together fact and fiction by superimposing stuccoes over frescoes. This decorative cycle culminates in the Loggia delle Rovine (or Loggia di Diana) by Paolo Gerolamo Piola. Fine portraits are displayed in these same rooms. The works by Van Dyck highlight the portraits of *Anton Giulio Brignole-Sale, Paolina Adorno Brignole-Sale* and *Geronima Brignole-Sale and her Daughter Aurelia*) were commissioned in the first half of the 17th century by Gio. Francesco II Brignole-Sale. It was the first major demonstration of the economic power that the family had acquired.

ROOMS 34-37: ROOMS WITH ALLEGORIES OF HUMAN LIFE

Geronima Brignole-Sale and her Daughter Aurelia, by Van Dyck

These rooms were frescoed in 1691–92 by Giovanni Andrea Carlone, Bartolomeo Guidobono, Carlo Antonio Tavella and Domenico Parodi. The paintings depict the allegories of the *Life of Man* (Room 34), the *Liberal Arts* (35) and *Youth in Peril* (37).

Room 36, Alcova, is a delightful space, decorated and furnished in full 18th-century style: delicate perspective wall paintings by Andrea Leoncino adorn the walls and the ceiling. The bridal bed was made by Gaetano Cantone in 1783.

San Siro ❼

Via San Siro 3. **Map** 5 B2.
Tel 010 246 16 74.
🕐 7:30am–noon, 4–7pm daily.

A church of ancient
foundation, San Siro was
mentioned in documents
in the 4th century. It was
Genoa's cathedral until the
9th century, when that title
passed to San Lorenzo.
Following a fire in 1580,
San Siro was reconstructed
under the supervision of the
Theatines, an order of Italian

The richly decorated interior of the church
of San Siro, once Genoa's cathedral

monks established to oppose
the Reformation by raising the
tone of piety in the Roman
Catholic church. The church's
current appearance dates
from this period, though the
façade was the work of Carlo
Barabino (1821).

Inside, there are three
broad aisles with frescoes and
stuccoes by Giovanni Battista
and Tommaso Carlone
respectively (second half
of the 17th century). In the
presbytery, adorned with
multicoloured marbles, is
a monumental high altar in
bronze and black marble,
a fine work by Pierre Puget
(1670). Also of interest in the
church is an *Annunciation*
by Orazio Gentileschi (1639).
Several side chapels were
decorated by Domenico
Fiasella, Domenico Piola and
Gregorio De Ferrari, who
also painted the canvases
in the church sacristy.

Santissima Annunziata del Vastato ❽

Piazza della Nunziata 4.
Map 5 B1. **Tel** 010 246 55 25.
🕐 9am–noon, 3–7pm daily. 🔲
during services. 📷

The name of this church
combines the two names,
one past and one present, of
the square that it looks onto.
Now Piazza della Nunziata,
the square was originally
Piazza del Vastato, a name
derived from *guastum*
or *vastinium*; these
terms referred to the
fact that the district,
which was not
enclosed within the
city walls, was free
from the restrictions
which could prevent its
use by the military.

The original church
dates from 1520, but it
was rebuilt in the 16th
and 17th centuries for
the powerful Lomellini
family. The façade has
two bell towers, with a
19th-century pronaos
(portico).

The rich interior
decoration is thought
to be the work of the
brothers Giovanni and
Giovan Battista Carlone in
1627–8, involving other
important artists such as
Gioacchino Assereto,
Giovanni Andrea Ansaldo
and Giulio Benso over the
ensuing decades. The central
nave is dedicated to
glorifying the divinity
of Christ and of the
Virgin Mary. In the
vaults of the transepts,
frescoes by Giovanni
Carlone depict the
Ascension and
Pentecost; the
Assumption of Mary
in the cupola was
painted by Andrea
Ansaldo and later
restored by Gregorio
De Ferrari.

In the side aisles
are frescoed scenes
from the Old and
New Testaments.
The frescoes in the
presbytery and the

apse *(Annunciation and
Assumption)*, by Giulio
Benso, are placed within
a grandiose painted
architectural framework.

Albergo dei Poveri ❾

Piazzale Brignole 2. **Map** 2 E1.

The grandiose white façade
of the vast Albergo dei
Poveri, with the Genoa city
coat of arms at the centre,
dominates your vision as you
approach along Via Brignole
De Ferrari. One of Italy's
earliest charitable institutions,
providing food, lodging and
medical care for the poor and
sickly, it was established in the
1600s under the patronage of
Emanuele Brignole.

The former poorhouse, an
emblem of the munificence
of the city's nobility, is laid
out around four courtyards,
with a church at the centre.
Works of art housed here
include paintings by Giovan
Battista Paggi, Pierre Puget
and Domenico Piola. The
building has been taken over
recently by the University of
Genoa, but may be open to
the public in the future.

Nearby are the **Salita
di San Bartolomeo del
Carmine** and the **Salita San
Nicolò**, perfectly preserved
narrow uphill streets *(creuze)*
that were once in the
outskirts but have now been
absorbed into the city centre.

The imposing façade of the Albergo
dei Poveri

For hotels and restaurants in this region see pp176–8 and pp188–91

The internal courtyard of one of the majestic palazzi on Via Balbi

Via Balbi ⑩

Map 2 E2.

This street, leading from Piazza della Nunziata, was one of the original Strade Nuove. Created in 1602 by Bartolomeo Bianco for the powerful Balbi family, its building was the result of a deal between the Balbi and the government, which ostensibly aimed to improve traffic flow in the area. (Ironically, Via Balbi can occasionally be clogged with traffic, though efforts have been made to rectify this.) By 1620, seven palazzi had been built, creating the Balbi's very own residential quarter. Sadly, none of the palazzi are open to the public.

At no. 1, **Palazzo Durazzo Pallavicini** (1618), one of the many residences to have been designed by Bianco, has a lovely atrium and a superb 18th-century staircase. **Palazzo Balbi Senarega**, another Bianco work at no. 4, is now a university faculty. Inside are fine frescoes by Gregorio De Ferrari.

Palazzo dell'Università ⑪

Via Balbi. **Map** 2 E2. **Tel** 010 209 91. ◯ 7am–7pm Mon–Fri; 7am–noon Sat.

Perhaps the most famous building on Via Balbi, this palazzo was built as a Jesuit college in 1634–36 to a design by Bartolomeo Bianco. It has functioned as the seat of the University of Genoa since 1775. Today it houses the rectorate and several faculties. Like the palazzi in Via Garibaldi (especially Palazzo Doria Tursi), this palazzo has the familiar succession of atrium, raised courtyard and hanging garden. The courtyard, with paired columns, is beautiful and airy. In the **Great Hall** (Aula Magna) there is a series of six statues personifying the theological and cardinal virtues by Giambologna (1579).

The **Biblioteca Universitaria** (university library), occupies the adjacent former church of saints Gerolamo and Francesco Saverio: the apse, with some fine frescoes by Domenico Piola, has been transformed into a reading room.

Palazzo Reale ⑫

Via Balbi 10. **Map** 5 A1. **Tel** 010 271 02 36. ◯ 9am–1:30pm Tue, Wed; 9am–7pm Thu–Sun. Ticket office closes 30 minutes before closure. ◉ 1 Jan, 1 May, 25 Dec. ◈ combined ticket valid for Palazzo Reale and Palazzo Spinola. **www**.palazzorealegenova.it

Constructed for the Balbi family in 1643–55, this fine palazzo was rebuilt for Eugenio Durazzo only 50 years later. Its new designer, Carlo Fontana, opted for a Baroque mansion, modelled on a Roman palazzo. The building acquired its present name in 1825, when it became the Genoa residence of the royal House of Savoy. Fontana's internal courtyard is striking: a combination of delightful architecture in red and yellow and fine views over the port. The superb mosaic pavement in the garden came from a monastery.

Vase on display in Palazzo Reale

The palazzo's magnificent rooms, decorated in the 18th and 19th centuries by the Durazzo family and by the Savoys, now form part of the **Galleria Nazionale**. They contain furniture, furnishings and tapestries, along with frescoes, paintings and sculpture. The 18th-century rooms include the lavish and breathtaking Galleria degli Specchi (hall of mirrors), with a ceiling frescoed by Domenico Parodi. Rooms created by the Savoys include the Sala del Trono (throne room), Sala delle Udienze (audience chamber) and the Salone da Ballo (ballroom). The most valuable works of art in the museum include paintings by Luca Giordano, Van Dyck, Bernardo Strozzi, il Grechetto and Valerio Castello; and sculptures by Francesco Schiaffino and Filippo Parodi.

The splendid Galleria degli Specchi in Palazzo Reale

Loggias on Piazza della Commenda

San Giovanni di Pré and La Commenda ⓭

Piazza della Commenda 1.
Map 2 D2. **Tel** 010 265 486.
⬜ **Upper church** 10am–5pm Tue–
Fri, 10am–7pm Sat & Sun. **Lower church** By appt only. 📷 on request.

A stone's throw from the main railway station, the church of San Giovanni di Pré was founded in 1180 by the Knights of the Order of St John. The original Romanesque church was largely rebuilt in the 14th century. The bell tower, adorned with a pyramidal spire, was left untouched and it is very attractive.

The main church consists, in fact, of two churches, one above the other. The lower one, which was always intended for public worship, has three aisles with cross vaults. The upper church was used by the Knights of the Order and opened to the public only in the 18th century. To do this, the church had to be re-oriented in the opposite direction, an entrance made in the apse and a second, artificial apse created from the opposite end. The upper church is similar in style to the lower church, though it is larger. Heavy columns support Gothic arches between the aisles and ribbed vaults, the bare stone making the interior

very atmospheric. There are paintings by Giulio Benso, Bernardo Castello and Lazzaro Tavarone.

La Commenda, next door, was founded by the Knights of St John in the 11th century to provide lodgings for pilgrims waiting to sail to the Holy Land; it also functioned as a hospital. Its portico, topped by two loggias, faces onto Piazza della Commenda. There are wonderful frescoes on the third floor. The complex was rebuilt in the 16th century, but restoration work in the 1970s revived its Romanesque appearance. Exhibitions and cultural events are held here.

A short walk eastwards, along Via di Pré (derived from "prati", meaning fields, a reminder of how rural this area once was), brings you to the **Porta dei Vacca** (or **Santa Fede**), a Gothic arch (1155) much altered by the addition of subsequent buildings.

Galata Museo del Mare ⓮

Calata De Mari 1, Darsena. **Map** 2 D3. **Tel** 010 234 5655. ⬜ Nov–Feb: 10am–6pm Tue–Sun (to 7:30pm Sat & Sun); Mar–Oct:10am–7:30pm Tue–Sun; Aug daily. Last entrance: 60 mins before closure. 📷 📷 (electronic guide for the blind available). ♿ 🅿 📷 🖥 www.galatamuseodelmare.it

Completed in 2004 and intrinsic to the revival of Genoa's port area, this museum of the sea is the largest museum of its kind in the Mediterranean. The complex combines 16th-century and Neo-Classical architecture with a stylish glass, wood and aluminium structure. It is located in the Darsena port area, alongside the Stazione Marittima and the historic Galata shipyards.

The museum illustrates Genoa's longstanding relationship with the sea,

from the Middle Ages to the present. The star exhibit and focal point is a beautifully restored 16th-century Genoese galley, eye-catching behind its glass veil, lit up at night and visible across the whole bay. As well as a fine display of maps and sailing instruments, the museum houses an original 17th-century launching berth and a reconstructed 17th-century pirate ship, which visitors can board.

Fully interactive, the museum enables visitors to taste life at sea at first hand: you can even experience what it is like to cross the Cape Horn in a storm.

The magnificent Fountain of Neptune, in the gardens of Palazzo Doria Pamphilj

Palazzo Doria Pamphilj or del Principe ⓯

Piazza del Principe 4.
Map 1 C1. **Tel** 010 255 509.
⬜ 10am–5pm Fri–Wed.
● 1 Jan, Easter, 1 May, Aug, 25 Dec. 📷 📷 book ahead.
♿ 📷 🚫
www.palazzodelprincipe.it

Constructed by Andrea Doria when he was at the height of his political power, this palazzo was conceived as a truly magnificent, princely residence, a demonstration of the admiral's power. It is still owned by the Doria Pamphilj family.

The building was begun in around 1529 and incorporated several existing buildings. When Charles V came as a

ANDREA DORIA

Andrea Doria as Neptune by Bronzino

This portrait of Andrea Doria (1468–1560), painted by Bronzino after 1540, and now in Palazzo Doria Pamphilj, is fitting. posing, despite his advanced years, in a heroic attitude, semi-nude, as the god of the sea, Neptune. Two fundamental themes in his life are concentrated in this work: the sea and the arts. A member of one of the most powerful families in Genoa, he did not, however, have an easy life. He made a successful career through warfare: initially serving the pope, then the king of France and, finally, emperor Charles V. A soldier and admiral of huge talent, he was one of the few to defeat feared pirates operating in the Mediterranean, to such an extent that he gained the deep respect of the Genoese, who declared him lord of the city in 1528. From this position of power he established an aristocratic constitution which lasted until 1798. He spent many years in his palazzo, built with the help of some of the great artists of the Renaissance.

Salone dei Giganti has a ceiling fresco by del Vaga showing **Giants struck by Jove** (1531). Fine tapestries depicting the *Battle of Lepanto*, in the **galleria**, were made in Brussels in 1591 to a design by Luca Cambiaso.

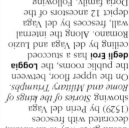

Detail from the Fontana del Tritone

As well as bringing new life to the palazzo's decoration, restoration work also made it possible for the public to visit the private apartments of Andrea Doria and his wife.

Around the palazzo, from the water's edge to Monte Granarolo to the rear, there was an enchanting garden,

guest in 1533, the decoration was largely complete. The principal artist involved was Perin del Vaga (c.1501–47), a pupil of Raphael summoned to Genoa by Andrea Doria. A marble entrance by Silvio Cosini gives way to an atrium, decorated with frescoes (1529) by Perin del Vaga showing *Stories of the kings of Rome and Military Triumphs*. On the upper floor, between the public rooms, the **Loggia degli Eroi** has a succeed ceiling by del Vaga and Luzio Romano. Along the internal wall, frescoes by del Vaga depict 12 ancestors of the Doria family. Following lengthy restoration work in the loggia, the splendour of the frescoes' original colours has been greatly revived. The

was created out of the Doria's private quay.

The nearby **Stazione Marittima**, a 1930s departure point for transatlantic liners, much altered in the 19th and 20th centuries to make way for a section of railway line and several road junctions. Damage during World War II didn't help, and there is now a project to return the garden to its 16th-century appearance. The garden's two main landmarks are the **Fontana del Tritone** by Montorsoli (a pupil of Michelangelo) and the **Fontana di Nettuno** by Taddeo Carlone, both made in the 16th century.

FURTHER AFIELD

Genoa sprawls westwards and eastwards from the city centre, taking in the Circonvallazione a Monte (mountain by-pass) and the old city walls and forts, as well as the towns annexed to the city with the creation of Greater Genoa in the 1920s. From Voltri, on the Riviera di Ponente to the west, to Nervi, on the Riviera di Levante to the east (the limits of Genoa's administrative territory), the steep landscape and beautiful coastline conceal all kinds of surprises: from the splendid 19th-century park of Villa Durazzo Pallavicini, at Pegli, to the sanctuaries just above Genoa, famous for their nativity scenes and the focus of pilgrimages. Genoa's city walls, which circle the regional capital some distance from the centre, date from

One of the cats fed by Boccadasse's fishermen

the 17th century and feature magnificent fortresses, still in a perfect state of preservation. Then there are medieval jewels such as the church of San Siro di Struppa, standing alone among vineyards and gardens. One sight that should not be missed is the Neo-Classical cemetery at Staglieno, regarded as one of Genoa's major attractions. East of the city centre, the residential district of Albaro is full of graceful villas set into an urban context, while Boccadasse is a picturesque, well-preserved fishing village, popular with visitors and locals alike. Nervi is a famous bathing resort with beautiful Art Nouveau buildings, a municipal park created out of the gardens of three villas, and the Passeggiata Anita Garibaldi, one of the loveliest coastal walks in Italy.

SIGHTS AT A GLANCE

Historic Buildings
Castello D'Albertis **6**
City Walls
 and Fortresses **9**

Residential Districts
Albaro **12**
Boccadasse **13**
Nervi **14**

Pegli **2**
Voltri **1**

Churches and Sanctuaries
Basilica di San Francesco
 di Paola **4**
San Bartolomeo degli
 Armeni **8**
San Siro di Struppa **11**
Santuario della Madonnetta **7**
Santuario di Oregina **5**

Parks and Gardens
Parco Durazzo Pallavicini **3**

Cemeteries
Cimitero di Staglieno **10**

KEY

▦	Central Genoa
▦	Greater Genoa
▬	Motorway
▬	Main road
═	Minor road
—	Railway line
⋯	Walls
⛴	Ferry terminal
✈	Airport

0 kilometres   5

0 miles   5

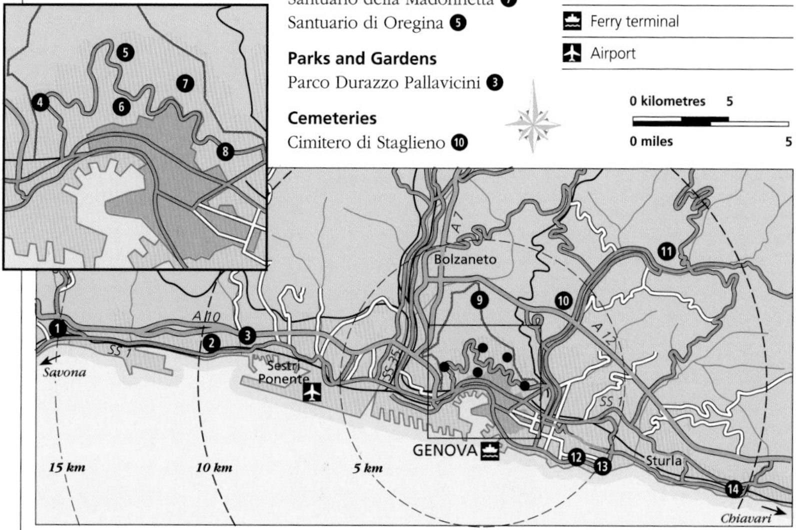

Bolzaneto
Savona
Sesti Ponente
GENOVA
Sturla
Chiavari

15 km   10 km   5 km

◁ The Egyptian obelisk overlooking one of the pools at the Parco Durazzo Pallavicini in Pegli

The Villa Brignole-Sale, surrounded by an English garden, at Voltri

Voltri ❶

Road Map D3.
FS Genoa–Savona line.

One of the most important towns in Greater Genoa, Voltri is more or less a continuation of the periphery of the city. The main sight of interest here is the **Villa Brignole-Sale**, also called the Villa della Duchessa di Galliera. Originally built in the 17th century, what you see was largely created in the 18th century. The palace became the home of Maria Brignole-Sale, Duchess of Galliera, in 1870. Her most striking contribution was the creation of an English-style garden, complete with pine trees, holm oaks and a deer park. The park extends for over 32 ha (80 acres) and is scattered with romantic follies and farmhouses. While the villa, with its lavish interior, is not open to the public, the grounds are a public park.

On the left of the villa, in a beautiful panoramic position, stands the **Sanctuary of Nostra Signora delle Grazie**. The Duchess of Galliera had it restored in Gothic style. She was buried here in 1888.

Pegli ❷

Road Map D3. **FS**

Annexed, like other nearby towns, to the city of Genoa in 1926, Pegli owes its fame to the aristocracy of Europe. From the end of the 19th century onwards, this was the aristocrats' preferred holiday place; it was also a popular retreat for the Genoese. Two villas hint at its former elegance.

Villa Durazzo Pallavicini, surrounded by a splendid park bursting with fanciful pagodas, arches and other follies *(see pp84–5)*, is the home of the **Museo Civico di Archeologia Ligure**. Objects from the paleontological, prehistoric, Etruscan and Roman eras are displayed alongside the collection of antique vases given to the city in 1866 by Prince Otto of Savoy. Among the more interesting finds are tools from the caves at Balzi Rossi *(see p169)* and the earliest known statue-stele from Lunigiana (c.3000 BC).

The 16th-century Villa Centurione Doria, featuring frescoes by Lazzaro Tavarone, is now home to the **Museo Civico Navale**. This traces Genoa's seafaring history using a fascinating array of objects. These include a portrait of Christopher Columbus by Ghirlandaio, models of three caravels, ship instruments such as astrolabes, and a famous view of Genoa by De Grassi, dating from 1481.

🏛 **Museo Civico di Archeologia Ligure**
Via Pallavicini 11. **Tel** 010 698 10 48. ◯ 9am–7pm Tue–Fri; 10am–7pm Sat, Sun & public hols. 🏷 🅿️ 📷 ✒ www.museoarcheologico.it

🏛 **Museo Civico Navale**
Piazza Bonavino 7. **Tel** 010 696 98 85. ◯ 9am–1pm Tue–Fri; 10am–7pm Sat &Sun. 🏷 🅿️ www.museonavale.it

Parco Durazzo Pallavicini ❸

See pp84–5.

Ex votos in the Basilica di San Francesco di Paola

Basilica di San Francesco di Paola ❹

Salita San Francesco di Paola 44. **Map** 1 C1. **Tel** 010 261 228. 📷 32, 35. ◯ Apr–Sep: 7:30am–noon, 3:30–7pm daily; Oct–Mar: 7:30am–noon, 3:30–6pm daily. 🅿️ 📷

This sanctuary is at one extreme of the Circonvallazione a Monte, the charming but tortuous panoramic road that snakes across the slopes just above the city. From the church courtyard, built on a rocky outcrop that dominates the district of Fassolo, visitors can enjoy a marvellous view of Genoa's Porto Antico,

Overlooking Pegli, with the airport in the background

which can be reached via a brick-paved road lined with the stations of the Cross. Dating from the early 16th century, the basilica took on an important role during the following century, when its patrons included powerful families such as the Doria, the Balbi and the Spinola. Also known as the Sanctuary of Sailors, the church contains numerous mariners' ex votos. Stuccoes and multicoloured marble embellish the spacious interior, and the side chapels contain some important works of art. In the third chapel on the right is a *Nativity* by Luca Cambiaso (1565), while the chapel at the end of the left aisle contains a *Washing of the Feet* signed by Orazio De Ferrari. Anton Maria Maragliano, one of the most active sculptors in Liguria in the 17th century, was responsible for the wooden statue of the Virgin Mary in the apse.

Detail from the funerary monument of Alessandro de Stefanis

including the addition of a dome and changes to the façade, some of which echoed motifs already used inside the church. The upper part of the façade features pilasters, Corinthian columns, a large window and a curvilinear pediment with succoes, following the dictates of Ligurian Baroque churches in hilly areas.

Inside the sanctuary, as well as a valuable painting by Andrea Carlone (1639–97), a *St Joseph with Baby Jesus* on the left-hand altar, there are mementoes of the era of the Risorgimento, including the funerary monument of Alessandro de Stefanis, a local hero who died in 1848, and, in the parish office, a case with flags of subalpine peoples. The church is also famous for its *Nativity* (*presepe*), which contains figures dating from the 1700s.

Santuario di Oregina ⑤

Salita Oregina 44. **Map** 2 D1.
Tel 010 212 024. 39, 40.
8am–noon, 4–7pm daily.
Sun pm; afternoons in Aug.

The history of this sanctuary is linked with worship of the Madonna di Loreto. It stands at the top of a flight of steps, preceded by a tree-filled square, in a gorgeous panoramic position looking over the city and the sea. A group of monks singled out this area, which still had a strongly rustic character at the time, as a place of hermitage in 1634. They immediately built a simple chapel, but this was taken over by the Franciscan Friars Minor in the following year. The sanctuary, as it appears today, was built in 1650–55, with further modifications being made in 1707.

Castello D'Albertis ⑥

Corso Dogali 18. **Map** 2 E1. **Tel** 010 272 38 20/34 64. 39, 40.
Apr–Sep: 10am–6pm Tue–Fri, 10am–7pm Sat & Sun; Oct–Mar: 10am–5pm Tue–Fri, 10am–6pm Sat & Sun.
www.museidigenova.it

This fortress, built in just six years, from 1886 to 1892, occupies a striking position on the bastion of Monte-galletto, not far from the city centre. The man behind the building was the captain Enrico Alberto D'Albertis, a curious figure who was a courageous explorer and passionate about the project and building. He was the great exponent of the Neo-Gothic revival of that time, under the leadership of Alfredo D'Andrade, employed a group of four architects.

One of the most emblematic symbols of revivalism in Genoa, Castello D'Albertis stands out for the forcefulness of the complex: from its mighty 16th-century base to the battlemented towers; the terracotta cladding echoes a style used in similar Genoese Romanesque monuments.

The captain bequeathed the building to the town council in 1932, together with the ethnographic collections that are now on display in the **Museo Etnografico** that now occupies the castle. Among items left by the captain are several sundials (made by D'Albertis himself), nautical instruments and geographical publications, as well as arms from that era. The museum also received a donation of finds from the American Committee of Catholic Missions in 1892. This included Native American costumes, crafts and jewellery and terracotta pieces, masks, stone sculptures and vases dating from the Mayan and Aztec civilizations. Other acquisitions include objects from South-East Asia, Oceania and New Guinea.

An aerial view of the impressive Castello D'Albertis

Parco Durazzo Pallavicini ❸

The man responsible for transforming the gardens of the Villa Durazzo Pallavicini was Michele Canzio, set designer at Genoa's Teatro Carlo Felice *(see p55)*. Between 1837 and 1846 he created a splendid English-style garden, following the romantic fashion of the time. He was commissioned by Marchese Ignazio Alessandro Pallavicini, who inherited the villa from his aunt Clelia Pallavicini Durazzo. She was passionate about plants and had begun a botanic garden here in the late 18th century. Today, more than 100 varieties of exotic species, including tropical carnivorous plants, are grown here. The park covers around 11 ha (27 acres).

One of the four Tritons around the Temple of Diana

Cappelletta della Madonna

Mausoleum of the captain

The 14th-century castle stands on the top of the hill, well concealed among trees. Squarely constructed around a circular, battlemented tower, the castle was conceived as the house of an imaginary lord of the time. The interior features fresco and stucco decoration, as do most of the other buildings in the park. The castle, sadly, is not open to the public.

Swiss chalet

THE PARK AS A STAGE SET

Frieze on the Temple of Flora

As a set designer, it is perhaps not surprising that Michele Canzio saw the park as a stage for a historical fairy tale, whose story unwinds en route through the grounds and evokes musings on the mystery of existence. The narrative, typical of a romantic melodrama, consists of a prologue and three acts of four scenes each. The prologue is made up of the Gothic Avenue and the Classic Avenue, while the first act, Return to Nature, develops through the hermitage, a pleasure garden, the old lake and the spring. The second act, representing the Recovery of History, passes from the shrine of the Madonna to the Swiss chalet and on to the captain's castle and the tombs and mausoleum of the captain. The third and final act, Purification, takes in the grottoes, the big lake, a statue of Flora (the goddess of flowers) and her charming temple, with a small square ("remembrance") surrounded by cypresses and a stream.

★ Temple of Diana

This circular Ionic-style temple, dedicated to the Graeco-Roman goddess of hunting, stands in a wonderful position at the centre of the lake. A statue of Diana, the work of Gian Battista Cevasco, poses elegantly beneath the dome, while four tritons stand guard in the water around the temple.

Turkish kiosk

Coffee house

Temple of Flora

This feminine, octagonal building could not be dedicated to anyone other than a goddess, the ancient protectress of the plant kingdom. Located just south of the lake, and surrounded by box hedges, the temple is a sign of the renewed interest in the Classical Greek and Roman periods that was so influential in the 19th century.

The Triumphal Arch bears

an inscription in Latin which invites the onlooker to forget city life and become immersed in the appreciation of nature. The reliefs and statues were by Gian Battista Cevasco.

The Chinese Pagoda

The pagoda roof is adorned with little bells and sculpted dragons. This Jun and exotic construction, one of the most charming in the entire park, is built on the lake and can be reached across a double iron bridge.

VISITORS' CHECKLIST

Via Pallavicini 13, Pegli.
Tel 010 698 1048. 📠 1, 2, 3.
🕐 9am–7pm (Oct–Mar: 9am–
5pm Tue–Sun. 🚫 25 Dec,
1 Jan. 📷 💷 🅿 🛍 🚻

Santuario della Madonnetta ❼

Salita della Madonnetta, 5. **Map** 2 F1. **Tel** 010 272 53 08. 🚠 *Zecca–Right funicular.* 🚌 33. ⏱ *9am–noon, 3:30–6pm daily.*

Lying at the end of a *creuza*, one of Liguria's distinctive steep narrow streets, paved with brick, this sanctuary is one of the highlights along the Circonvallazione a Monte. The complex Baroque building was erected in 1696 for the Augustine Order. The delightful area paved with black and white pebbles outside dates from the 18th century. On one side a niche contains a marble sculpture of a *Pietà* by Domenico Parodi. The interior is also charming, with a light-filled central chamber in the form of an irregular octagon linked to the presbytery by two side staircases. Another ramp leads beneath the presbytery down to the so-called "scurolo", an underground chamber on whose altar stands a revered statue of the *Madonnetta* (17th century), from which the current

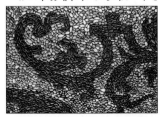

Paving at the Santuario della Madonnetta

the sanctuary takes its name; it is the work of Giovanni Romano. In the chapel alongside is a wooden *Pietà* (1733), by Anton Maria Maragliano.

The sanctuary's crypt houses some of Genoa's best-loved nativity scenes (*presepi*), of particular interest because of their faithful reproduction of parts of the old city centre. The wooden figures were carved mainly in the 17th and 18th centuries, including some by Maragliano and others by the Gagini, a hugely talented family of sculptors originally from Lombardy.

In the sacristy visitors can see an interesting rendition of the *Annunciation* (1490), attributed to Ludovico Brea, a native of Nice who was active in Liguria from around 1475 to 1520 (*see p159*).

San Bartolomeo degli Armeni ❽

Piazza San Bartolomeo degli Armeni 2. **Map** 6 F1. **Tel** 010 839 24 96. 🚌 33. ⏱ *7:30–11:30am, 4–6:30pm daily.* 📷

This church was founded in 1308 by Basilian monks (followers of St Basil) and then passed to the Barnabites, who rebuilt it in 1775 and are the current

occupants. The church is almost completely enclosed by a 19th-century building, but still has its bell tower, dating from 1300.

San Bartolomeo owes its fame to the fact that it is home to the relic of Santo Volto (Holy Face), a piece of linen with an image of the face of Jesus Christ. People also call it "Santo Sudario", or "Mandillo" (handkerchief in the local dialect). This relic was given to Leonardo Montaldo, doge of Genoa, in 1362 by the Constantinople emperor Giovanni V Paleologo, in return for military assistance. The doge, in turn, gave the relic to the Basilian monks. Much of the decoration inside the church relates to the tradition of the relic. The Santo Volto itself is set against a background of gold and silver filigree (a masterpiece of Byzantine goldsmithery), with ten embossed tiles describing the origins of the portrait and later episodes in its history.

Triptych depicting the Madonna and Saints in San Bartolomeo, 1415

THE NATIVITY SCENES TRADITION

The spread of the cult of the nativity scene (*presepe*) may date back to the Jesuits, who were particularly active in Genoa in the first half of the 17th century. Although the tradition was not as strong here as in Naples, it was nonetheless very popular. During the 17th and 18th centuries, aristocratic houses assembled *presepi* but kept them in private family chapels. The scenes were eventually made public and bourgeois families of the late 19th century and early 20th century became accustomed to making special visits to the *presepi* at Christmas.

Today, it is possible to follow the 19th-century custom all year round. Several churches still display nativity scenes, including the Madonnetta and Oregina sanctuaries. Typical figures, usually carved from wood, sometimes made of coloured wax or plaster, included those of a young, smiling peasant girl, an old peasant woman with a grotesque expression, and a lame beggar (*to zoppo*); the latter became a famous symbol of poverty and need.

Nativity scene at the Santuario della Madonnetta

The most valuable work of art is the triptych on the high altar, *Madonna and Saints*, by Turino Vanni (1415).

City Walls and Fortresses 9

Parco Urbano delle Mura.
FS Genova–Casella line. 🚌 40, 64.
🚋 Zecca–Right funicular (terminus).
ℹ️ organized by Cooperativa DAFNE (010 247 39 25).

Genoa's defensive walls have been rebuilt or moved several times over the centuries. Traces remain of the 1155 and 1536 walls, but the impressive 13-km (8-mile) triangle of walls that still encloses the city dates from the 1600s. These fortifications, which became known as La Nuova Mura ("the new wall"), were designed in part by Bartolomeo Bianco, and became one of the city's outstanding features. Major alterations had to be made to the walls in the 1800s, after attacks by Austrian troops made clear their inadequacy; most of the forts along their length date from this period. The best way to explore the old walls is to drive along the scenic Strada delle Mura, which begins at Piazza Manin, north of the Centro Storico, and follows the line of what remains of the 17th-century walls (and which also defines the boundaries of the Parco Urbano delle Mura). Piazza Manin itself is home to the

fanciful **Castello Mackenzie** (1896–1906), the work of Gino Coppedè, which embraces medieval, Renaissance and even Art Nouveau influences. Travelling along the line of the walls in an anti-clockwise direction, you reach **Forte Castellaccio**, mentioned in the 13th century but rebuilt in the 16th century by Andrea Doria and again altered in the 1830s; within its ring of bastions is the Torre della Specola, where condemned men were once hanged. **Forte Sperone** juts out on the top of Monte Peralto, at the apex of the triangle. Originally 16th-century, the massive citadel you see today was built in 1826–7 by the House of Savoy. Inland from Forte Sperone, off the line of the city walls, lies **Forte Puin** (accessible by train from the Genoa–Casella line), completed in 1828. Its square tower is one of the key landmarks in the Parco Urbano delle Mura. Polygonal **Forte Diamante**, the furthest inland of the forts, is in a high and delightful position. Dating from 1758, it has survived almost intact. Back along the walls, **Forte Begato** has a rectangular layout, with robust buttresses supporting bastions from which there are fine views. **Forte Tenaglia**, which dominates the Valle del Polcevera, was first recorded in the 16th century; its horn-shaped structure, acquired in the 19th century, was badly damaged in World War II.

Aerial view of Forte Diamante, along the line of the old city walls

Cimitero di Staglieno 10

Piazzale Resasco 1.
Tel 010 870 184. 🚌 12, 14, 34, 48. 🕐 7:30am–5pm daily. 🔴 1 Jan, Easter Monday, 1 May, 24 Jun, 15 Aug, 8 Dec, 26 Dec. www.comunegenova.it

This vast and extraordinary monumental Neo-Classical cemetery on the bank of the River Bisagno, northeast of the city centre, was designed by Carlo Barabino, but he died before the grand project was carried out (1844–51). Containing a great panoply of grandiose and exuberant monuments to the dead, the cemetery fills an area of 160 ha (395 acres), hence the shuttle bus which ferries people around. In a dominant position, on the side of the hill, stands the circular Cappella dei Suffragi, adorned with statues by Cevasco, sculptor of the statues in the Parco Durazzo Pallavicini (*see pp84–5*). Other works of note include the colossal 19th-century marble statue of *Faith* by Santo Varni, and, probably the best-known monument at Staglieno, the tomb of Giuseppe Mazzini, the great philosopher of the Risorgimento. Also buried here, in the Protestant section, is the wife of Lord Byron, Constance Mary Lloyd. Two wooded areas – the broad Boschetto Regolare and an area of winding paths known as the Boschetto Irregolare – enhance the atmosphere of the place.

The funerary monument to Giuseppe Mazzini at Staglieno

GIUSEPPE MAZZINI

San Siro di Struppa ⓫

Via di Creto 64.
Tel 010 809 000. 🚌 12, 14. ⏱ summer:8am-8pm daily; winter: 8am-6:30pm. 🚗 ⓖ

This abbey church sits in an isolated position among pretty gardens and rows of vines in the district of Struppa, the most north-easterly part of Genoa. Mentioned in 13th-century documents, it was built around 1000 and named after the bishop of Genoa, San Siro, who was born here in the 4th century. From the late 16th century onwards, the church was tampered with periodically, by the end of which its early Romanesque appearance had greatly suffered. Separate projects to restore the building, carried out in the 1920s and 1960s, have restored San Siro to its original form, including the decorative masonry in grey sandstone and the pavement of black and white pebbles outside the church. The façade, pierced by a rose window, is divided by pilasters into three sections

Wooden statue of San Siro, 1640

Inside, traces of the original fresco decoration are still visible, and the columns in the nave have interesting capitals. On the wall in the right-hand aisle is an almost jaunty, heavily gilded wooden statue of *San Siro*, dating from 1640 and much restored. The high altar is modern, but visitors should notice that the front part was the architrave of a door from a 16th-century palazzo in Genoa.
The splendid *Polyptych of San Siro* (depicting the saint enthroned, eight scenes from his life and the Virgin and Child) dates from 1516. It is possibly the work of Pier Francesco Sacchi and hangs in the left-hand aisle.

Polyptych of San Siro (1516), San Siro di Struppa

Albaro ⓬

Road Map D3.

Albaro was one of the towns annexed to the city in 1926. It marks the start of the eastern, Levante zone of Greater Genoa, an almost unbroken succession of settlements rich in both artistic and historical interest, extending as far as Nervi. The scenic Corso d'Italia road hugs the coast along the way.
Since the Middle Ages, Albaro has been a popular spot for Genoa's high nobility to build their country houses. It remains the residential district par excellence of the city. Though now rather over-developed, it boasts a series of beautiful suburban villas. One of these is the 16th-century **Villa Saluzzo Bombrini**, also known as "il Paradiso". Its charming Renaissance garden features in *Trattenimento in un Giardino di Albaro* (1735), the famous painting by Alessandro Magnasco, now in Palazzo Bianco *(see p71)*. **Villa Saluzzo Mongiardino**, dating from the early 18th century, played host to the English poet Lord Byron in 1823. **Villa Giustiniani Cambiaso** (1548) is the work of the great Renaissance architect Galeazzo Alessi, and was highly influential at the time. Set in an elevated position, surrounded by

---

THE CASELLA TRAIN

FS Genova-Casella
Via alla Stazione per Casella 15, Genova. **Tel** 010 837 321. 🚌 33. www.ferroviagenovacasella.it

First opened in 1929, the Genova–Casella line is one of the few narrow-gauge railway tracks remaining in Italy. It takes around 55 minutes to make the 24-km (15-mile) journey from Piazza Manin in Genoa to the Apennine hinterland. The route passes through forests, over viaducts and through tunnels and reaches its highest point (458 m/1,503 ft) at Crocetta, the ancient border of the Genoese republic; Casella, at 410 m (1,345 ft), is the head of the line. This mountain railway follows a steep gradient and is known as the "tre valli", after three valleys, the Val Bisagno, Val Polcevera and Valle Scrivia. The small stations along the way (Trensasco, Campi, Pino, Torrazza, Sardorella, Vicomorasso and Sant'Olcese) are starting points for walking and biking trails (bikes can be hired at the stations), and have trattorias eager to feed hungry travellers. You can choose to travel either in a modern or period carriage; either way, you should book.

The Casella train crossing a viaduct

extensive grounds, it is now houses the university's faculty of engineering. Inside are decorative reliefs which are reminiscent of Classicism and Roman Mannerism. Two frescoes by the Bergamo artist Gian Battista Castello and Luca Cambiaso embellish the upstairs loggia.

The picturesque fishing village of Boccadasse

Boccadasse ⑬

Road Map D3.

At the start of the Riviera di Levante, but still within Greater Genoa, Boccadasse is a fishing village which has managed to retain its picturesque charm. The houses, their façades painted in lively colours, are tightly packed around the small harbour. This is one of the most popular destinations for the Genoese, who come for day trips, especially at the weekends. It has also become very popular with tourists, for whom Boccadasse has the air of a place where time has stood still.

Nervi ⑭

Road Map D3. **FS**
www.nervi.ge.it

Nervi was, from the second half of the 19th century, a major holiday destination for the European aristocracy, especially the English. These days it is better known for its international dance festival, held in the summer.

The town's seaside location, gardens and art are the main attractions. A path called the Passeggiata Anita Garibaldi, created for Marchese Gaetano Groppallo in the 19th century, offers one of the most beautiful panoramas in Italy, with views along Nervi's own rocky shore and, beyond, the entire Riviera di Levante as far as Monte di Portofino. The 2-km (1-mile) path passes the 16th-century Torre Groppallo, which was later modified by the Marchese in Neo-Medieval style.

In the town, the gardens of three villas have been combined to form a single park, planted with exotic or typically Mediterranean species and extending over 9 ha (22 acres).

Portrait of Miss Bell, by Boldini, Raccolte Frugone

The first of these, Villa Groppallo, houses the town library, while Villa Serra contains the **Galleria d'Arte Moderna**, a gallery with a fine gathering of Ligurian paintings from the last two centuries. Villa Grimaldi Fassio houses the **Raccolte Frugone**, with mainly figurative works from the 19th and 20th centuries.

The **Museo Giannettino Luxoro** has three paintings by Alessandro Magnasco, but is best known for its decorative arts, including ceramics, clocks and nativity scene figures.

▥ Galleria d'Arte Moderna
Villa Serra, Via Capolungo 3. **Tel** 010 372 60 25.
◷ 10am–7pm Tue–Sun. ♿

▥ Raccolte Frugone
Villa Grimaldi Fassio, Via Capolungo 9. **Tel** 010 322 396. ◷ 9am–7pm Tue–Fri, 10am–7pm Sat & Sun. ♿ 🖾

▥ Museo Giannettino Luxoro
Villa Luxoro, Via Mafalda di Savoia 3. **Tel** 010 322 673. ◷ 9am–1pm Tue–Fri, 10am–1pm Sat. 📷 with permission. 🖾
www.museodigenova.it

The Villa Luxoro at Nervi, home to the Museo Giannettino Luxoro

GENOA STREET FINDER

The attractions described in the Genoa section of this guide, as well as the city's restaurants and hotels (listed in the Travellers' Needs section), all carry a map reference, which refers to the six maps in this Street Finder. The page grid below shows which parts of Genoa are covered by these maps. A complete index of the names of streets and squares marked on the maps can be found on the following pages. In addition, the maps show other sights and useful institutions (including ones not mentioned in this guide), including post offices, police stations, hospitals, bus stations and railway termini, sports grounds, public parks, and the principal places of worship in the Ligurian capital. The medieval part of Genoa is made up of an intricate web of narrow streets and alleys, and therefore maps 5 and 6 feature an enlarged map of the Centro Storico, in order to help visitors orientate themselves within this complicated labyrinth.

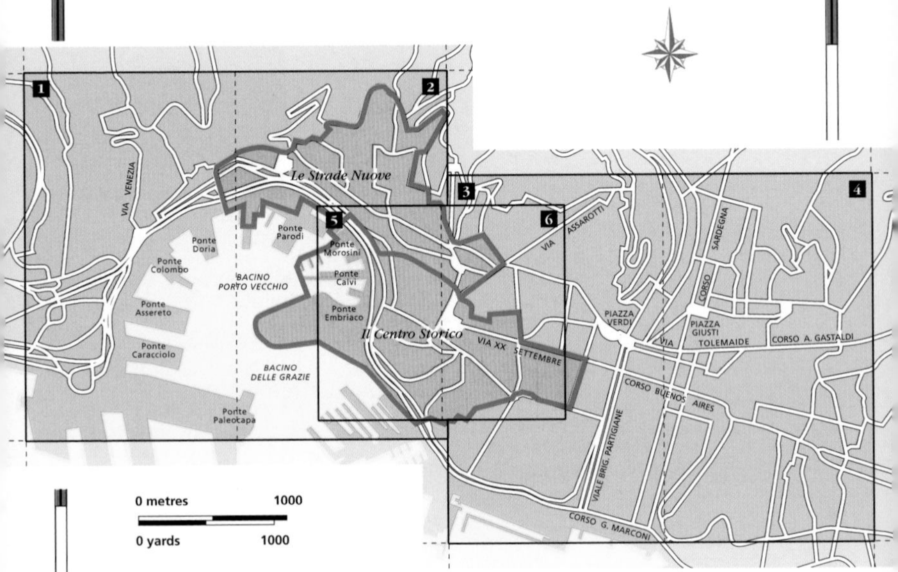

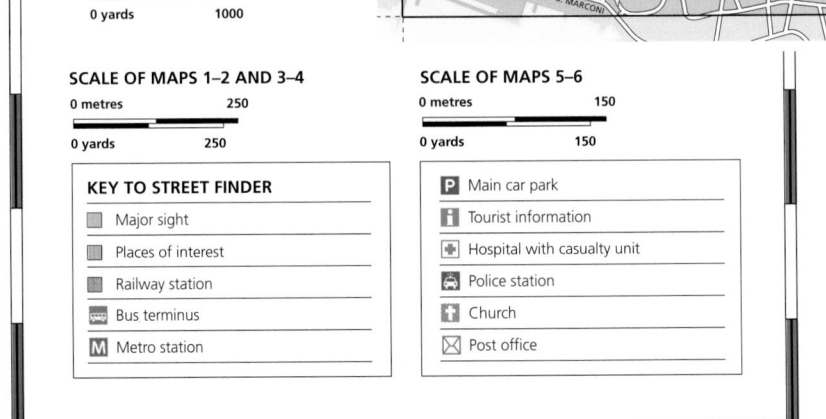

| 0 metres | 1000 |
| 0 yards | 1000 |

SCALE OF MAPS 1–2 AND 3–4

| 0 metres | 250 |
| 0 yards | 250 |

SCALE OF MAPS 5–6

| 0 metres | 150 |
| 0 yards | 150 |

KEY TO STREET FINDER

▨	Major sight
▨	Places of interest
▨	Railway station
🚌	Bus terminus
Ⓜ	Metro station

🅿	Main car park
ℹ	Tourist information
✚	Hospital with casualty unit
🚓	Police station
✝	Church
⊠	Post office

Street Finder Index

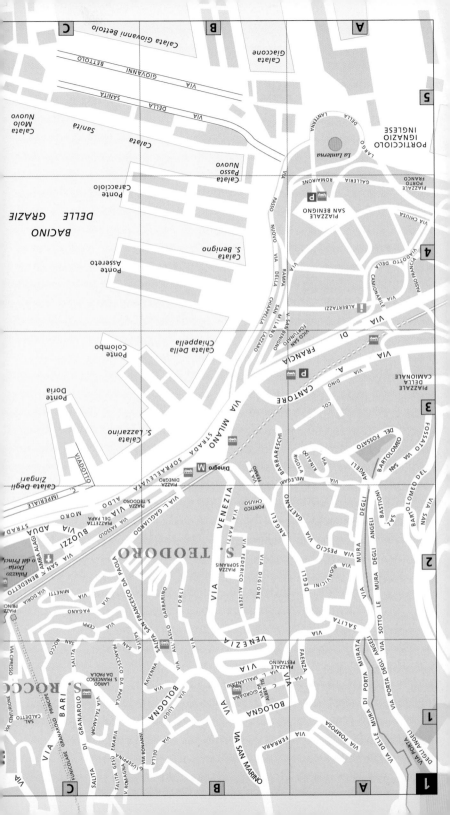

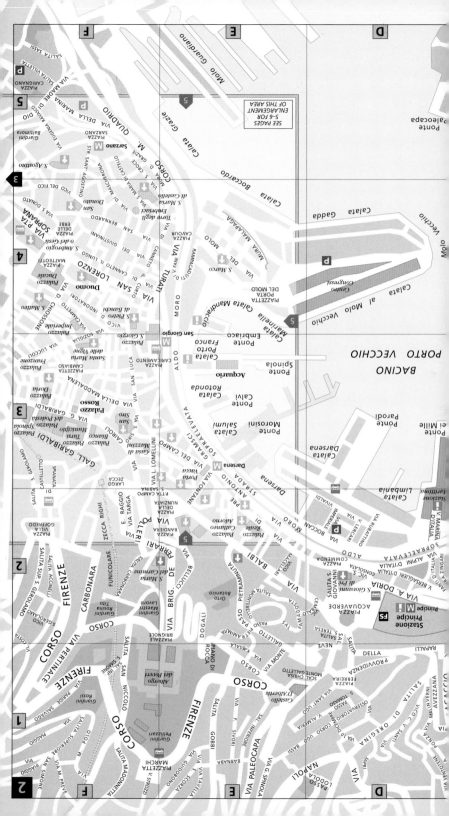

SEE PAGES 5–6 FOR
ENLARGEMENT
OF THIS AREA

BACINO
PORTO VECCHIO

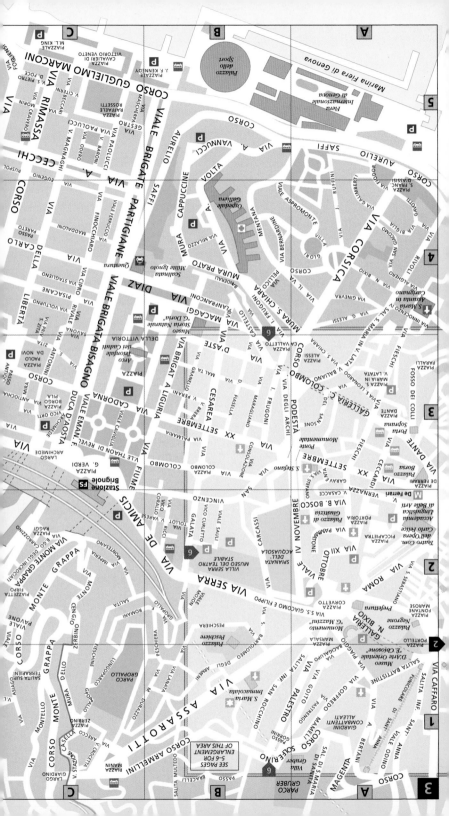

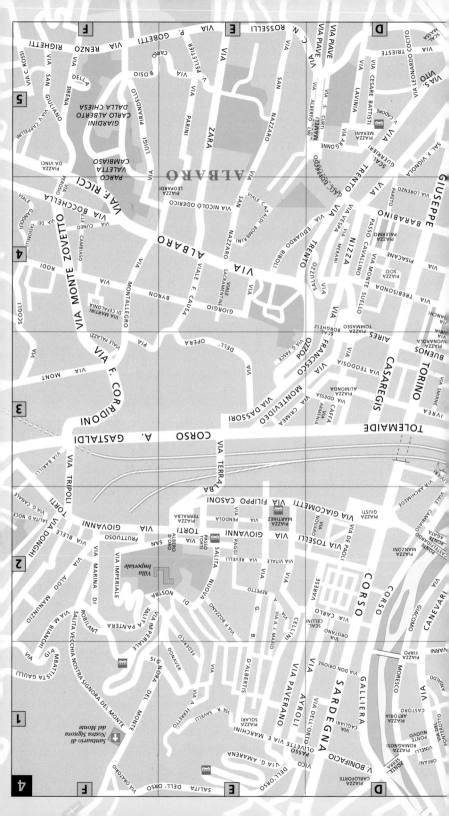

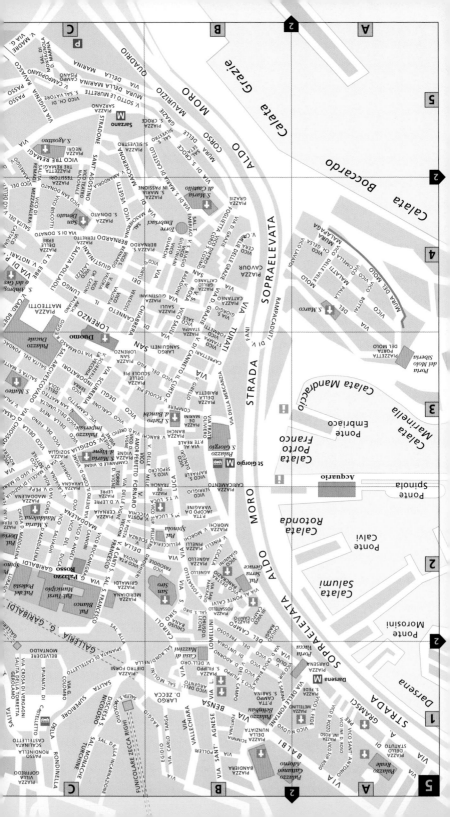

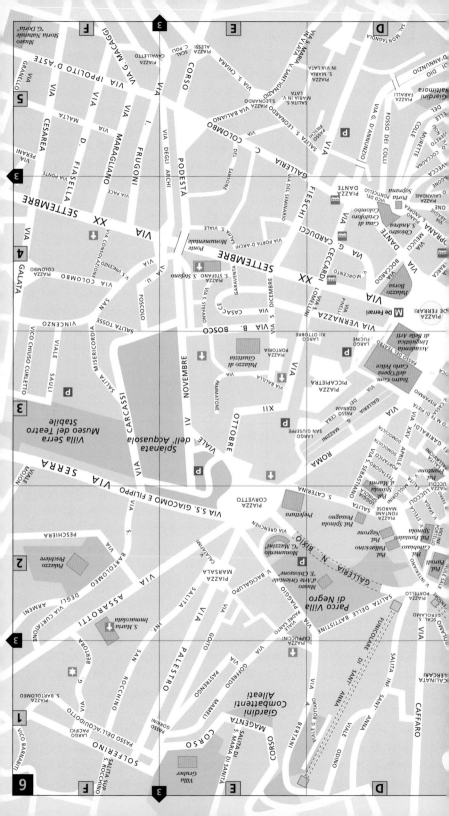

THE ITALIAN
RIVIERA AREA
BY AREA

The Italian Riviera at a Glance

Liguria may be one of the smallest regions in Italy but it still has plenty to offer. As well as dramatic landscapes, both along the coast and in the mountains behind, the region has a rich cultural history. Genoa, the Ligurian capital, lies midway along the coast. To the east of the city lies the Riviera di Levante (which includes La Spezia, a provincial capital), bordering the regions of Tuscany and Emilia-Romagna. To the west is the Riviera di Ponente, which meets the border with France, and has two more provincial capitals, Savona and Imperia. Liguria's long, rocky coast is often superbly picturesque, particularly in the Cinque Terre and the headland of Portofino, both on the Riviera di Levante. Punctuating the shores are seaside resorts which are buzzing with life in summer, as well as towns of historic interest such as Albenga and Bordighera. The often forested and mountainous hinterland (the so-called *entroterra*) is also home to some fascinating medieval towns, such as Pieve di Teco, Pigna and Dolceacqua.

Albenga (see pp148–51) *shelters within its historic centre some of the oldest and most significant monuments in the region, such as the cathedral of San Michele (above) and the Early Christian baptistry.*

THE RIVIERA DI PONENTE
(see pp130–171)

The Casino (see p164) *in San Remo is an example of the Art Nouveau style so popular in the heyday of this wonderful and old-fashioned seaside resort. San Remo is also known for its Festival of Italian Song.*

The town of Cervo (see p153) *clings to a peak and is overlooked by the lovely parish church of San Giovanni Battista (1686–1734). This fine example of Ligurian Baroque has a great concave façade embellished with stuccoes.*

◁ The seafront at Camogli, on the Riviera di Levante, with its brightly painted palazzi

**The town of
Portofino** (see pp110–11)
*is packed with tall, narrow,
pastel-coloured houses
gathered around a small
harbour. This is one of the
most appealing sites in the
entire region, on one of
Italy's most famous
stretches of coastline.*

Luni (see p127), *close to
the border with
Tuscany, is an
important
archaeological site
with a large Roman
amphitheatre. It is
also the source of
these prehistoric
statue-stelae.*

THE RIVIERA DI LEVANTE
(see pp104–129)

0 kilometres   20

0 miles   20

The church of San Pietro
(see p120) *at Portovenere
stands on a rocky promontory
overlooking the sea. The
striped church dates from
the 6th century.*

THE RIVIERA DI LEVANTE

*T*houghts turn, inevitably, when considering this part of the world, to the great poets who have lauded it, including the romantic poets Percy Bysshe Shelley and Lord Byron; there is even a gulf named in their honour. These poets and other writers have celebrated the enchantment of the Riviera di Levante, the gentleness of the climate, the colourful flowers and the beautiful coves.

This stunningly beautiful area genuinely deserves their praise. The often beautifully positioned coastal resorts and villages are truly delightful, the result of the combined efforts of man and nature. The contrast between the sea and the steep mountains immediately behind adds to the fascination, which only increases as you head inland, into the jagged valleys and ravines where villages cling to hilltops.

The Riviera di Levante is home to a number of chic resorts – including Portofino, Santa Margherita Ligure and Rapallo – once the haunt of European, and particularly English aristocrats, but now frequented mainly by Italians. Tourism has thrived in this area since the 1800s, though this formidable success has meant the arrival of mass tourism and, with it, inevitably, over-development in some areas and periods of overcrowding (both on the beaches and the roads). But what may seem like high-season chaos to some, is liveliness and fun to others.

Largely in response to the effects of increased development, including pollution and erosion, nature reserves, national parks and other protected areas have been founded both along the coast (such as the Cinque Terre) and inland, and are a vital contribution to the conservation of this precious landscape.

The way of life in the interior is a world away from the bustling scene on the coast. Steep valleys, formed by the rivers Magra, Vara and Aveto, cut deep into the landscape and are carpeted with dense forest. There is a serious problem of population decline in some areas (a problem common to all parts of the Italian Apennines), but village communities do survive in the hinterland, dependent mostly on agriculture.

Green shutters and flower-filled balconies, a feature of Ligurian houses

◁ The church of San Pietro at Portovenere, in a lovely position by the sea

Exploring the Riviera di Levante

This slim tongue of land starts just south of Genoa and runs as far as the easterly region of Lunigiana. Dotted along the coast are famous beaches and pretty resorts, from Camogli, Rapallo and Portofino in the west to Portovenere in the east. The inland mountains and valleys are less visited, but shelter attractive towns of both historical and architectural interest, such as Varese Ligure and Sarzana, and the archeological ruins at Luni; walks through chestnut woods reveal the contrast with the exuberant Mediterranean flora of the coast. Important monuments in the region include the forts of Sarzana, the churches of San Salvatore dei Fieschi and Sant'Andrea di Borzone and the abbey of San Fruttuoso, examples of the magnificent Romanesque and Gothic architecture which developed in the 3rd and 4th centuries in the region.

SEE ALSO

- *Where to Stay* pp178–81
- *Where to Eat* pp191–4

Tellaro at sunset

Fishing boats at Manarola, one of the villages in the Cinque Terre

SIGHTS AT A GLANCE

The seafront at La Spezia, the easternmost city on the Riviera di Levante

KEY

═══	Motorway
──	Main road
····	Minor road
⌁	Railway
──	Regional border
△	Summit

GETTING AROUND

The main communication routes in the Riviera di Levante are the A12 (the motorway linking Livorno with Genoa) and the A15, linking Parma to La Spezia. Running the length of the coast is the Via Aurelia (Strada Statale 1). Numerous roads link the coast to the hinterland, often travelling through spectacular landscapes. The Genoa–Livorno railway line provides train links, with regional and local train services connecting all towns and villages, with the important exception of Portofino. Efficient coach services ensure daily links between all the towns on the coast and those inland. In high season, there are also ferry services running between the key centres along the coast between Portofino and La Spezia, including the Cinque Terre, as well as to the most popular offshore islands.

Bogliasco ❶

Genoa. Road Map D4. 🚉 4,600. 🚌
FS 🚉 **ℹ️** *Via Aurelia 106, 010 347
04 29.* 🎉 *Festa Patronale della
Madonna del Carmine (Jul).* **www**
.prolocobogliasco.it

On the aptly named Golfo
di Paradiso east of Genoa,
Bogliasco is an elegant
residential and tourist town
with a few small beaches.
It retains the look of a
traditional fishing village,
though, with painted houses
arranged prettily around the
mouth of the River Bogliasco
(crossed by a medieval bridge
known as the Ponte Romano).
The town is dominated by
the 1,000-year-old **Castello,**
a defensive tower built by the
Republic of Genoa. To the
west, high up on a cliff, is the
18th-century parish church,
with a terrace of black and
white pebbles in front. The
Oratory of Santa Chiara
(15th century) is also of note.
Inside are several traditional,
highly ornate, processional
crosses, among them one
by Maragliano (1713).

Typically painted façades in
Bogliasco

Torriglia ❷

Genoa. Road Map D3. 🚉 2,300. **FS**
🚌 **ℹ️** **Ente Parco d'Antola.**
*Via Nostra Signora della Providenza 3,
010 944 931.* 🎉 *Presepe di Pentema
(Dec–Jan).* **www**.parcoantola.it

This small summer holiday
resort is distinguished by its
position among the forested
Antola mountains. In the
Roman period it was a

significant commercial centre,
located as it was at an
important crossroads on the
main route between Genoa
and Emilia-Romagna.

The town is overlooked
by the imposing ruins of a
medieval **castle.** Built by the
Malaspina family, it was later
occupied by the Fieschi
family and, from the second
half of the 16th century, by
the Doria dynasty.

Environs

Two pleasant trips can be
made from Torriglia. The
first is to **Pentema**, about
6 km (4 miles) north of the
town along a winding road.
Having crossed a totally
unspoilt landscape of hills
and mountains covered in
dense forest, you reach one
of the loveliest villages inland
from the Riviera di Levante.
Pentema consists of a handful
of houses scattered on a sun-
facing hill, with a church at
the top. The houses, set on
terraces, are identical, all very
simple and with chalet-style
roofs. The village streets are
still paved with river stones,
or simply earth.

Absolute silence seems
to reign at the wonderfully
peaceful **Lago del Brugneto,**
some 8 km (5 miles) east of
Torriglia. An artificial basin
created as a reservoir for
Genoa, the lake lies within
the **Parco Regionale del
Monte Antola** and is entirely
surrounded by hills and
mountains. A scenic walking
trail snakes around the shores
of the lake: some 13 km
(8 miles) long, the walk takes
about six hours to complete.

Camogli ❸

Genoa. Road Map D4. 🚉 5,900.
FS 🚌 **ℹ️** *Via XX Settembre 33,
0185 771 066.* 🎉 *Sagra del Pesce
(second Sun in May; 0185 729 01).*
www.camogli.it

An old fishing and seafaring
village on the Golfo di
Paradiso, Camogli is named
after the women (*moglie*)
who ran the town while their
husbands were at sea. It has
an enchanting medieval heart,
with tall, narrow houses
(some are over six storeys
high) crowded around the
harbour and along the maze
of alleys and steps behind.
A small promontory, known
as the "Isola" (island) because
it was once separated from
the mainland, is home to the
**Basilica di Santa Maria
Assunta.** Founded in the 12th
century but much modified,
it has a Neo-Classical façade
and a 17th-century pebbled
courtyard. The interior is
richly decorated: the vault in
the central nave has a fresco
by Francesco Semino and
Nicolò Barabino, and the
high altar has a sculpture of
the Virgin Mary by Bernardo
Schiaffino (18th century).
On a cliff overlooking the
sea stands **Castel Dragone,**
medieval but much altered.
The **Museo Marinaro Gio
Bono Ferrari,** at the end of
the seafront, documents a
glorious period in Camogli's
history that seems almost
unthinkable today: namely,
the 18th and 19th centuries,
when Camogli supplied a
fleet of some 3,000 merchant
ships under contract to the

The seafront at Camogli with the "Isola " in the background

For hotels and restaurants in this region see pp178–81 and pp191–4

The seafront at Santa Margherita Ligure

major European states; they even fought with Napoleon. Camogli's fishing fleet today is tiny by comparison.

The museum contains models of ships, navigational instruments and also paintings of ships (often by the ships' owners), which served as ex votos. The cloister next to the sanctuary of **Nostra Signora del Boschetto**, just outside Camogli, is also full of sailors' ex votos.

If you are in the area in May, don't miss the famous Sagra del Pesce, when vast numbers of fish are cooked in a giant frying pan *(see p28).*

🏛 **Museo Gio Bono Ferrari**
Via GB Ferrari, 41.
Tel *0185 729 049.*
☐ *9am–noon Mon, Thu & Fri; 9am–noon, 3–6pm Wed, Sat, Sun & hols (4–7pm Jun–Sep).*

Portofino Peninsula ➍

See pp110–13.

Santa Margherita Ligure ➎

Genoa. **Road Map** E4. 🏯 *10,800.*
🚆 🚌 ℹ *Via XXV Aprile 2/B, 0185 287 485.* 🎭 *Nostra Signora della Rosa (Jul).* **www**.turismoinliguria.it

Built along an inlet on the Golfo del Tigullio, Santa Margherita is a lively resort with a beautiful harbour and grand hotels and villas. The lavish rococo church of Santa Margherita d'Antiochia gave the town its name.

Santa Margherita emerged in its own right only in the 19th century, when it was created out of the two villages of Pescino and Corte. It soon became a popular destination among the (mainly British) holidaying elite.

The hill between the two old villages has been transformed into the public **Parco di Villa Durazzo**. The villa at the top, begun in the mid-16th century, still has its original furnishings as well as an art collection. The large Italian-style garden offers lovely views of the city and the sea.

At the foot of the hill, in the district known as Corte, is the 17th-century church of the Cappuccini, with a 15th-century wooden cross.

Rapallo ➏

Genoa. **Road Map** E4. 🏯 *29,300.*
🚆 🚌 ℹ *Lungomare Vittorio Veneto 7, 0185 230 346.* 🎭 *Mostra Internazionale dei Cartoonists (Nov–Dec); Festa della Madonna di Montallegro (Jul).* **www**.turismoinliguria.it

Rapallo enjoys a gorgeous position on the Golfo del Tigullio and is perhaps the best-known resort along the Riviera di Levante. It has a large marina, swimming pool, sailing, tennis and riding schools, as well as an 18-hole golf course.

The climate was a big draw for aristocrats from the 19th century, as can be seen from the Art Nouveau cafés and hotels lining **Lungomare Vittorio Veneto**. Max Beerbohm (1872–1956), the English wit and critic, was a resident for many years.
In the centre, the parallel

streets Via Venezia, Via Mazzini and Via Marsala define the medieval "borgo murato" (walled village), so-named because of the way the buildings are closely packed together. Historic monuments include the old parish church of Santo Stefano (mostly 17th century) and the adjacent 15th-century civic tower, and the medieval Ponte di Annibale (Hannibal's bridge), with a single-span arch of 15 m (49 ft).

From Piazza Pastene, on the seafront, you can reach the **Castello**, built in 1551 on a cliff to defend the settlement against pirate raids. There is also a highly enjoyable funicular ride up to the **Santuario di Montallegro** (16th century), from where there are superb views of the coast and sea.

Villa Tigullio is home to the **Museo del Merletto**, a museum of lace with more than 1,400 pieces from the 16th to 19th centuries. Among these are lace clothing,

The castle at Rapallo, a defensive structure dating from 1551

lace for furnishing, and several 18–19th century pillows. There is also a collection of designs.

Environs
Just east of Rapallo, **Zoagli** is a small resort which still feels like a fishing village despite being bombed in World War II.

🏛 **Museo del Merletto**
Villa Tigullio, Parco Casale.
Tel *0185 633 05.*
☐ *3–6pm Tue, Wed, Fri & Sat; 10–11:30am Thu & Sun.* 🎦

Portofino Peninsula ④

This headland extends for around 3 km (2 miles) out to
sea and separates the Paradiso and Tigullio gulfs. The
southern part, hot and dry, has high cliffs that enclose
gorgeous inlets hidden in the Mediterranean maquis;
on the northern side, woods of chestnut trees
dominate. The small area is extraordinarily rich
botanically, and its favourable position has drawn
human settlements since antiquity: *Portus Delphini*
(the bay was, and still is, known for its large dolphin
population) was an important settlement in the Roman
era. Today, the peninsula is dotted with impossibly
picturesque hamlets and villages, including the
world-famous port and celebrity mecca of Portofino.
There are also magnificent
walks to be done, as well as
all kinds of maritime sports,
including some great diving.

A splendid view of the rocky coast
close to Portofino

Camogli
(see p108)

San Fruttuoso →

Cristo degli Abissi

*This bronze statue by Guido Galletti was
lowered into the sea at San Fruttuoso in
1954, a symbol of the attachment of the
Ligurian people to the sea. Every year, on
the last Sunday in July, garlands of flowers
are given to the statue in memory of those
who have lost their lives at sea. Divers pay
homage to the statue at all times of the year.*

★ San Fruttuoso

*A symbol of the Italian
heritage and conservation
organization FAI, to which it
has belonged since 1983, San
Fruttuoso is a delightful village
with houses grouped around a
Benedictine abbey, built by the
Doria family in the 1200s.
It is dominated by the church's
octagonal bell tower. Alongside is
the cloister and mausoleum of the
Doria family. San Fruttuoso is
accessible only by boat or on
foot: it is 30 minutes by boat from
Camogli, for example, or 75
minutes' walk from Portofino.*

For hotels and restaurants in this region see pp178–81 and pp191–4

Paraggi

In Paraggi, a short distance from Portofino, multicoloured houses are gathered around a small sandy cove, with terraces rising up the mountain behind. Nowadays, the once-flourishing trades of fishing and olive-pressing have given way to tourism. The views from here are beautiful.

VISITORS' CHECKLIST

Genoa. **Road Map** D4. ⚲ 590.

🚌 Santa Margherita Ligure.

🚢 Santa Margherita Ligure to Portofino. 🚢 boats around the Golfo del Tigullio and to Cinque Terre (Apr–Sep); 0185 284 670. 🛈 Via Roma 35, 0185 269 024. **Abbey of San Fruttuoso** *Tel* 0185 772 703. ◻ Mar, Apr & Sep: 10am–5:45pm daily, May– Oct: 10am–5:45pm daily, Jan, Feb, Nov & Dec: 10am–3:45pm Tue–Sun. ● Nov. 🚫

Santa Margherita Ligure (see p109)

STAR SIGHTS

★ Portofino

★ San Fruttuoso

Paraggi

0 kilometres 50

0 miles 50

KEY

- - - Boat Routes

Punta di Portofino can be reached on foot. Beyond the 16th-century Fortezza di San Giorgio, known as "Castle Brown", is the lighthouse and the Madonnina del Capo statue.

Fortezza di San Giorgio

Portofino

★ Portofino

The town, with its lovely harbour and rows of coloured houses facing the piazzetta, is best viewed from the headland opposite. The cove is sheltered both by its position and by the mountain range, which rises to a height of 600m (1,970 ft) and forms a 3-km (2-mile) long cliff behind the town. While small, the port still has space for 300 mooring berths.

◁ **View of Portofino's unmistakeable little harbour**

Chiavari ⑦

Genoa. **Road Map** E4.
🚃 *28,200*. 🚉
ℹ️ *Corso Assarotti 1, 0185 325 198.* 🎉 *Festa Patronale di Nostra Signora dell'Orto (2 Jul).*
www.provincia.genova.it

One of the principal cities in Liguria, Chiavari stands on an alluvial plan on the eastern shores of the Golfo del Tigullio and on the west bank of the Entella torrent. Called Clavarium ("Key to the valleys") by the Romans, the town was once known for its old crafts, particularly ship-building, chair-making and macramé. Nowadays, tourism is the most important source of income. The marina has space for some 450 boats.

The ruins of a necropolis, dating from the 8th–7th centuries BC, now held in the local archaeological museum, demonstrate that the area was inhabited by the Liguri Tigulli people in the pre-Roman era. The fortified town of Chiavari dates from 1178, when the Genoese expanded into the Riviera di Levante in their struggle with the power of the Fieschi family (arch rivals of the Doria dynasty).

The heart of Chiavari is Piazza Mazzini, around which the arcaded streets of the old city are laid out. One of these, Via dei Martiri della Liberazione, is a straight alleyway known as a

The old centre of Chiavari, with its characteristic arcaded streets

"carruggiu dritu"; it was occupied by the bourgeoisie from the 14th century. This street, Via Rivarola and Via Ravaschieri have porticoes made of the local slate. The cathedral, **Nostra Signora dell'Orto**, has 17th-century origins but many alterations were carried out in the 19th–20th centuries. The interior, richly decorated with gilded stucco and marble inlay, contains works by Orazio De Ferrari and Anton Maria Maragliano. The parish church of San Giovanni Battista was founded in 1182 but was rebuilt in 1624.

In the outskirts, at Bacezza, is the 15th-century **Santuario della Madonna delle Grazie**, from where there is a lovely view stretching from Porto-fino to Sestri Levante. Inside is a 16th-century cycle of frescoes by Teramo Piaggio and Luca Cambiaso.

Abbazia di Sant'Andrea di Borzone ⑧

Via Abbazia 63, Borzonasca.
Road Map E3. 🚃 *Chiavari.* 📷 *Tel 0185 342 503.* 🕐 *until sunset daily.* 📷 ♿

The lovely abbey of Sant'Andrea di Borzone can be reached along a winding road that runs eastwards from the centre of Borzonasca, an inland town some 16 km (10 miles) from Chiavari. Standing in splendid isolation, Sant'Andrea is one of the oldest Benedictine

The abbey of Sant'Andrea di Borzone, in a stunning position

settlements in Italy. It was founded in the 12th century by the monks of San Colombano in Bobbio (in Emilia-Romagna) and donated in 1184 to the Benedictines of Marseille, who reclaimed the land and used it for cultivation. The monks undertook a programme of terracing and irrigation: even today, despite the fact that the woods have begun to encroach, the remains of dry stone walls can still be seen along the paths. The abbey was rebuilt in the 13th century, at the behest of the Fieschi counts, but has managed to retain its original Romanesque look.

The church, with a square bell tower, is built of brick and stone. It has a single nave and a semicircular apse, and a cornice of terracotta arches. Several cloister columns survive from the old monastery. In the presbytery is a polyptych dating from 1484, by an unknown Genoese artist, and a slate tabernacle from 1513.

Santo Stefano d'Aveto ⑨

Genoa. **Road Map** E3. 🚃 *1,250.* 🚉 *Piazza del Popolo 6, 0185 880 46.* 🎉 *Cantamaggio (2 May).* www.provincia.genova.it and www.parks.it

Situated in an almost Alpine-looking hollow, dominated by Monte Maggiorasca, Santo Stefano is both a summer and a winter holiday resort. It is a popular centre for cross-country skiing. In summer, you can enjoy the simple pleasure of strolling around the pretty historic centre, with its winding alleys and small squares.

Close to the village are the isolated, imposing ruins of **Castello Malaspina**, built by the local nobles in the 12th century, and subsequently passed to the Fieschi and Doria families.

The Val d'Aveto was formed by the Aveto torrent, which carves out an upland plain southwest of the town, where pastures are enclosed by mountains covered in forests of silver fir, Norway spruce, and beech and ash trees. Much of this is now part of the **Parco Naturale Regionale dell'Aveto**.

From Santo Stefano, you can reach Monte Aiona, the tallest peak in the park at 1,700 m (5,576 ft), along trails that show off the beauty of this wild, unspoilt area. Note that the western slopes form part of the **Riserva Naturale delle Agoraie** and are open only to those doing scientific research.

Another area of interest is the great forest of Le Lame, where there are marshes and small lakes of glacial origin. The icy cold water has perfectly preserved some 2,500-year-old fir trunks, which can be seen lying on the bottom of Lago degli Abeti.

Logo of the Parco Naturale dell'Aveto

Lavagna ⑩

Genoa. **Road Map** E4. 🚗 12,900. 🚉 **i** *Piazza della Libertà 48/A, 0185 395 070.* 🎉 *Torta dei Fieschi (7–14 Aug).* www.provincia.genova.it

The town of Lavagna lies across the Entella from Chiavari, to which it is linked by several bridges, including the fine medieval Ponte della Maddalena.

In the Middle Ages this coastal town was a stronghold of the local Fieschi counts. Historically, its prosperity has been due largely to the local slate quarries. Nowadays, the town depends more on its beach and marina, which has space for more than 1,500 yachts. The town's medieval heart developed inland from the sea, from what is now Via Nuova Italia. Historic monuments include the church of **Santo Stefano**, dating from the 10th century, but rebuilt in 1653, when a Baroque staircase and asymmetrical bell towers were added, the imposing 17th-century Palazzo Franzone, now the town hall, and the church of **Santa Giulia di Centaura** (1654), reached along a scenic road from Viale Mazzini and with panoramic views along the coast.

Environs

A short drive or 30 minutes' walk inland from Lavagna lies the village of San Salvatore di Cogorno, from where you can reach the **Basilica di San Salvatore dei Fieschi**, one of the most important Romanesque-Gothic monuments in Liguria. It was commissioned in 1245 by Ottobono Fieschi, the future Pope Hadrian V and nephew of Pope Innocent IV (another Fieschi), who made it a basilica in 1252. The building lies in a particularly lovely setting, on the top of a hill covered in olive groves, and surrounded by ancient buildings, among them the ruined 13th-century Palazzo dei Conti Fieschi.

The church is dominated by a powerful square tower which rises over the crossing. It has cornices of blind arches and four-mullioned windows, and is crowned with a tall spire with four pinnacles. The upper façade features alternating bands of marble and slate, and a large rose window. The marble and slate striped bands are repeated inside the rather austere interior, and slate is used elsewhere, too, in the form of tiles in the transept and presbytery.

i **Basilica di San Salvatore dei Fieschi**
Piazza Innocenzo IV, San Salvatore di Cogorno. **Tel** *0185 380245.* 🕐 *8am–noon, 1.30–6pm daily (7pm in summer).*

San Salvatore dei Fieschi, Lavagna

THE SLATE ROAD

For information on the Via dell'Ardesia: GAL Fontanabuona e Sviluppo, Via Chiappanino 26, Cicagna. **Tel** *0185 971 091.* www.fontanabuona.com

From the black stripes of San Salvatore dei Fieschi to the roofs of numerous houses, slate is a characteristic element of many buildings in the Riviera di Levante. It is still quarried in the hinterland behind Chiavari (not far, in fact, from the town of Lavagna, the Italian for blackboard). To visit the quarries, take the SS225 road from Chiavari to the Fontanabuona valley. There are six itineraries to follow as part of the so-called Via dell'Ardesia ("slate road"). You can visit a slate quarry at Isolana di Orero, and there is a slate museum in nearby Cicagna, 20 km (12 miles) from Lavagna.

Sculpture in slate

Sestri Levante **⓫**

Genoa. **Road Map** E4.
🏛 *19,000.* FS 🚌 🛈 *Piazza
Sant'Antonio 10, 0185 457 011.*
🎭 *Premio Letterario per la Fiaba
Hans Christian Andersen (end May).*
www.provincia.genova.it

At the far western point
of the Golfo del Tigullio,
Sestri Levante is one of the
liveliest resorts on the coast.

**Fishing boats on the Baia del
Silenzio at Sestri Levante**

The resort clusters around a
rocky peninsula known as the
"Isola". In the heart of the old
town, the most interesting
monuments are the **Basilica
of Santa Maria di Nazareth**
by Giovan Battista Carlone
(1604–16); the **Palazzo
Durazzo Pallavicini** (17th
century), which is now the
town hall; and the lovely
Romanesque church of **San
Nicolò dell'Isola** (12th century).
Of much greater appeal
altogether, however, is the
wonderful Grand Hotel dei
Castelli *(see p181)*, at the tip
of the peninsula. Built in the
1920s on the site of an old
castle, the hotel has a magnificent park overlooking two
bays: the sandy **Baia delle
Favole**, named after Hans
Christian Andersen, who
stayed here in 1833 *(favole*
means fairy tales), is now
rather built up; but the smaller and more secluded **Baia
del Silenzio**, framed by multicoloured houses and dotted
with fishing boats, is utterly
charming. Also in the grounds
is the tower where Marconi

carried out some of his
radio experiments in 1934.
Back in the old town, the
Galleria Rizzi has paintings,
sculptures, ceramics and
furniture collected by the
local Rizzi family. The
paintings include works by
Giovanni Andrea De Ferrari
and Alessandro Magnasco.

🏛 **Galleria Rizzi**
Via dei Cappuccini 4. **Tel** *0185 413
00.* 🕐 *Apr–Oct: 10:30am–1pm
Sun; May–Sep: 4–7pm Wed (mid-
Jun–Sep: 9:30–11:30pm Fri, Sat).* 🌐

Varese Ligure **⓬**

La Spezia. **Road Map** E4.
🏛 *2,500.* 🚌 *from Sestri Levante.*
🛈 *Via Portici 19, 0187 842 094 (in
high season).*
www.comune.vareseligure.sp.it

This pretty, inland summer
resort was, for centuries, an
important market town and
stopping place on the route
north to Parma, in Emilia-
Romagna. After the decline in
traffic across the mountains in
the 19th century, the town
acquired the rural role it still
has today. Agriculture is the
main trade in this region.
Varese Ligure was a
possession of the Fieschi
family, who obtained it in fief
from Emperor Frederick I
(Barbarossa) in 1161. They
built the rather splendid 15th-
century castle. This stands in
a piazza which was once the
market square, around which
the so-called **Borgo Rotondo**
was built: almost perfectly
circular, with a continuous
screen of buildings, this ring
of shops and houses around
the market was an ingenious

defensive idea dreamt up by
the Fieschis. Charming to look
at, the multicoloured façades
are supported by arches and
porticoes. The 16th-century
Borgo Nuovo, which grew up
alongside, features aristocratic
palazzi dating from the 16th
to 19th centuries, a long,
affluent period for the town.
Nearby, crossed by a
medieval bridge, is the River
Crovana. This is one of the
tributaries of the Vara, whose
valley, the **Val di Vara**, extends
for more than 60 km (37
miles) and has a varied
landscape, among the best
preserved in the region. The
upper reaches of the river
flow through wonderful
mountain scenery, among
woods of beech and chestnut,
interspersed by meadows
where cows and horses graze;
elsewhere there are scenic
stretches where the river is
confined between rocks.
Towards the coast the valley
widens and the river flows
through the Parco Naturale
Regionale di Montemarcello-
Magra *(see p126)*.

Moneglia **⓭**

Genova. **Road Map** E4.
🏛 *2,700.* FS 🚌 🛈 *Corso Longhi
32, 0185 490 576.* 🎭 *Mostra-
Mercato dell'Olio d'Oliva (Easter
Mon).* **www**.prolocomoneglia.it

The town once known as
Monilia faces a small gulf
which interrupts the high,
jagged cliff extending
between Sestri Levante and
Deiva Marina. Moneglia is
a typical fishing town, with
picturesque *carruggi* and
slate roofs, and a thoroughly

View of the unusual Borgo Rotondo in Varese Ligure

The beach at Monegrila in summer, crowded with tourists

gentle pace. Long years of loyalty to the Republic of Genoa have left many traces: among them, the **Fortezza Monleone**, dating from 1173, and the 16th-century **Castello di Villafranca**, on the slopes above the town centre. The striped parish church of **Santa Croce** (1726) has a *Last Supper* by Luca Cambiaso, the great 16th-century artist who was born in Monegrila. Inside, there are also two links from the chain that once closed the gates of Pisa, trophies from the battle of Meloria (*see p38*), in which the Monegliese helped Genoa to defeat Pisa.

There is lots of scope for swimming at Monegrila, especially beneath the cliffs, and you can go on lovely walks through the maquis west towards Punta Baffe and Punta Manara, or through hillside villages and scenic vineyards towards the Bracco mountain pass.

Bonassola ⑭

La Spezia. **Road Map** E4. 1,000. **FS** *Via Fratelli Rezzano, 0187 813 500.* Madonna del Rosario (first weekend in Oct). **www**.prolocobonassola.it

Built around a cove, in a splendid spot, Bonassola was selected by the Genoese in the 13th century as the site for a defensive naval base.

These days, Bonassola has no marina, but it is not difficult to land small boats here. The town also has a wide beach, mostly pebbles, and the sea bed is varied and suited to dives of medium difficulty. Sights of interest include the parish church of **Santa Caterina** (16th century), with sumptuous Baroque decoration and numerous ex votos, evidence of the busy seafaring lives of the inhabitants.

The tiny church of **Madonna della Punta**, built on a cliff jutting out over the sea to the west of the village, is the focus of a popular sunset walk. Several old villages in the vicinity are

Santa Croce bell tower, in Monegrila

worth exploring, either on foot or by car. One path, following a route through vineyards and olive groves, takes walkers the 9 km (6 miles) to **Montaretto**, known for its production (albeit limited) of good white wine.

Levanto ⑮

La Spezia. **Road Map** E4. 5,800. **FS** *Piazza Mazzini, 0187 808 125.* Festa del Mare (24–25 Jul). **www**.levanto.com

Over the years, Levanto has been a centre for trade, agriculture and, most recently, tourism: it has a long and lovely beach. The small town is divided into Borgo Antico, the

medieval district around the church of Sant'Andrea and the hill of San Giacomo, and the Borgo Nuovo, which grew up in the 15th century on the nearby plain. In the medieval district is the lovely Loggia del Comune (13th century), the Casa Restani, with a 13th–14th-century portico, a castle (privately owned) and a stretch of the old town walls, dating from 1265.

The principal monument is the parish church of **Sant' Andrea**, a lovely example of Ligurian Gothic. The façade is striped with white marble and local serpentine (a softish green stone), with a finely carved rose window. Serpentine is also used in the capitals of the columns in the nave. Works of art inside include two canvases from a polyptych by Carlo Braccesco (1495) depicting *Saints Augustine and Jerome* and *Saints Blaise and Pantaleon*.

In the ex-oratory of the church is a **Museo Permanente della Cultura Materiale**, which reconstructs various aspects of the rural and seafaring life of the Riviera di Levante.

Among vestiges of Levanto's more recent past are several important palazzi (often with painted façades) dating from the 17th and 18th centuries, when many Genoese noble families chose to build their summer residences here: **Palazzo Vannoni**, facing on to Piazza Cavour, is the most important one.

Museo Permanente della Cultura Materiale
Piazzetta Massola 4.
Tel 0187 817 776.
Jul & Aug: 9–11pm Tue–Sun; at other times by request.

Sant'Andrea in Levanto

The Cinque Terre ⑯

Translucent sea and cliffs plunging into the water; towns clinging to rocky slopes, and terraces dug into the contours of the mountains directly behind the coast. These are the Cinque Terre (Five Lands), today a national park encompassing some 20 km (12 miles) of coast and the immediate hinterland. A UNESCO World Heritage site, this is a place where the relationship between man and the environment is preserved in miraculous equilibrium. The five small towns on the coast that give the area its name are Monterosso al Mare, Vernazza, Corniglia, Manarola and Riomaggiore. The coastal paths are great for both walking and horse riding (see p201), and you can go diving, too. Access is primarily by foot, boat or train (rather than car), and note that accommodation gets very booked up in high season.

Monterosso al Mare ①

For Italians, the words of writer Eugenio Montale (1896–1981), who holidayed here as a child, capture the atmosphere of Monterosso. Alongside the old town is the popular tourist area of Fegina, with a sandy beach.

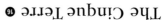

Lontani andremo e serberemo un'eco
della tua voce, come si ricorda
del sole l'erba grigia
nelle conti scurite, Tra le nasce.

The Terraces ②

The steep-sided landscape of the Cinque Terre is an extraordinary example of an architectural landscape. The terraces sculpted out of the mountain slopes have been used primarily to cultivate olives and vines (from which the highly covered Sciacchetrà fortified wine – see p187 – is made).

Vernazza ③

With its colourful houses clustered around an inlet, Vernazza is the only town in the Cinque Terre to have a harbour; this is known to have been in use in antiquity. The port has made Vernazza the richest village in the area, while the combination of the surroundings and architectural grace also make it the prettiest place in the Cinque Terre.

For hotels and restaurants in this region see pp178–81 and pp191–4

0 kilometres   1

0 miles   1

PIGNONE

PIGNONE

S. Antonia
Semáforo

LEVANTO

KEY

▬▬	Coastal Tour route
—	Mountain route
═	Other roads
▬	Railway
—	River
--	Ferry

Riomaggiore ⑦

The headquarters of the national park, Riomaggiore has two rows of tall narrow houses and lots of seafood restaurants. You can go diving off nearby Punta di Montenero.

Via dell'Amore ⑥

Constructed in the 1920s, the Via dell'Amore (Path of Love) traces a route from Manarola to Riomaggiore. The path, cut into the steep cliffs, is just 2 km (1 mile) long and easy to walk, but is scenic, thrilling and justifiably renowned.

Manarola ⑤

Clinging to a cliff overlooking the sea, the village of Manarola makes a striking sight with its compact, coloured houses.

The Strada dei Santuari ⑧

This tortuous path across often cultivated land is cut into the mountainside and links the five coastal towns. It can be covered on foot, by bicycle or on horseback, and offers superlative views.

Corniglia ④

This town, built high on a ridge, 100 m (320 ft) above a beautiful and sheltered beach, was called Cornelia by the Romans. The beach has a history almost totally separate from that of the town above, which has always been an agricultural centre. The local vineyards produce limited quantities of white Cinque Terre and Sciacchetrà wine.

Map labels: Menhir di M. Capri, Volastra, Groppo

VISITORS' CHECKLIST

La Spezia. **Map** E-F4. **FS** **Corniglia** station, 0187 812 523; **Manarola** station, 0187 760 511; **Monterosso al Mare** station, 0187 817 059; **Riomaggiore** station, 0187 920 633; **Vernazza** station, 0187 812 533. Compulsory *Carta Cinque Terre* gives access to transport, paths and maps. **www**.parconazionale5terre.it

The church in the pretty medieval village of Campiglia

Campiglia ⓱

La Spezia. **Road Map** F5. 🚶 150.
🚆 La Spezia. 🚌 from La Spezia.
🛈 IAT Cinque Terre, 0187 770 900.
www.campiglia.net and
www.tramontidicampiglia.it

This rural village, founded in the Middle Ages and occupying a precipitous position near the coast only a short distance from La Spezia, is fascinating and magical.

Campiglia was built on an old mule road along the ridge between Portovenere and Levanto, and it is still a great starting point for walks. The most beautiful, and hardest, walk is along CAI (Italian Alpine Club) path no. 11. This takes visitors through the spectacular terrain of the **Tramonti**, a continuation of the Cinque Terre with terraces of vines, until you descend a steep flight of 2,000 steps, as far as the small beach of Punta del Persico: the landscape open to the sea is genuinely breathtaking.

Portovenere ⓲

La Spezia. **Road Map** F5.
🚶 4,600. 🚆 La Spezia. 🚌
🛈 Piazza Bastreri 7, 0187 790 691.
🎪 Festa della Madonna Bianca
(17 Aug). **www**.portovenere.it and
www.comune.portovenere.sp.it

Portus Veneris (the port of Venus) was fêted for its beauty as far back as Roman times. Nowadays, its beauty and cachet even rival those of Portofino.

Lying at the base of the rocky cliff that fringes the western side of the Golfo della Spezia, Portovenere

looks like a typical fortified fishing village, with rows of gaily painted houses on the slope down to the harbour. Behind is a maze of narrow alleys and vaulted staircases, populated by Portovenere's famous cats.

At the tip of the headland is the striped church of **San Pietro**, built in 1277 in honour of the patron saint of fishermen. It incorporates elements of a 6th-century, early Christian church and has a small Romanesque loggia, open to the sea.

Also worth visiting is **San Lorenzo**, a short walk up an alley from the harbour. This beautiful Romanesque church was built in the 12th century, but reworked in the Gothic and Renaissance eras. It has a wonderfully rustic font inside.

Further up the alley (it's a steep climb), visitors will reach the 16th-century **castello**. Built by the Genoese, this is a grandiose example of military architecture, and also offers fantastic views. It is linked to the town by a line of walls with square towers. The remains of various medieval fortifications are still visible around Portovenere.

Le Grazie, along the winding route north from Portovenere to La Spezia, is another place of great beauty. Monte Muzzerone nearby is hugely popular among free-climbers. The village itself is home to the church of Santa Maria delle Grazie (15th century) and the 16th-century monastery of the Olivetans. By the inlet of Varignano, nearby, is a ruined **Roman**

villa (2nd to 1st centuries BC), with a mosaic pavement and a small museum, known as the **Antiquarium**.

⚓ **Castello**
Tel 0187 791 106. 🕐 9am–
12:30pm, 3–5:30pm daily. 🌙
during events & in winter. 🎫

🏛 **Antiquarium del Varignano**
Le Grazie. **Tel** 0187 790 307.
🕐 on request.

The church of San Pietro at Portovenere, overlooking the sea

Palmaria, Tino and Tinetto ⓳

La Spezia. **Road Map** F5. 🚢 from
La Spezia or Portovenere for Isola
Palmaria, 0187 732 987. 🛈 IAT
Portovenere, 0187 790 691.

Liguria's only archipelago once formed part of the headland of Portovenere.

The largest island, **Isola Palmaria**, is divided from the mainland by just a narrow channel. It is covered in dense vegetation on one side, and has steep cliffs and caves on the other. In the past, Portor marble, a valuable black stone used in some

The harbour at Portovenere, with its characteristic painted houses

The island of Palmaria, the largest in the Ligurian archipelago

buildings in Portovenere, was quarried here, which has partially disfigured the island. Palmaria is a popular among the locals, who come for day trips, but the island's appeal can't compete with that of the mainland.

The much smaller islands of Tino and Tinetto are in a military zone. Access to **Tino** is allowed only on the 13th of September, for the Festa di San Venerio. There is a ruined 11th-century abbey, built on the site of a chapel where the hermit saint lived in solitude. The island light-house guides ships into the gulf.

Tinetto is an inhospitable rock, but the rich diversity of the sea beds make this a popular diving area. The ruins of two religious buildings on the island confirm the earliest known Christian presence in the area (5th century).

La Spezia ⓴

See pp124–5.

San Terenzo ㉑

La Spezia. **Road Map** F5.
🚉 *La Spezia.* 🚌
ℹ️ *Lerici, 0187 967 346.*

San Terenzo lies on the northern side of the Golfo della Spezia, overlooking the pretty bay of Lerici. Once a small group of fishermen's houses clustered on the shore, San Terenzo was a favourite among certain 19th-century poets, including Percy Bysshe Shelley. (Casa Magni, the last home Shelley shared with his wife Mary, is nearby.) Today, sadly, the village is suffering from the effects of mass tourism.

Sights to visit include a castle on a rocky promontory nearby; the church of Santa Maria Assunta; and Villa Marigola, with lovely gardens.

Lerici ㉒

La Spezia. **Road Map** F5.
🚶 *12,000.* 🚉 *La Spezia.* 🚌
ℹ️ *Via Biaggini 6, 0187 967 346.*
🎭 *Festa di Sant'Erasmo (Jul).*

In the Middle Ages Lerici was a major port, and enjoyed both commercial and strategic importance. Today, it is a

popular tourist town, but one that manages to still feel like a working community with a strong identity.

The old centre is dominated by the **Castello**, the most important example of military architecture in the region. Built by the Pisans in the 13th century to counter a Genoese fort at Portovenere, it was taken by Genoa shortly afterwards; they enlarged it in the 15th century. It is still in a remarkably good state, with its pentagonal tower and massive walls. There is an archaeological museum inside.

Below the castle is the lovely (and sandy) Baia di Maralunga, good for a swim.

⚓ Castello and Museo
Piazza San Giorgio. *Tel* 0187 969 042. ⏰ mid-Oct–mid-Mar: 10:30am–12:30pm Tue–Fri; 10:30am–12:30pm, 2:30–5:30pm Sat, Sun, public hols; mid-Mar–Jun, Sep–mid-Oct: 10:30am–1pm, 2:30–6pm Tue–Sun; Jul–Aug: 10:30am–12:30pm, 6:30pm–midnight Tue–Sun. ⏰ Mon. 🎫

The port of Lerici, dominated by an imposing castle

THE GULF OF POETS
It was the Italian playwright Sem Benelli who first described the Gulf of Lerici as the "Gulf of Poets" in 1919. It is an evocative and romantic epithet, and not inaccurate given the personalities who came here in the 19th and 20th centuries: including Percy Bysshe Shelley (who drowned at sea en route to La Spezia from Livorno, in 1822, and was cremated at Viareggio) and his wife Mary (author of *Frankenstein*), Lord Byron, DH Lawrence and Virginia Woolf. The gulf still has strong appeal today and attracts artists and intellectuals, mainly Italians. As a consequence a "cultural park" has been established, called the Parco Culturale Golfo dei Poeti, joining similar parks dedicated to Eugenio Montale, in the Cinque Terre, and in the Val di Magra and Terra di Luni. For more information contact the tourist office APT Cinque Terre-Golfo dei Poeti in La Spezia (*see p207*).

Shelley

La Spezia ⑳

One of the cannons on the seafront at La Spezia

The port of La Spezia has been important since antiquity as a trading centre for produce from all over the world, especially spices (*la spezia* means spice in Italian). In the 13th century, the Fieschi family transformed what had been a fishing village into a fortress surrounded by walls. The city expanded and a second defensive ring was built in the 1600s. This city was lauded by poets in the 19th century, and attracted generations of European travellers, drawn by La Spezia's elegance and attractive position on the gulf. The city, and its role, changed radically after 1861, when the Savoy government began construction of a naval base. Today, traces of the distant past are tucked away amid the sprawling metropolis. The naval base and port are still thriving.

🏛 Arsenale Militare and Museo Navale

Viale Amendola 1.
Tel 0187 784 693. ◯
8am–6:45pm Mon–Sat,
8am–1pm Sun. ● 1 Jan,
15 Aug, 8, 24–26 Dec. 📷
📷 no flash. **www.**
turismoprovincia.laspezia.it
In exile on St Helena, Napoleon, tracing a portrait of the Italian peninsula, wrote of La Spezia that "it is the most beautiful port in the universe; its defence by land and by sea is easy… maritime institutions would be sheltered here". It was not Napoleon, however, who transferred the naval base from Genoa to La Spezia, but the Savoy government under Camillo Cavour.

Construction of the colossal site began in 1861. The city inevitably expanded as a result of the building of the base, and from 1861 to 1881 the number of inhabitants tripled. Badly damaged by bombing in World War II and further damaged by German troops, who occupied the site between 1943 and 1945, the base was reconstructed with meticulous care.

Today the structure illustrates how the designer, colonel Domenico Chiodo, responded carefully to the practical requirements: the workshops are located close to the entrance for the

Figurehead, Museo Navale

convenience of the workers, the general warehouse and offices are placed at the centre of the entire complex, and so on. The predominant style is Neo-Classical. It is possible to visit parts of the base, including the old workshops, sailmakers' yards, masonry docks and the swing bridge.
The **Museo Tecnico Navale della Marina Militare** is one of Italy's oldest and most important naval museums. The core of its collection dates back to the 16th century, and was started by Emanuele Filiberto of Savoy, who gathered mementoes from the Battle of Lepanto (1571). Models help to illustrate the history of the port; there is also a fine collection of anchors (around 120 different ones) and a good display of 28 figureheads from old sailing ships.

🏛 Museo Amedeo Lia

Via Prione 234. *Tel* 0187 731 100.
◯ 10am–6pm Tue–Sun. ● 1 Jan,
15 Aug, 25 Dec. 📷 ♿ 📷 📷
http://mal.spezianet.it
This excellent and award-winning museum, opened in 1996, is based around the works donated by Amedeo Lia and his family. It is housed in part of the ancient church and monastery of the

monks of San Francesco da Paola, restored for the purpose. The museum includes paintings and miniatures, medieval ivory, Limoges enamels, medals and numerous archaeological finds from excavations around the Mediterranean basin.

Paintings are the collection's most significant element: indeed, the 13th- and 14th-century paintings form one of the finest private collections in Europe.

Besides fine works by Paolo di Giovanni Fei, Pietro Lorenzetti, Sassetta and Lippo di Benivieni, there are two 16th-century highlights: a presumed *Self Portrait* (1520) by Pontormo, painted, unusually, using tempera on terracotta, and a *Portrait of a Gentleman* (1510) by Titian.

The 17th-century paintings by followers of Caravaggio are also worth seeking out, as are the Venetian views by Canaletto, Bellotto, Marieschi and Guardi. There are also bronzes from the 16th and 17th centuries.

***Self Portrait* by Pontormo, Museo Amedeo Lia**

♟ Castello di San Giorgio

Via XXVII Marzo. *Tel* 0187 751 142.
◯ see Museo Archeologico.
The oldest architectural vestige of centuries past, the Castello di San Giorgio occupies a commanding position overlooking the city. The imposing fortification was commissioned by the Fieschi family in the 13th century, though what you see today dates from a reconstruction that took place

Castello di San Giorgio, home to the Museo Archeologico

in the 14th century, and from defence work carried out in the 17th century. Following major restoration work, the castle is now home to the Museo Civico Archeologico.

🏛 Museo Civico Archeologico Ubaldo Formentini

Castello di San Giorgio, Via XXVII Marzo. *Tel 0187 751 142.*
⏰ summer: 9:30am–12:30pm, 5–8pm daily; winter: 9:30am–12:30pm, 2–5pm. ⏰ Tue (except hols), 1 Jan, 24, 25 Dec. 🗐 ⚆ ✔ ⬜
www.castagna.it/sangiorgio

This museum was established in the 19th century as a home for the many archaeological finds and fossils discovered in the city environs, mainly as a

result of excavation work carried out when the naval base was being built.

Some of these finds provide evidence of the first human settlements in the Lunigiana area: coins and ceramics dating from the prehistoric, Etruscan and Roman eras are among the objects found near the ancient city of Luni *(see p127)*. Also of interest are paleolithic finds from the Grotta dei Colombi on the island of Palmaria.

The most significant section of the museum is, however, the collection of statue-stelae, sculptures in sandstone dating from the Bronze and Iron ages, depicting in stylized form warriors grasping weapons and figures of women. Although typical art of the Lunigiana, their function and significance are unclear.

🔒 Chiesa di Santa Maria dell'Assunta

Piazza Beverini.
⏰ 9:30–11am, 3–5:30pm daily.
This 14th-century church has been modified more than once. Its appearance today, with its black and white façade, owes

Statue-stele at the Museo Archeologico

much to reconstruction after the war. It contains a *Coronation of the Virgin,* a glazed terracotta relief by Andrea Della Robbia and a *Martyrdom of St Bartholomew* (16th century) by Luca Cambiaso.

🔒 Pieve di San Venerio

This charming Parish church dates from the 11th century, although excavations carried out in the last century have revealed much earlier, even Roman, origins. The façade is decorated with a two-mullioned window and is flanked by a bell tower. The interior has two aisles, the older of which ends, unusually, in two apses.

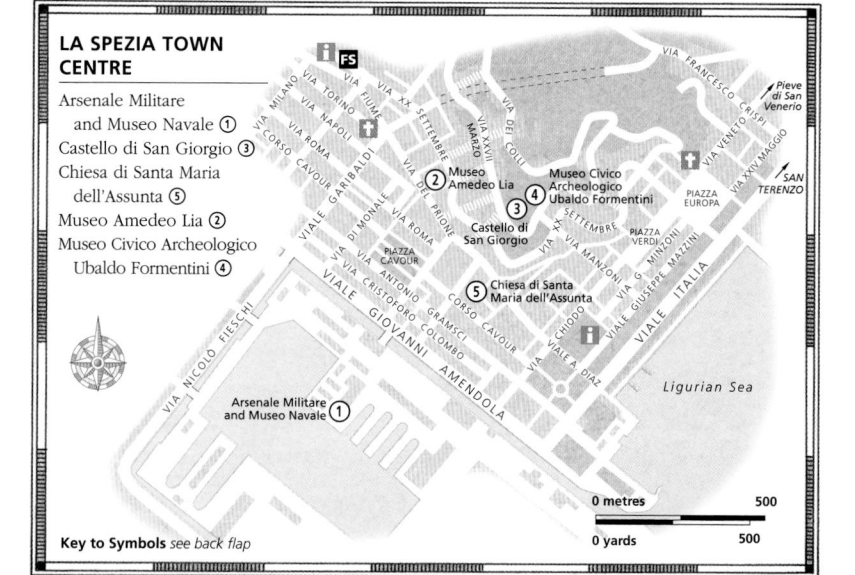

LA SPEZIA TOWN CENTRE

Arsenale Militare and Museo Navale ①
Castello di San Giorgio ③
Chiesa di Santa Maria dell'Assunta ⑤
Museo Amedeo Lia ②
Museo Civico Archeologico Ubaldo Formentini ④

Key to Symbols *see back flap*

0 metres 500
0 yards 500

A picturesque alley in Tellaro

Fiascherino and Tellaro ㉓

La Spezia. **Road Map** F5.
🏚 800. FS La Spezia. 🚌
ℹ️ Lerici, 0187 967 346.
🎭 Natale Subacqueo (24 Dec).
www.tellaro.net

These two pretty fishing villages of painted houses lie next to each other, just south of Lerici. Both face small bays, with verdant hills behind.

Tiny **Fiascherino** has a lovely beach, and the cliffs conceal enchanting coves accessible only by boat. The writer DH Lawrence lived in the village from 1913–14.

Thanks to its position on the cliffs high above the sea, medieval **Tellaro** has preserved its original features almost intact, though the instability of the rock itself has caused some damage. The oldest part is built on a promontory that marks the furthermost limit of the Riviera di Levante: the tall houses here had to be built on different levels in order to accommodate the terrain. The village's extremely narrow streets are linked by flights of steps and tunnels. The Baroque church of San Giorgio overlooks the sea, while the Oratory of In Selàa has a lovely courtyard, which also faces the water.

Montemarcello ㉔

La Spezia. **Road Map** F5. 🏚 4,600.
FS La Spezia. 🚌 ℹ️ Via Nuova 48,
0187 691 071 (seasonal). **Parco N R
Montemarcello-Magra**, Via Paci
Agostino 2, Sarzana, 0187 600 324.
www.parcomagra.it

This town on the eastern fringes of the Golfo della Spezia offers fantastic views, both west towards the gulf and east towards the Versilia coast.

Montemarcello doesn't share the structure common to hilltowns: lacking the traditional concentric arrangement, it is instead laid out on a square network, echoing the layout of the original Roman military camp, or *castrum*. The houses in the oldest part, still partially enclosed by the remains of the town walls, are painted in the bright colours usually seen in coastal towns, an anomaly in a mountain village. Indeed, the street layout and the architectural style of the houses give Montemarcello a particular and unusual atmosphere, more akin to an elegant holiday resort than a rural village. As such, it has become a discreet haven for Italian intellectuals and artists – a situation that has, in effect, saved Montemarcello from attempts at major development.

Logo of the Parco di Montemarcello

The landscape around the town is delightful: this is the southern tract of the **Parco Naturale Regionale Montemarcello-Magra**, Liguria's only river park, which offers great opportunities for walks, with several marked walking trails. The park extends from the summit of the eastern headland of the Golfo della Spezia as far as the plain of the river Magra. In the southern stretches, near Bocca di Magra, the vegetation and the wildlife are typically Mediterranean, while in the northern part of the park cultivated fields and wetlands alternate.

Ameglia ㉕

La Spezia. **Road Map** F5. 🏚 4,500.
FS Sarzana, Santo Stefano Magra.
🚌 ℹ️ Via della Mura 7, 0187 691
071. 🎭 Carnevale Amegliese (Feb).
www.comune.ameglia.sp.it

Although it is not far from the mouth of the river Magra, Ameglia still has the look of a hill town. Tall, narrow houses are packed together around a hilltop where a castle once stood. Its ruins include a round tower and parts of the original walls; the main part was replaced in the Renaissance period by the Palazzo del Podestà, later the Palazzo Comunale (town hall).

From the summit, alleys extend in concentric circles, broken up by small squares, several of which have a view of the Carrara marble mountains. The piazza in front of the church of Santi Vincenzo e Anastasio is lovely, with views over the lower Lunigiana and the Apuan Alps. The church has a 16th-century marble door.

Bocca di Magra ㉖

La Spezia. **Road Map** F5. 🏚 4,300.
FS Sarzana, Santo Stefano Magra. 🚌
ℹ️ Via Fabbricotti, 0187 608 037.

Originally a fishing village at the mouth (*bocca*) of the river Magra, this town manages to keep a grip on its heritage, despite its role as a tourist resort. In addition to numerous holiday homes,

A glimpse of Montemarcello

The ancient Roman amphitheatre at Luni

there is a small beach, a spa and a well-equipped marina.

The coast here is very different from that of the Cinque Terre and the Golfo della Spezia: it is near here that the low-lying, sandy stretch, known as the Versilia coast, begins.

The appeal of Bocca di Magra, which stems largely from its combined seaside and riverside location, was not lost on writers, poets and other demanding holidaymakers, who were attracted to Bocca in the first half of the 20th century, just as they were to other towns in the area.

Nearby are the remains of a **Roman villa** dating from the 1st century AD. It is built on sloping terraces on the cliff, in a panoramic position above the mouth of the river.

Luni ②⑦

Via Luni 37, Ortonovo (La Spezia). **Road Map** F5. **Tel** 0187 668 11. **Site and museum** ◯ 8:30am–7:30pm Tue–Sun. ◉ 25 Dec, 1 Jan, 1 May.

The Roman colony of *Portus Lunae* was founded in 177 BC in an effort to counter the native Ligurians. Its role as an important port grew as Luni became a major channel for the shipping of marble from the nearby Apuan Alps (known as Luni marble) to all corners of the Roman empire.

Luni's prosperity faltered during the early centuries of the Middle Ages, due to the tailing-off of the marble trade, with full-blown decline accompanying the silting-up of the harbour. (The coast is now 2 km/1 mile away.) In 1204, the bishopric was moved to nearby Sarzana, and soon, all that was left of Luni was its name, which had also given the surrounding area its title, the Lunigiana.

The archaeological site at Luni is the most important in northern Italy. Surrounded by walls, the city was built to a perfectly regular layout, with the public buildings equally neatly placed. A great temple and several prestigious houses stood near the huge, marble-paved Forum. Nearby was the Capitolium, a temple dedicated to Jove, Juno and Minerva, encircled by a marble-edged basin and with a flight of steps in front. Remains of these buildings are still visible.

Nearby was the Casa dei Mosaici, with an atrium in Corinthian style surrounded by rooms with mosaic floors; some of these 3rd–4th century AD mosaics survive. The vast Casa degli Affreschi was built around a garden and had numerous rooms with fine floors and frescoes. Inside the walls there are also the ruins of the Early Christian basilica of Santa Maria, including the remains of three early Romanesque apses and the base of a bell tower.

Outside the walls is the amphitheatre, built in the Antonine era (1st–2nd centuries AD) and the scene of bloody gladiatorial fights. The lower section of stepped seats, as well as part of a covered portico, survives. The complex system of steps and corridors that led to the seating is still visible.

On the site of the Forum is an **archaeological museum**, with displays of Imperial-era marble statues, busts, fragments of frescoes, jewellery, tools, stamps and ceramics.

Castelnuovo di Magra ②⑧

La Spezia. **Road Map** F5.
🏛 8,000. 🚆 Sarzana, Santo Stefano Magra. 🚌
ℹ Via Aurelia 241, 0187 693 306.
🎭 Corteo Storico "A Pace de Dante" (end Aug).

It seems probable that the origins of this inland town coincided with the decline of nearby Luni and the abandonment of the port by its inhabitants.

Castelnuovo, built on a hilltop in view of the mouth of the River Magra, is spread out attractively along a ridge, with the church at one end and the bishop's palace (a 13th-century castle) at the other. Linking these two landmarks is Via Dante, lined with handsome palazzi with elegant façades. Sections of the old town walls and two 15th-century towers are still visible.

The church at one end of Via Dante is **Santa Maria Maddalena**, built in the late 16th century but with a 19th-century façade. The marble columns inside are thought to have come from Santa Maria Assunta at Luni. Inside is a *Calvary* by Brueghel the Younger.

Between Castelnuovo and Luni, up a very winding road, is **Nicola**, a pretty medieval hilltop village centred around the church of Santi Filippo e Giacomo.

Nicola, near Castelnuovo

Sarzana ㉙

This lively agricultural and commercial centre has a splendid historic centre which has remained almost intact, despite being bombed during the war. Built by the River Magra and on the Via Francigena, the main land route between Rome and northern Europe, Sarzana was of strategic importance both under the Romans and in the Middle Ages. It is no surprise that such a desirable town was fought over at length by its most powerful neighbours, including Pisa and Florence, until in 1572 the town became a stable possession (and the easternmost outpost) of the Republic of Genoa. A sophisticated town, Sarzana has a famous antiques market and great shops.

Statue of the *Procellaria* **in Piazza Matteotti**

Church of Sant'Andrea
This ancient Romanesque church has a sober stone façade with an unusual 16th-century door decorated with caryatids.

PIAZZA MATTEOTTI

VIA BONAPARTE

VIA MAS

VIA FIASELLA

VIA MAZZINI

VIA ROSSI

PIAZZA CALANDRIN

VIA DEI GIARDIN

PIAZZA NICOLÒ

Piazza Matteotti, with its distinctively tapered corner

★ Cathedral
The cathedral of Santa Maria Assunta, begun in 1204 after the transfer of the bishopric from Luni to Sarzana, was completed in the 15th century and modified in the 17th century. The 14th-century door, the finely carved marble rose window and the bell tower are all enchanting. Inside are two marble altarpieces (mid-1400s) by Leonardo Riccomanni.

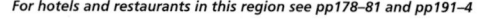

For hotels and restaurants in this region see pp178–81 and pp191–4

LA FORTEZZA DI SARZANELLO

Just north of Sarzana, the Fortress of Sarzanello rises on a hill in an excellent strategic position from which to control the lower Lunigiana. Built for Castruccio Castracani, a lord of Lucca, in around 1322, it was altered in later centuries, including in 1493, when it was restored by the Florentines. The fortress is built on a triangular plan and has three cylindrical corner towers. Access is over a bridge, which straddles a deep moat.

VISITORS' CHECKLIST

La Spezia. **Road Map** F4–5.
👥 20,000. **FS** 🚌 **ℹ** *Piazza San Giorgio, 0187 620 419.*
📷 *"Soffitta in Strada", crafts and antiques market (first 3 weeks of Aug).*
www.aptcinqueterre.sp.it

KEY

– – – Suggested route

★ Cittadella
This imposing fortress was built by Lorenzo the Magnificent, the powerful Medici ruler of Florence, from 1488–92. It is built on a rectangular plan with six round towers and a moat. The 16th-century walls were constructed by the Genoese.

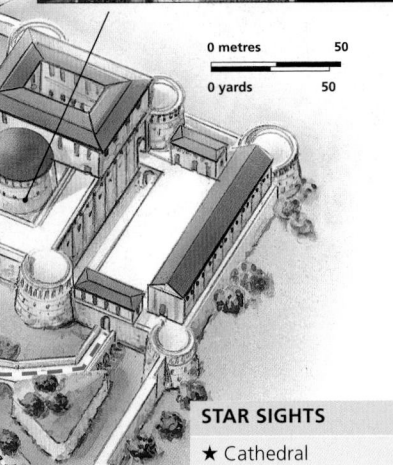

0 metres   50
0 yards   50

STAR SIGHTS

★ Cathedral

★ Cittadella

Via Mazzini
corresponds to the ancient Via Francigena, which links the Neo-Classical Porta Romana and Porta Parma.

The Cross of Maestro Guglielmo, the work of a Tuscan artist, dated 1138, can be seen in the Cathedral. A key work, it was a prototype for the crucifixes painted in Tuscany and Umbria in the following two centuries.

Sarzanello

THE RIVIERA DI PONENTE

W*ith the capital city of Genoa at one end and Ventimiglia, on the border with France, at the other, the Riviera di Ponente extends for around 150 km (93 miles). There is spectacular scenery in the interior, and the coast is so green and lush that it is divided, fittingly, into the Riviera delle Palme (of palm trees) and the Riviera dei Fiori (of flowers).*

Any visitor to this area cannot fail to appreciate the mild climate of the coast, which has been exploited in the past for the cultivation of citrus fruits and is now used in the growing of cut flowers and house plants, adapting customs as well as the landscape in the creation of a new industry. Liguria is now one of the most important flower-growing areas in the world. It is no coincidence that San Remo, one of the main towns along this coast, is known as the "città dei fiori", or city of flowers. Olives are the other major crop, particularly around Imperia.

Like the Riviera di Levante, the Riviera di Ponente became a favourite holiday destination among the European aristocracy, particularly the British and the Russians, from the late 19th century. Hotels and Art Nouveau villas are still in evidence almost everywhere.

The western part of Liguria also has a rich history, evoked by numerous atmospheric towns and villages. You need head only a short distance inland to discover fascinating medieval towns which are in stark contrast to the touristy coastal towns. Traces of the Romans can also be found both on the coast and in the interior, such as the five Roman bridges in the Parco del Finalese (in whose limestone caves paleolithic utensils and burial tombs have been found), or the excavations of Albintimilium, ancient Ventimiglia.

In between excursions, as well as spending time on the beach or swimming in the sea, visitors can relax and breathe fresh clean air in one of the region's parks: such as the Parco Naturale del Monte Beigua, above Savona, with trees and plants of tremendous variety and numerous animal species.

Triora, in the hinterland behind Imperia, also known as the "village of witches"

◁ Palm trees in the gardens of Villa Ormond in San Remo

Exploring the Riviera di Ponente

The two provincial capitals on the Riviera di Ponente are Savona and Imperia. San Remo, with its grand Art Nouveau architecture, is the main holiday resort. New developments have spoilt the coast closest to Genoa, but there are many interesting places to visit elsewhere along the coast: these range from Noli, with its church of San Paragorio, one of the key monuments of Ligurian Romanesque, and Albenga, with its well-preserved historic centre and its Early Christian baptistry, to the splendid English gardens at Hanbury Botanical Gardens, close to the French border, and the nearby caves at Balzi Rossi, a fascinating prehistoric site. In the hinterland, the delightful medieval village of Dolceacqua is especially worth a visit, as is Triora, famous for a witch trial held here at the end of the 16th century. The luxuriant vegetation and mild climate make this part of the Ligurian coast a pleasure to explore.

Hanbury Botanical Gardens

SIGHTS AT A GLANCE

Bardinet

Erli

Ponte de Nava

Nava

Monesi

S28

Borghetto d'Arroscia

S453

Arroscia

Realdo

PIEVE DI TECO 18

Rezzo

TRIORA 21

Testico

Merula

S548

Chiusavecchia

Pontedassio

PIGNA **25**

Monte Ceppo
1629m

**DOLCEDO
20**

Monte Merlo
1014m

Montalto
Ligure

S28

ANDORA 1

Cuneo

Baiardo

23

Ceriana

CERVO 17

Apricale

Diano
Marina

Airole   S20

Perinaldo

**IMPERIA
19**

Oneglia

DOLCEACQUA 26

TOUR OF THE
ARMEA AND
CROSIA VALLEYS

22 TAGGIA

Porto
Maurizio

A10

Nice

Vallecrosia
Alta

Seborga

24

Santo Stefano

**BALZI
29 30
ROSSI**

28

SAN REMO

Bussana
Vecchia

HANBURY   VENTIMIGLIA   27
BOTANICAL   **BORDIGHERA**
GARDENS

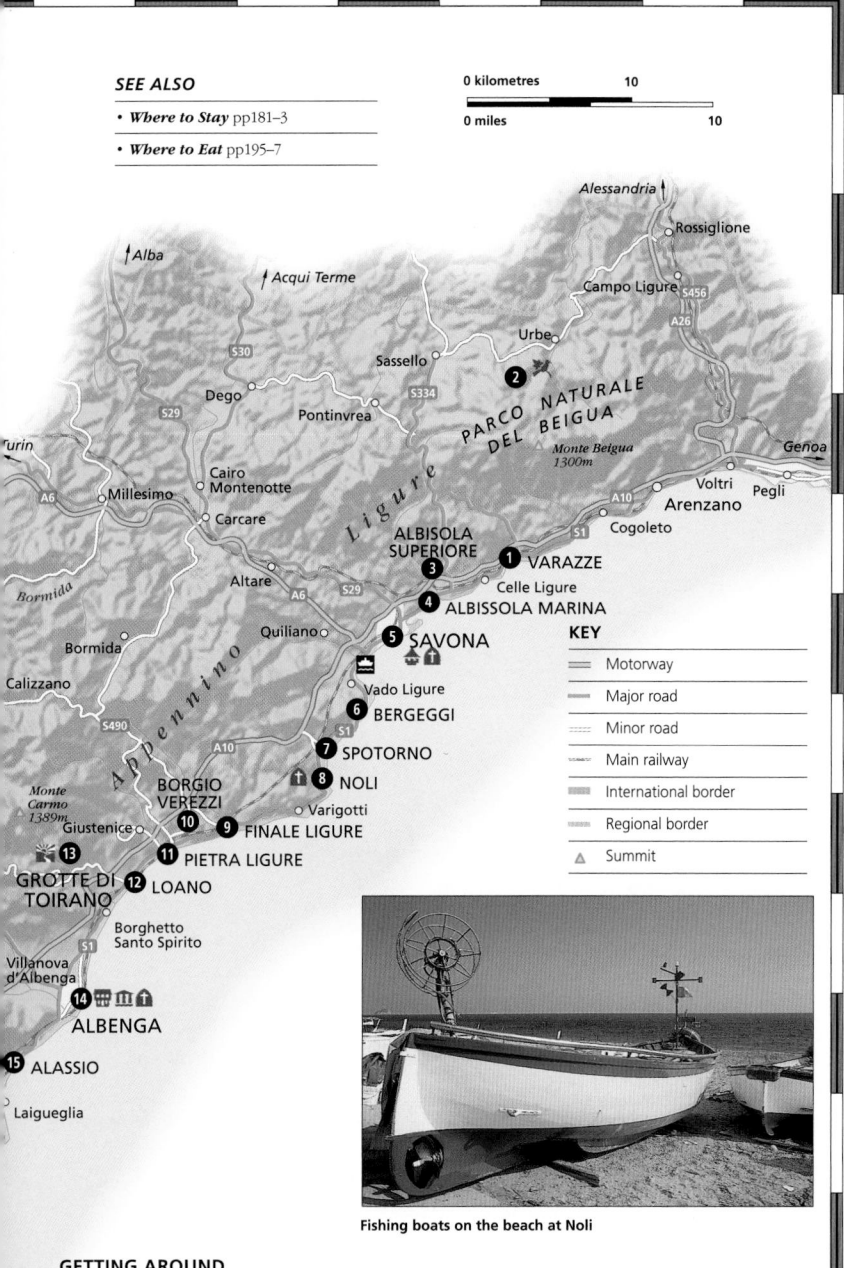

0 kilometres   10

0 miles   10

Alessandria

Rossiglione

Alba

Acqui Terme

Campo Ligure   S456

Urbe   A26

Sassello   **2** PARCO NATURALE DEL BEIGUA

Dego   S30   Pontinvrea   S334

Monte Beigua 1300m   Genoa

Turin   Cairo Montenotte   Voltri   Pegli

Millesimo   A6   Carcare   Arenzano

Bormida   Altare   A6   S29   ALBISOLA SUPERIORE   **3**   Cogoleto   A10   S1

Bormida   Quiliano   **5** SAVONA   Celle Ligure   **1** VARAZZE   **4** ALBISSOLA MARINA

Calizzano   Vado Ligure   **6** BERGEGGI

S490   A10   **7** SPOTORNO

Monte Carmo 1389m   BORGIO VEREZZI   **8** NOLI

Giustenice   **10**   Varigotti   **9** FINALE LIGURE

13   **11** PIETRA LIGURE

GROTTE DI TOIRANO   **12** LOANO

Borghetto Santo Spirito

Villanova d'Albenga   S1

14

ALBENGA

15 ALASSIO

Laigueglia

KEY

═══ Motorway

─── Major road

┄┄┄ Minor road

▬▬▬ Main railway

▭▭▭ International border

═══ Regional border

△ Summit

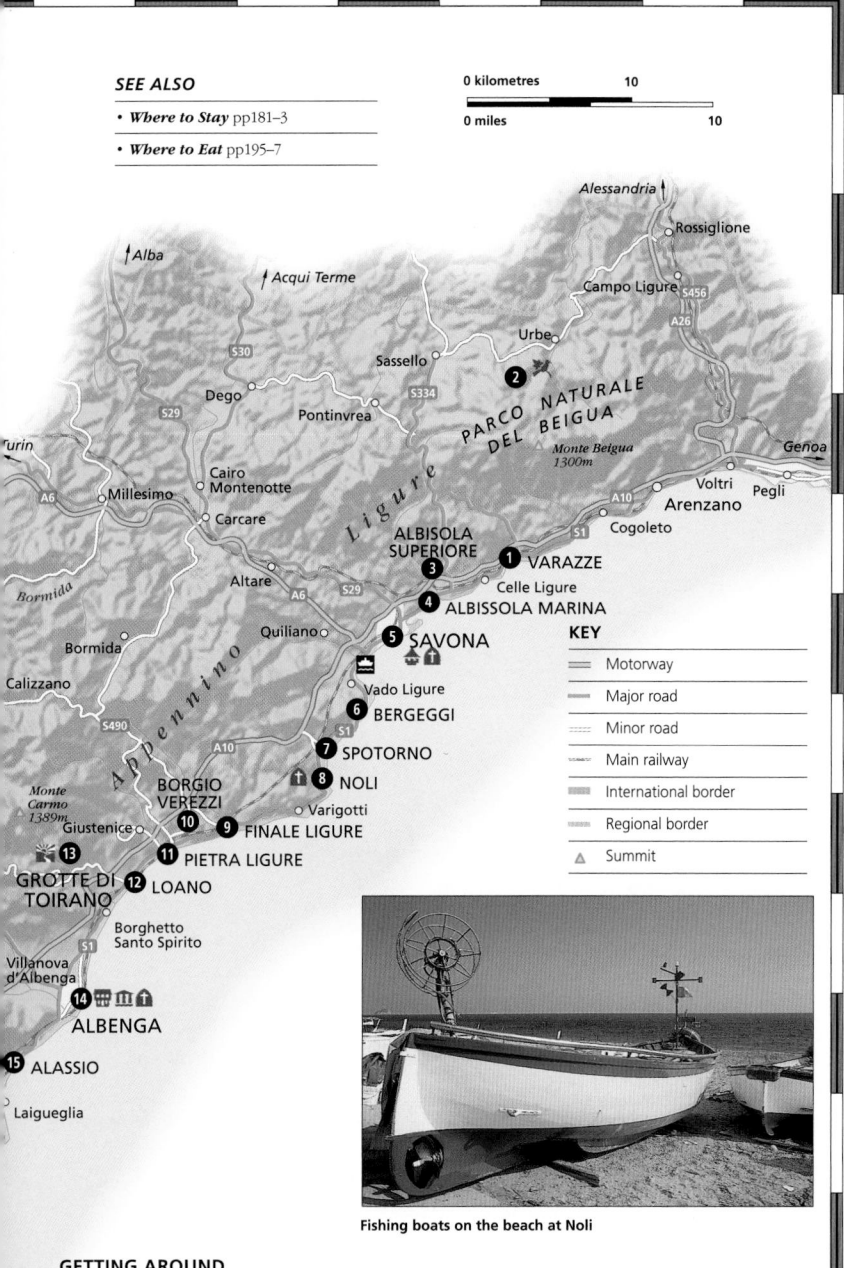

Fishing boats on the beach at Noli

GETTING AROUND

The main communication routes along the Riviera di Ponente are the A10, the motorway between Genoa and Ventimiglia, and the SS1, or Via Aurelia (once a Roman road), which runs parallel to the motorway at sea level, passing by all the main towns. The roads leading into the interior are narrow and twisting, although they do pass through very beautiful countryside. The A6, the motorway from Savona to Turin, gives access to Altare, Carcare and other towns located inland from the Riviera delle Palme. Regional, inter-regional and intercity trains connect Genoa and Ventimiglia (with up to 15 trains a day). It is also possible to get around using coaches, particularly if heading inland; the provincial coach companies operate a good network of services.

Varazze ❶

Savona. **Road Map** C3.
14,000. FS
Corso Matteotti 56, 019 935 043. Processione e Corteo Storico di Santa Caterina da Siena (30 Apr); Festa del Mare (early Aug).
www.turismo.provincia.savona.it

At the eastern end of the Riviera di Ponente, Varazze is a major seaside resort, complete with a beach and palm-shaded promenade.

The town's name derives from the Roman name of *Varagine* ("trees"), though it was later known as *Ad Navalia* ("At the shipyards"). Both names were appropriate since much of the local wood was used for boat-building. The town was the birthplace of Jacopo da Varagine, a famous 13th-century friar and writer, and later a saint.

In the old centre, sights of interest include the church of **Sant'Ambrogio**, dating from 1535. Remaining from an earlier 14th-century construction is an imposing brick bell tower in the Lombard style, complete with a spire. The Neo-Renaissance façade, in Finale stone, was built in 1916. The courtyard is paved in beach pebbles, laid out in a pretty geometrical design. The façade of an earlier, Romanesque church dedicated to Sant'Ambrogio has been incorporated, curiously, into the **town walls**, an impressive work dating from the 12th century.

Built in 1419, but much modified since, the church of **San Domenico** is famous as the home of the silver urn containing the remains of Jacopo da Varagine. There is also a polyptych (16th century) depicting *Blessed Jacopo and other saints*, by Simone da Pavia, and a 12th-century fresco, probably of the Sienese school, with a *Madonna delle Grazie*. A cannon ball, fired from a French ship in 1746, is embedded in the church façade.

The Romanesque church of Sant'Ambrogio at Varazze

From San Domenico visitors can go on a lovely seafront walk along disused railway tracks; various paths en route cut inland up to Monte Beigua.

The seafront at Varazze

Environs

Celle Ligure, 3 km (2 miles) west of Varazze, is a small fishing village with twisting *carruggi* (narrow streets) and a wall of hills behind. The tradition of painting the houses bright colours began so that sailors could make them out while still at sea.

The **Deserto di Varazze**, 9 km (6 miles) inland from Celle Ligure, is another lovely spot. It is a simple 17th-century hermitage associated with the barefoot Carmelite friars, surrounded by a dense wood.

Parco Naturale del Beigua ❷

Genoa/Savona. **Road Map** C3.
FS **Ente Parco del Beigua** *Via G Marconi 165, Arenzano, 010 859 03 00.* **www**.parks.it

This densely forested park covers an area of 17,000 ha (42,000 acres) and runs from the border with Piemonte down to the coast, east of Varazze. It is the biggest of the region's three national parks and takes its name from Monte Beigua (1,300 m/4,265 ft), which is accessible by road. The grassy plain at the mountain summit provides a platform for wonderful views stretching for miles in all directions, and is a starting point for numerous walks.

Scented daphne, symbol of the Parco del Beigua

The park's rocky heart is typically composed of ophiolites, also known as "green rocks" (mainly serpentine) – metamorphic rocks deriving from changes which occurred in the original igneous rock. Prehistoric axes found in this area are on display, along with other prehistoric utensils, at the Museo Civico Archeologico in Pegli, near Genoa *(see p82)*. Prehistoric as well as more recent graffiti have also been discovered in Monte Beigua.

The flora and fauna in the park are extremely varied. In terms of the plant life, there are vast numbers of beeches, and the Alpine aster *(Aster alpinus)* is also common; drosera *(Drosera rotundifolia)*, an insect-eating carnivorous plant, can be found in the wetland area known as the Riserva del Laione. And there is the scented daphne *(Daphne cneorum)*, too, whose characteristic pink flowers have been chosen as the symbol of the park.

The wildlife is varied, too, and includes foxes, badgers, weasels, wild boar and roe deer. Two endemic species of amphibian – *Salamandrina terdigitata* and *Triturus vulgaris meridionalis* – have also been seen, here at their westernmost limit. From the southern slopes you can also see migratory birds in spring.

The park headquarters is in Sassello, a pretty town on the park's western fringes.

Albisola Superiore ❸

Savona. **Road Map** C3. 🏘 *12,000.* 🚇 🚌 🛈 *IAT Albissola Marina, Piazza Lam, Albissola Marina, 019 400 25 25.* **www**.turismo. provincia.savona.it

Known to the Romans as Alba Docilia, Albisola consists, in fact, of two parts: Albissola Marina, on the coast, and Albisola Superiore, a short way inland. The different spelling of Albisola perhaps indicates the towns' wish to reinforce their separation, but since the 15th century they have both enjoyed fame for their ceramics, made from the local clay and typically decorated in blue and white.

Albisola's ancient heritage can be seen in traces of a vast Roman **villa**, occupied from the 1st to 5th centuries AD. The parish church of **San**

The remains of an Imperial-era Roman villa at Albisola Superiore

Nicolò was reconstructed in 1600 in the shadow of the castle, now in ruins. The Baroque wooden statues inside were carved by Maragliano and Schiaffino. A 17th-century oratory stands alongside. Within a large park, adorned with fountains and statuary, stands **Villa Gavotti**, built in 1739–53 for the last doge of Genoa, Francesco Maria Della Rovere, replacing a 15th-century building. The sumptuous interior contains stuccoes by the Lombard school and local ceramics. The villa is home to the **Museo della Ceramica Manlio Trucco**, which is devoted to ceramics from the 16th century onwards. Displays include work by artists from Albisola and elsewhere in Liguria, as well as tools of the trade.

Ceramic plate from Albisola

🏛 **Museo della Ceramica Manlio Trucco**
Corso Ferrari 193. **Tel** *019 48 22 95.* 🕐 *8:30am–12:30pm Wed–Fri, 8:30am–12:30pm, 5:30–7:30pm Sat.*

Albissola Marina ❹

Savona. **Road Map** C3. 🏘 *5,600.* 🚇 🚌 🛈 *IAT Albissola Marina, Piazza Lam, 019 400 25 25.* 🎨 *Mostre Nazionali di Ceramica d'Arte (biennial, next in Jun 2006).* **www**.turismo.provincia.savona.it

Separated from Albisola Superiore since 1615, this coastal town is also known as Borgo Basso (or "lower town"). Like its neighbour, Albissola Marina has prospered historically thanks to its ceramics industry, but it is also now a well-known seaside resort.

Of interest in the old town is the **Forte di Sant'Antonio**, known as the Castello, built in 1563 against a Saracen invasion, and **Piazza della Concordia**, attractively paved with concentric circles of black and white pebbles, in front of the parish church.

The unmissable sight is the handsome 18th-century **Villa Faraggiana** (named after its last owner, who gave it to the town in 1961), formerly Palazzo Durazzo. The lavishly furnished interior includes some lovely local majolica tiles, while the delightful gardens feature grottoes and statuary, including nymphs and sculptures of the god Bacchus and goddess Diana.

On **Lungomare degli Artisti**, the mosaic paving dating from 1963 was created with works by contemporary painters and sculptors, among them the artists Lucio Fontana and Aligi Sassu.

🏛 **Villa Faraggiana**
Via Salomoni 117–119. **Tel** *019 480 622.* 🕐 *Apr–Sep: 3–7pm daily.* ⚫ *occasional Sat & Sun for private functions.* 🎨 **www**.villafaraggiana.it

The 18th-century Villa Faraggiana at Albissola Marina

Savona ❺

Majolica jar, Pinacoteca

One's first impression of Savona tends to be of a sprawling and industrial port. Yet this thriving, untouristy city has a lovely historic centre. Savona (the name derives from the Ligurian tribe of the Sabates) is the largest town on the Riviera di Ponente, and a provincial capital. Its history has always been linked with that of Genoa: the rivalry between the two has existed since ancient times, when, during Hannibal's Punic wars, Savona sided with Carthage, and Genoa with Rome. The port (destroyed by the Genoese in 1528) was rebuilt only in the 1800s. It was heavily bombed in World War II. There is lots to see here. The Fortezza del Priamàr, a symbol of the city, is now a vast museum complex; you can stroll around the medieval centre and port; or explore the arcades and the Art Nouveau palazzi in Via Paleocapa, jewels of 19th-century architecture.

The imposing bulk of the Fortezza del Priamàr

🏛 Il Priamàr

Corso Mazzini (access from Ponte di San Giorgio). **Tel** 019 8310 325.
⏱ summer: 9am–midnight; winter: 9am–6:30pm daily. **Pinacoteca Civica** Palazzo Gavotti, Piazza Chabrol. **Tel** 019 811 520.
⏱ 8:30am–1:30pm Mon, 8:30am–1pm Wed & Fri, 2–7pm Tue & Thu, 8:30am–1pm, 8:30–11:30pm Sat (winter: 3:30–6pm), 10am–1:30pm Sun. 📷 ♿ **Civico Museo Storico-Archeologico Tel** 019 822 708.
⏱ Sep–Jun: 10am–12:30pm, 3–5pm Wed–Fri, 10:30am–3pm Sat–Mon; Jun–Sep: 10:30am–3pm daily.

The Roman writer Livy records the building of an early fortress here. Today's fort was erected on the site of the first Savona settlement (destroyed by the Romans following the war against Hannibal) in the 16th century, in a bid by Genoa to establish its hold over the port. It wasn't completed until 1680. During the 19th century, the Priamàr (derived from *pietra sul mare*, or "stone above the sea") was used as a prison: Giuseppe Mazzini, a key figure in the Risorgimento, was imprisoned here in 1830–31. Now restored, the Priamàr houses two of Liguria's most important museums, but it is also well worth a visit as a work of military architecture.

The entrance is across the San Giorgio bridge. To the left is the keep, from which visitors can reach, via ramps and embankments, the Bastione dell'Angelo, the Bastione di San Carlo and the so-called Cavallo Superiore, from which there are stunning views over the city.

Palazzo Gavotti (also known as Palazzo della Loggia), between the Angelo and San Carlo bastions, was built in the middle of the 16th century on medieval foundations, and modified in the 19th century. The

building houses two interesting museums. The most important one is the **Pinacoteca Civica**; spread over 22 rooms on the second and third floors, it is dedicated to works by Ligurian artists from the Middle Ages to the 20th century. Highlights on the third floor include *Crucifixions* by Donato de' Bardi and Giovanni Mazone, who were active in the 14th and 15th centuries. There is also a lovely polyptych (a part of which is in the Paris Louvre) by Mazone entitled *Christ on the Cross between the Marys and St John the Baptist* (1460s).

Many other painters from the 17th and 18th centuries, who were working in both Genoa and Savona, are represented, including Fiasella, Robatto, Guidobono, Brusco, Agostino and Bozzano. Among the contemporary art on display, Eso Peluzzi's works from the 1920s stand out.

The third floor also houses a collection of ceramics ranging from the 12th to the 20th centuries. Among the items on display are a particularly fine majolica jar decorated with historical scenes, ornamental vases and a 172-piece collection of apothecary jars created for a hospital that used to be located on this very site around the 16th century.

The second floor is taken up by the art collection of the late Italian president Sandro Pertini. It includes around 90 works by modern artists, such as Arnaldo and Giò Pomodoro, De Chirico, Guttuso, Manzù, Morandi, Sassu and Sironi. Some of the works, including those of Henry Moore and Joan Miró, bear a dedication.

Palazzo Pavoni on Via Paleocapa

*Crucifixion by Donato de' Bardi,
an early painting on canvas*

Also on the third floor are the four rooms of the Foundation Museum of Contemporary Art Milena Milani, with works by the likes of Magritte, Mirò, Picasso and Man Ray.

On the first floor of the palazzo is the **Civico Museo Storico-Archeologico**. The focus of the exhibits here is the original Savonese settlement, with finds gathered mostly from other (Roman or pre-Roman) collections, as well as items discovered in the city environs. Ceramics, amphorae and funerary objects from the Bronze and

Iron ages are on display, along with medieval weaving tools, ornamental objects and eating and drinking vessels. Well worth seeking out are the superb Arab- and Byzantine-influenced ceramics and the multicoloured and Savona majolica (typically coloured blue and white). There are also cooking pots and metal, bone and glass objects from local excavations, as well as a 5–6th-century burial ground.

🚩 Torre del Brandale

Piazza del Brandale.
The old port is one of the most attractive parts of the city, not so much for the mass of boats that moor here but for the backdrop of medieval towers.

Dating from the 12th century, the Torre del Brandadlei is one of the most interesting of Savona's old towers. It owes its name to the flagstaff on top, commonly known as the "brandale". Inside, traces of frescoes

The Torre del Brandale

VISITORS' CHECKLIST

Road Map C4. 🏠 *69,000.* FS
🚌 ℹ️ *Corso Italia, 157r,
019 840 23 21.*
🎭 *Good Friday procession,
Pasqua Musicale Savonese;
Concorso Nazionale della
Ceramica d'Arte (biennial
ceramics fair shared with
Albissola Marina; next in
2012); Confuoco (Sun before
Christmas).* **www**.turismo.
provincia.savona.it

from the same era can be seen, while on the façade there is a ceramic relief, entitled *Apparition*: first carved in 1513, what you see today dates from the 1960s. The tower's great bell is known to the Savonesi as "*a campanassa*" – a name used by a local history association which has its head-quarters in the adjacent Palazzo degli Anziani, formerly the seat of the podestà. Built in the 14th century, its façade dates from the 1600s.

SAVONA TOWN CENTRE

Cattedrale di Nostra Signora
    Assunta ⑧
Chiesa di Sant'Andrea ⑤
Il Priamàr ①
Nostra Signora di
    Castello ⑨
Oratorio del Cristo
    Risorto ⑦
Palazzo Della Rovere ⑥
Piazza Salineri ③
Torre del Brandale ②
Torre di Leon Pancaldo ④

0 metres   300
0 yards   300

Key to Symbols *see back flap*

Piazza Salineri

The heart of mercantile trading in the Middle Ages, thanks to its position by the sea, this lovely square still has traces of its former splendour, especially in the splendid, opening on to it: Via Orefici and Via Quarda Superiore.

Two interesting towers rise up above the piazza: the Ghibellina (dated 1200) and the tower of the Aliberti (1100). Nearby stands the dilapidated 16th-century Palazzo Martinengo, which bears a curious conundrum. Five proverbs have been muddled up to create a word game, and the onlooker is invited to reconstruct the sayings.

Torre di Leon Pancaldo

Piazza Leon Pancaldo

This small tower at one end of the harbour (by the cruise ship terminal) is the last remnant of the 14th-century walls. It is dedicated to the Savona-born navigator who accompanied Magellan on his voyages to the Americas, and who died on the Rio della Plata in 1537.

The tower features an effigy of the *Madonna della Misericordia*, patron saint of the city, dated 1662. Beneath it is a verse by the local poet Gabriello Chiabrera, dedicated to the Madonna: "In mare irato/In subita procella/Invoco Te/Nostra benigna stella", unusual

The Torre di Leon Pancaldo, known as the "Torretta"

For hotels and restaurants in this region see pp181-3 and pp195-7

Chiesa di Sant'Andrea

Via Palecapa. **Tel** 019 851 952.
☐ 8:30am–noon daily.

The lovely arcaded Via Palecapa, Savona's main shopping street, runs inland from the Torre di Leon Pancaldo. Notice the lovely Palazzo dei Pavoni at no. 3, designed by Alessandro Martinengo.

A short distance along the street, a broad flight of steps leads up to the church of Sant'Andrea. This was built at the beginning of the 18th century as the Jesuit church of Sant'Ignazio, on the site of a medieval church. It has an elegant façade, while inside there is an *Immaculate Conception* (1749) by Ratti and a *Madonna* (1500s) by Defendente Ferrari. In the sacristy is an icon of *St Nicholas* from Constantinople, and a *Madonna della Misericordia* (1800s), sculpted by Antonio Brilla.

Oratorio del Cristo Risorto

Via Palecapa. **Tel** 019 838 63 06.
☐ 4–7pm Mon–Sat; 8:30am–noon Sun.

Further along Via Palecapa, this oratory was reconstructed in the early 17th century as part of an existing convent of Augustinian nuns, the Santissima Annunziata. The façade is typical of many Baroque buildings in the region, which have richly painted architectural decoration instead of more sculptural motifs.

The interior, where chapels face onto a single room with a barrel vault, is charming. Liberally adorning the place are 18th-century trompe l'oeil frescoes and stuccoes, which create a wonderfully illusionistic background. Traditionally, the high altar is attributed to Francesco Parodi, but he may have been responsible only for the design; in the presbytery, the powerful statue of *Christ Arisen* (*Cristo Risorto*) to whom the oratory is dedicated, is by an unknown artist. The organ dates from 1757, and there are also some fine 15th-century carved choir stalls.

Maragliano's *Annunciation* (1722), the *Addolorata* (1795) by Filippo Martinengo and the *Deposition* (1866) by Antonio Brilla are three processional floats for which the oratory is famous. (Many churches in Savona have floats featuring scenes from the Passion which go onto the streets on Good Friday.)

Palazzo Della Rovere

Via Pia 28.

The ancient Via Pia, which begins near the oratory, is one of the most charming streets in the old city. Hemmed in and full of shops of every description, its medieval layout has lost none of its original fascination.

Fishing boats in the harbour, with the Torre del Brandale behind

At the far end of Via Pia, at no. 28, is Palazzo Della Rovere, now the police headquarters. This fine palace, begun in 1495, was designed by Giuliano da Sangallo (one of the architects of St Peter's in Rome) for Cardinal Giuliano Della Rovere, later Pope Julius II.

It became the property of the Spinola family and then, in 1673, was acquired by the Order of the Poor Clares. The nuns covered up the magnificent interior decoration with plaster and renamed it Palazzo Santa Chiara. (At one stage it was the Napoleonic prefecture.) With its façade divided into three storeys with pilasters, its two-tone marble cladding, and its vast courtyard, this palazzo is a clear example of Tuscan architecture, a rarity in the region. Only a very few of the splendid original frescoes are now visible inside.

⌂ Cattedrale di Nostra Signora Assunta

Piazza del Duomo.
Museo del Tesoro della Cattedrale *Tel 019 813 003.*
⏲ *10am–noon, 4–5:30pm Sat.*

This church was built in the late 16th century to replace the old cathedral of Santa Maria del Castello, which had been demolished (along with other buildings) to make space for the Priamàr fortress. Many of the contents of the old building were transferred to the new, including the splendid baptismal font, made from a beautifully carved Byzantine capital and a late 15th-century marble *Crucifixion*, both are found in the central nave, behind the façade. The imposing marble façade dates from the late 19th century and features, above the central door, an *Assumption* by the Carrara artist, Cibel (1706–84). Inside, the three aisles are divided

Adoration of the Magi by the Master of Hoogstraeten, Museo del Tesoro

by imposing columns and flanked by chapels. The frescoes in the central nave, like those of the presbytery and the transept, were produced between 1847 and 1951; the walls and the cupola (dated 1840) were decorated between 1891 and 1893.

In the presbytery is a masterpiece by Albertino Piazza, *Enthroned Madonna with Child and saints Peter and Paul*, and *Presentation of Mary at the Temple*, a marble relief dating from the 16th century. Also in the presbytery stand the splendid wooden choir stalls, dated 1515. Commissioned and financed by the Republic of Savona and Cardinal Giuliano Della Rovere for the new cathedral, they were removed from their original setting and then remodelled for the new semicircular apse.

In one of the chapels in the left-hand aisle is a notable fresco of the *Madonna della Colonna* (early 15th century), originally on a column in the Franciscan monastery on whose site the current cathedral was constructed. Also of note is the pulpit of the Evangelists (1522).

To the left of the presbytery there is access to the **Museo del Tesoro della Cattedrale**, a treasury museum with works from different sources. The core of the collection dates from the first half of the 14th century. Other works

Statue of the Assumption on the cathedral

include a polyptych, *Assumption and Saints*, by Ludovico Brea (1495), a *Madonna and saints* by Tuccio d'Andria (1487), and an *Adoration of the Magi* (early 16th century) by the Master of Hoogstraeten.

In the cloister alongside the church are 21 marble statues of saints. At the far end is Savona's own **Cappella Sistina**, built in 1481 for another Della Rovere pope, Sixtus IV (for whom the Sistine Chapel in the Vatican was built), as a resting place for his parents. The interior of the chapel was transformed in the 18th century, when rococo decoration in the form of multicoloured stucco was introduced. The marble tomb of Sixtus IV's parents (1483) is on the left-hand side.

⌂ Nostra Signora di Castello

Corso Italia. *Tel 019 804 892.*
⏲ *Sun am, for Mass.*

This small oratory is almost hidden from view on Corso Italia, a long street of elegant shops which, along with Via Paleocapa, was the most important road built during the expansion of Savona in the 19th century. It houses one of the finest paintings in the city – a late 15th-century polyptych of the *Madonna and Saints*, by the Lombard artist Vincenzo Foppa, completed by Ludovico Brea (one of Liguria's most active painters at that time).

The oratory also contains what is claimed to be the world's tallest processional float, a *Deposition* built by Filippo Martinengo in 1795.

The Ponte della Gaietta at Millesimo

Environs

Heading inland from Savona the first place of interest, about 14 km (9 miles) from the coast, is **Altare** in the Apennines. This town has been famous for the production of glass since at least the 11th century (before Murano glass from Venice came onto the scene.) The **Museo del Vetro e dell'Arte Vetraria** houses both antique and modern examples, as well as objects from the local school of engraved glass, and documents and books related to the subject, some as much as 800 years old. The displays include some splendid vases in blue crystal decorated in pure gold.

Also in the town is the church of the Annunziata (late 15th century), with a bell tower belonging to an earlier Roman building, and the late 17th-century Baroque church of Sant'Eugenio, whose façade is flanked by two bell towers. On the nearby hill of Cadibona is the Forte Napoleonico della Bocchetta, built in the late 18th century.

Nine km (6 miles) beyond Altare, on the left bank of the River Bormida di Spigno, lies **Cairo Montenotte**, important historically because Austro-Piemontese troops were defeated here by Napoleon Bonaparte in 1796.

Within the town, a large tower, called the Torrione, and the ogival Porta Soprana are all that remain of the original circle of 14th-century walls. On the hill overlooking the village are the ruins of an old castle, also dating from the 14th century and belonging originally to the Del Carretto family, local lords during the Middle Ages.

The parish church of San Lorenzo, with a tall bell tower, dates from 1630–40, though it was modified later. Local gastronomic specialities are fruit-flavoured amaretti and black truffles, best tasted with a glass of the local Dolcetto wine.

Millesimo, 27 km (17 miles) from Savona, is a charming hill town and the main centre in the upper Valle Bormida. It retains well-preserved traces of the late Middle Ages. The ruined castle (1206), on the edge of the town, dominates from on high, and once belonged to the Del Carretto family; the castle, like the town, later passed to the Spanish, and eventually ended up in the hands of the House of Savoy.

The central **Piazza Italia**, much of it arcaded, is very pretty; the so-called **Torre**, now the town hall, dates from around 1300 and was a Del Carretto residence.

The most striking monument in the town is the **Ponte della Gaietta**, whose simple design, complete with watch tower, dates from the 12th to 13th centuries.

🏛 **Museo del Vetro e dell'Arte Vetraria**
Villa Rosa, Piazza Consolato 4, Altare. ⬜ 4–7pm Tue–Fri & Sun, 3–7pm Sat.
www.museodelvetro.org

Bergeggi ❻

Savona. **Road Map** C4.
👥 1,200. FS 🚌 🛈 Pro Loco, Via Aurelia 1, 019 859 777 (seasonal).
www.turismo.provincia.savona.it

This small but busy coastal resort lies in a lovely spot on the slopes of Monte Sant'Elena. Records of a settlement on this site date back to Roman times. Its strategic position and its defences enabled the town to fend off Saracen raids in the 10th and 11th centuries. In 1385, Bergeggi became the seat of a colony of deportees set up by the Republic of Genoa, which governed the town at that time.

The town is distinctive for its houses with roof terraces overlooking the sea, and famous for its Claudio restaurant, which serves some of the best (and dearest) seafood on the entire Riviera.

Traces of the Middle Ages can be seen in two look-out towers, the **Torri di Avvistamento**, at the top of the town; the parish church of **San Martino** dates from the early 18th century.

The ruins of two ancient churches, a monastery and a tower can be seen on the nearby island of **Bergeggi**, an important religious centre in the Middle Ages. Now uninhabited, and also a nature reserve, the island is covered in thick vegetation. The entrance to a cave, 37 m

Coat of arms on the Porta Soprana, Cairo Montenotte

Bergeggi rooftops, with Bergeggi island in the background

For hotels and restaurants in this region see pp181–3 and pp195–7

The castle on Monte Ursino at Noli, with its tall central tower

The small island of Bergeggi, a tiny natural oasis a short distance from the coast ◁

(121 ft) long and 17 m (23 ft) wide, is visible at sea level. There are boats to Bergeggi from Savona and Finale Ligure in high season.

Spotorno ❼

Savona. **Road Map** C4.
👥 **4,300.** 🚉 *Piazza Matteotti 6, 019 741 50 08.* 🎭 *Festival del Vento (end Mar–early Apr); Rassegna Nazionale di Musica Etnica (Jul & Aug).* **www**.comune.spotorno.it

Despite the growth of tourism in this part of the region, which has transformed Spotorno into a large resort, the historic nucleus of this town has not lost the appearance of a Ligurian fishing village, with buildings scattered along the waterfront. There is also a good beach that is popular with locals and tourists.

Once the possession of the bishops of Savona, and later of the Del Carretto family, Spotorno was destroyed by neighbouring Noli in 1227. At the centre of the old town, focused around Via Mazzini and Via Garibaldi, rises the 17th-century parish church of the **Assunta.** Inside, the chapels feature frescoes by artists such as Andrea and Gregorio De Ferrari, Domenico Piola and Giovanni Agostino Ratti. There is more to see at the **Oratorio della Santissima Annunziata,** which contains works by the Genoese school (17th century) and a wooden sculpture by Maragliano (18th century).

Noli ❽

Savona. **Road Map** C4.
👥 **2,900.** 🚉 *Corso Italia 8, 019 749 90 03.* 🎭 *Regatta Storica dei Rioni (first or second Sun in Sep).* **www**.inforiviera.it

This is one of the best preserved medieval towns in the entire region. Its good fortune began in 1097, when it assisted in the first Crusade, thereby setting itself up to become a maritime power. In the early 13th century Noli allied itself with Genoa, and fought at her side against Pisa and Venice.

In the old town, the narrow alleys with suspended arches between the houses are reminiscent of the Centro

Storico in Genoa. Several of the once-numerous medieval towers survive. On Corso Italia, Noli's main street, look out for the 13th-century Torre Comunale and, next door, the **Palazzo Comunale** (15th century); the loggia that forms part of this palace recalls the arcades that once lined the Corso Italia. The **Cattedrale di San Pietro** is medieval beneath its Baroque shell. Inside, the apse contains a *Madonna enthroned with Child, angels and saints,* a polyptych by the school of Ludovico Brea (late 1400s). Also of note is the altar, which incorporates a Roman sarcophagus.

The wooden cross in the church of San Paragorio

as well as curious maritime ex votos. Above the town are the ruins of the 14th-century castello.

The key monument in Noli is, however, the church of **San Paragorio,** one of the finest examples of Romanesque in Liguria, originally built in the 11th century and beautifully restored in the late 19th. Blind arches and pilasters decorate the façade, adorned with exotic majolica. On the left are several Gothic tombs in Finale stone.

Inside, the church has three aisles with semicircular apses, also Romanesque. Highlights include a vast wooden cross (Romanesque), a 12th-century bishop's cathedra in wood, fragments of 14th-century frescoes, and a marble pulpit. On the slopes of Monte Ursino rise the ruins of a 12th-century **castello.** Battlemented walls connect the castle to the town below.

The arching beach overlooked by the resort of Spotorno

Finale Ligure ❾

Savona. **Road Map** C4. *13,000.*
FS *Pro Loco, Via San Pietro 14, Finale Marina, 019 681 019.*
Festa dell'Assunta at Finalpia (15–20 Aug); historic re-enactment of the exploits of the Marchesi Del Carretto (Aug & Sep).
www.turismo,provincia.savona.it and **www**.comunefinaleligure.it

Finale Ligure consists of the three separate communities of Pia, Marina and Borgo, united in 1927 to form one of the main towns on the Riviera di Ponente. Finale Marina, the buzzing resort overlooking pebbly beaches, with a smattering of smart 16th–18th century palazzi, is the newest part, while nearby Finale Pia and Finalborgo, just inland and protected from the worst of the modern development along the coast, grew up in the Middle Ages.

Finale Pia, across the river Sciusa from Finale Marina, developed around the church of **Santa Maria di Pia**, which is the most important monument in the town and was first documented in 1170. The rococo-style façade dates from the 18th century, and the interior is also Baroque. The bell tower is medieval. The grandiose 16th-century Benedictine abbey next door contains some coloured terracottas by the Tuscan Della Robbia school (15th–16th centuries).

The bell tower of San Biagio

The most interesting of the three villages is Finalborgo, whose old centre remains almost intact within its 15th-century walls. Elegant houses and palazzi abound, many now housing shops, small cafés and restaurants. (Finalborgo is famous for its basil, so pasta with pesto is a speciality here and should not be missed.)

THE PARCO DEL FINALESE

Grotto in the Parco del Finalese

Limestone rock with reddish veining is found in abundance in the hinterland behind Finale, and forms an amphitheatre of cliffs that is the focus of the Parco del Finalese. Some 20 million years old, the cliffs are riddled with caves in which evidence of paleolithic life has been found. To reach the area, take the road to Manie, which runs inland from Finale Pia. Fans of freeclimbing will find the upland plain of Le Manie an absolute paradise. There are traces of Roman and even pre-Roman roads in this area. A Roman road, the Via Julia Augusta, ran through the tiny Val Ponci, just north of Manie, and you can still see the remains of five Roman bridges, some of which are in excellent condition.

The church of **San Biagio** dates largely from the 17th century, but retains its Gothic bell tower, the symbol of Finalborgo. Inside is a marble pulpit by Schiaffino, a fine example of Genoese Baroque.

The ex-convent of **Santa Caterina**, founded in 1359, is home to the **Civico Museo del Finale**, which exhibits archaeological finds from prehistoric times to the Middle Ages, including Roman-era objects.

One of the best examples of Ligurian Baroque is the basilica of **San Giovanni Battista** in Finale Marina. Its façade is flanked by two bell towers, and inside there is a wooden *Crucifixion* by Maragliano (18th century).

Civico Museo del Finale
Chiostri di Santa Caterina, Finalborgo. ***Tel*** *019 690 020. Jul & Aug: 10am–noon, 4–7pm Tue–Sun (to 10pm Wed & Fri); Sep–Jun: 9am–noon, 2:30–5pm Tue–Sun.*

Environs

Varigotti, some 6 km (4 miles) up the coast towards Noli, is almost impossibly pretty, with its colourful houses and a truly gorgeous setting overlooking a broad sandy beach. The fishermen's houses, painted in all shades of ochre and pink, are of particular interest since they date from the 14th-century settlement founded by the Del Carretto, a local dynasty all-powerful in the Middle Ages.

On Capo di Varigotti, you can see the ruins of the Byzantine-Lombard fortifications (Varigotti was originally a Byzantine settlement, destroyed in the 7th century by the Lombards), as well as the remains of a castle built by the Del Carretto. North of the old town is the church of San Lorenzo Vecchio, of medieval origin. It stands in a dramatic position, facing a precipice jutting over the sea.

Typical fishermen's houses on the beach at Varigotti

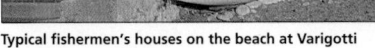

Borgio Verezzi ⑩

Savona. **Road Map** C4.
🏠 *2,200*. **FS** 🚌 **ℹ** *Via Matteotti
158, 019 610 412 (seasonal)*.
🎭 *open-air and classic
theatre seasons (summer;*
www.festivalverezzi.it
www.comuneborgioverezzi.it

This town is formed by
the two distinct centres of
Borgio, on the coast, and
Verezzi, on the slope above.
The medieval heart of Borgio
has remained virtually intact:
old cobbled streets alternate
with gardens and orchards,
rising up to the 17th-century
parish church of **San Pietro**.
Near the cemetery is the

Piazza Sant'Agostino in Borgio Verezzi

pretty medieval church of
Santo Stefano, with a bell
tower of decorative brick.
    A winding scenic road leads
up to Verezzi. Of the four
groups of houses that make
up the village, all on different
levels, the best preserved is
Piazza, which still displays
some Saracen influence. At
the centre stands the church
of **Sant'Agostino** (1626).
There is a view over the sea
from one side of the pretty
church square.

Environs

Inside the limestone caves
of the nearby **Grotte di
Valdemino** are stalactites so
slim that they vibrate at the
sound of a voice, as well as
magical underground lakes.
Fossils of saber-tooth tigers,
cave bears and elephants
have been discovered here.

🐾 **Grotte di Valdemino**
Via Battorezza. **Tel** *019 610 150*.
📅 *Jun–Sep: 9:30am, 10:30am,
11:30am, 3:20pm, 4:20pm, 5:20pm;
Oct–May: 9:30am, 10:30am,
11:30am, 3pm, 4pm, 5pm.* ⬤ *25
Dec, 1 Jan.* 📷 *with permission.*

Pietra Ligure ⑪

Savona. **Road Map** B4. 🏠 *9,400*.
FS 🚌 **ℹ** *Piazza Martin Liberté
31, 019 629 003*. 🎭 *Processione
di San Nicolò (8 Jul); Confoëgu
(24 Dec).* **www**.turismo.provincia.
savona.it

The name of this delightful
beach resort translates as
"Ligurian stone" and derives
from the rocky outcrop to
the northeast of the old town,
where a fortified site stood
in the Byzantine era. The
medieval town grew up
around the base of the
castello, a Genoese stronghold that underwent
alterations in the 16th century
and again in later
centuries. The so-called
Borgo Vecchio was
planned on a regular
layout with five streets
running parallel to the
coastline. As you stroll
along these streets
today, you notice how
both medieval houses
and 16–17th century
palazzi rub shoulders,
an unusual architectural
combination that resulted from
a programme of partial reconstruction in the 16th century.
    The 10th-century **Oratorio
dei Bianchi** stands in Piazza
Vecchia (also known as Piazza
del Mercato). In the bell
tower is the "holy bronze" –
according to local legend, the
bell rang in 1525 to announce
the end of the plague. In
Piazza XX Settembre, not far
from the sea, stands the 18th-
century church of **San Nicolò
di Bari**, its façade flanked by
two bell towers.

Environs

Just inland, high up above
Pietra Ligure, is the village
of **Giustenice**, from where
there are superb views over
the coast. This former Del
Carretto stronghold lost its
castle in the 15th century.

Loano ⑫

Savona. **Road Map** B4.
🏠 *11,000*. **FS** 🚌
ℹ *Corso Europa 19, 019 676 007*.
🎭 *Carnevalöa, Liguria's largest
carnival (in summer)*.
www.turismo.provincia.savona.it
and **www**.cai.loano.com *(for up-to-
date information on walking in the
Loano and Finalese areas)*.

Ever since Roman times,
Loano has been a desirable
place to live. It has been the
property of, among others,
the bishops of Albenga, the
Doria family and the Republic
of Genoa. (It was also the site
of Napoleon's first victory in
Italy.) These days Loano is
an extremely pleasant town
with an extensive beach.
    The most interesting build-
ing is the 16th-century **Palazzo
Comunale**, built for the Doria
family. Its austere appearance
is softened by balconies and
loggias, while a gallery links it
to a watch tower (1602) that
features a beautiful Roman
mosaic pavement.
    In 1603, the Doria family
founded the **Convento di
Monte Carmelo**, in a lovely
spot in the hills above Loano.
The complex includes a
church full of Doria tombs
and the Casotto, a favourite
Doria residence.

The medieval castle dominating Pietra Ligure

Grotte di Toirano ⑬

Logo of the
Grotte di Toirano

These caves, a real wonder of nature, are among the most beautiful in Italy. They are situated in the karst area of the Val Varatella, between Albenga and Pietra Ligure. Discovered by young researchers and speleologists from Toirano in 1950, these subterranean caves, full of broad caverns, stalactites and stalagmites of all sizes and rare crystal formations, are reminiscent of images of hell. Of prime importance is the beautiful Grotta della Basura ("Cave of the Witch" in Ligurian dialect), where traces of Paleolithic man and also the extinct cave bear have been found. The caves are also the habitat of the largest ocellated lizards in Europe. The site, which is about 1.3 km (0.8 miles) in length and can be toured in around 90 minutes, is one of the greatest attractions of the Riviera di Ponente.

★ Sala dei Misteri
Traces of prehistoric man are still visible here. The balls of clay buried at the cave walls were probably concerned with propitiatory rites or hunting ceremonies. The Sala dei Misteri is currently closed to the public.

The Antro di Cibele
offers the extremely rare spectacle of rounded concretions, spherical even, which have been shaped by rhythmical but continuous fluctuations in the water level.

Sala Morelli
The route within the Grotta della Basura starts in this room. A little further ahead is the Torre di Pisa (left), an impressive central stalagmite formed when water ceased to flow on the cave floor.

Entrance

In the Bear Cemetery
visitors can see footprints of *Ursus spelaeus* (cave bear).

★ Salotto
Venturing further into the cave system, you reach the area known as the Salotto ("drawing room"). Here, stalactites, stalagmites and wall concretions create a truly fairytale environment, mirrored in the waters of an underground pool, with light playing off the surfaces.

For hotels and restaurants in this region see pp181–3 and pp195–7

STAR FEATURES

★ Grotta di Santa Lucia Inferiore

★ Sala dei Misteri

★ Salotto

The Landscape
Toirano is in the high Val Varatella, characterized by steep-sided walls of karst rock. There are lovely views of the landscape from the road leading to the caves.

KEY

① Grotta della Bàsura

② Grotta di Santa Lucia Inferiore

③ Grotta di Santa Lucia Superiore (open only 13 Dec for patron saint's day)

④ Grotta del Colombo (closed to the public)

★ Grotta di Santa Lucia Inferiore
This cave shows no human or animal traces but contains beautiful and rare crystallized deposits, including these aragonite flowers.

In the Corridoio delle Colonne evidence of ancient earthquakes can be seen in the fracture lines which split numerous formations in half.

Sala del Pantheon
This cavern contains a stalagmite which reaches the great height of 8m (26 ft) and which, in its vast scale and visual impact, evokes images of Dante's Inferno. Aragonite flowers cover it like a light dusting of sugar on a biscuit.

VISITORS' CHECKLIST

Toirano (Savona). Road Map B4.
Piazzale Grotte, Toirano.
Tel 0182 980 62. Caves and
Museo Etnografico Toirano
Oct–Jun: 9:30am–12:30pm, 2–
5pm; Jul, Aug: 9:30am–12:30pm,
2–5:30pm. Night excursions:
9pm Thu (book ahead). toirano.it and
www.toiranogrotte.it

Street-by-Street: Albenga ⑭

In the province of Savona, Albenga is one of the Riviera di Ponente's most important cities. It owes its fame not only to its historic centre, one of the best-preserved in Liguria, but also to the mildness of its climate and the fertility of the surrounding plain, which has been under cultivation since the Roman era and produces a wide range of fruit and vegetables. The Roman town of *Albingaunum* was founded on the site of a port built by the Ingauni, a Ligurian tribe. For centuries, Albenga's prosperity depended on the River Centa, but its role as a major sea power declined after Genoa asserted itself, and following the silting-up of the port. A long avenue links the old city to the coast, now a short distance away.

Porta Molino
is the largest of the gates in the city walls.

Porta Torlaro
A solid bastion called Il Torracco, once used as a prison, projects from the northwest corner of the city wall. Alongside is 17th-century Porta Torlaro.

Lengueglia Doria Tower and House lie at the end of Via Ricci. The tower dates from the 13th century, while the brickwork house was built in the 15th century.

Via Bernardo Ricci, lined with intact or restored medieval houses, is Albenga's most picturesque long street. In the Roman era it formed part of the main road or *decumanus maximus*, as did its continuation Via Enrico d'Aste.

Loggia dei Quattro Canti
Set at the corner of Via Ricci and Via Medaglie d'Oro, this loggia features one rounded arch and one ogival arch and dates from the transitional period between the Romanesque and Gothic styles. In the Middle Ages, it served to increase visibility and ease the traffic flow at the crossroads.

★ Baptistry
This is the only example of late Roman architecture left intact in Albenga. Built by the general Costanzo in the early 5th century, the baptistry is the foremost Early Christian monument in Liguria.

★ Piazza dei Leoni

This square, the most charming spot in the city, is named after three stone lions (leoni) which were brought here from Rome in 1608 by the local counts Costa. Medieval houses overlook the piazza, one side of which is formed by the apse of the cathedral.

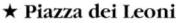

KEY

– – – Recommended route

★ Cathedral

Rebuilt in the Middle Ages on the site of an early Christian basilica (from the same era as the Baptistry), the cathedral is dedicated to St Michael. The fine bell tower dates from the late Gothic period.

| 0 metres | 50 |
| 0 yards | 50 |

VICO A P ZA S. FRANCESCO

PIAZZA DEI LEONI

PIAZZA SAN FRANCESCO

PIAZZA IV NOVEMBRE

HELE

VIA ENRICO D'ASTE

PIAZZA D'ERBE

LARGO DORIA

VIA SANTA EULALLIA

Santa Maria in Fontibus
This church on Via Enrico d'Aste has medieval origins but was remodelled in 1600. The façade has a 14th-century stone door.

STAR SIGHTS

★ Baptistry
_____

★ Cathedral
_____

★ Piazza dei Leoni

Exploring Albenga

Detail of the Baptistry mosaics

In the old heart of Albenga, with its superb collection of medieval piazzas, palazzi and churches, the streets are set at intersecting right angles, reflecting the grid layout of the *castrum* (or military camp) of the early Roman town. With its plethora of red-brick tower-houses, some still standing proud, some now much reduced, and many now restored, the historic centre of Albenga is utterly delightful. This rare example of a medieval city built on Roman foundations is undoubtedly one of the top places to visit in the whole of Liguria and should not be missed. There are two excellent museums, the Museo Navale Romano and the Civico Museo Ingauno, but a stroll along Via Enrico d'Aste, Via Bernardo Ricci and Via Medaglie d'Oro is sufficient to appreciate the beauty of the place.

Medieval fresco in the loggia of Palazzo Vecchio del Comune

Roman amphorae at the Museo Navale in Palazzo Peloso Cepolla

🏛 Palazzo Peloso Cepolla
Piazza San Michele.
Museo Navale Romano
Tel 0182 512 15. ◻ *winter:*
10am–12:30pm, 2:30–6pm Tue–Sun;
summer 9.30am–12:30pm, 3:30–
7:30pm Tue–Sun. 🎫 🅿
Originally made up of several buildings – the medieval part of the palazzo came to light only recently – the Palazzo Peloso Cepolla was unified in a single late Renaissance building in the 17th century. The building is dominated by a Romanesque tower.

The palazzo is home to the **Museo Navale Romano**. Its most important finds include more than 1,000 amphorae, vases and other objects found on board the wreck of a Roman ship which sank off the coast of Albenga in the 1st century BC.

Pharmacy jars from the hospital of Albenga, dating from between 1500 and 1700, are made of the white and blue pottery typical of Savona and Albisola.

🄰 Cathedral of San Michele
Piazza San Michele.
◻ *7:30am–8pm daily.*
Overlooking Albenga's lovely main square, the cathedral is the old seat of both civil and religious authority. It has been remodelled several times since its construction in the Middle Ages (on the site of an Early Christian church), but remnants of the Romanesque building survive: including blind arches in the lower part of the façade, and elements of the apse. The fine bell tower, rebuilt in the late 14th century, is Gothic, but its base of large stone blocks is Romanesque.

The interior was returned to its simple 13th-century form by restoration work carried out in the 1960s. Highlights inside include a fresco of the *Crucifixion with Saints* (1500), the 19th-century frescoes

Decoration on the façade of the cathedral

in the central nave, an enormous 19th-century organ, and the Carolingian crypt.

🏛 Palazzo Vecchio del Comune
Via Nino Lamboglia 1.
Civico Museo Ingauno
Tel 0182 512 15. ◻ *winter:*
10am–12:30pm, 2:30–6pm Tue–Sun;
summer: 9:30am–12:30pm, 3:30–
7:30pm Tue–Sun. 🎫 🅿
This building dates from the early 14th century and, with the contemporaneous Torre Comunale, forms a truly impressive medieval complex. The cathedral tower, the Torre Comunale and the tower of the Palazzo Vecchio itself are known as "Preghiera" (prayer), "Governo" (government) and "Giustizia" (justice) respectively.

The side of the palazzo facing Via Ricci has the great Loggia Comunale (1421), built of brick and with sturdy round pillars supporting the heavy arches. On the rear façade, facing the Baptistry, are decorative Ghibelline (swallowtail) battlements and a steep double staircase. At the top of the tower is a big bell known as the *campanone*, cast in 1303.

The Palazzo Vecchio del Comune houses the **Civico Museo Ingauno**, with finds from around Albenga, dating from the pre-Roman era to the Middle Ages. Objects include mosaics, tomb-stones, sculptures and Roman ceramics. Make sure you carry on right to the top floor, from where there is a lovely view of the city.

🔒 Baptistry

Piazza San Michele. ☐ *combined ticket with the Museo Ingauno.*
Albenga's most important monument is also the only remaining evidence of the Early Christian era in the whole of Liguria. It is thought to have been founded by Constantius, general to the emperor Honorius, in the 5th century. Restoration work in the 20th century returned the building to its original appearance.

Unusually, the Baptistry takes the form of an irregular decagon outside and a regular octagon inside. There is a niche in each of these eight sides, with columns of Corsican granite topped by Corinthian capitals supporting the arches above. The entrance to the Baptistry is through one of these niches, while others function as windows; two of the latter feature beautiful sandstone transennas. In another niche, part of its original blue and white mosaic decoration is still visible.

On the altar niche is a *Trinity and the apostles*, a 5–6th century mosaic in Byzantine style; in another is a Romanesque fresco of the *Baptism of Christ*. The Baptistry also contains some interesting medieval tombs with Lombard-style reliefs, and at the centre is an octagonal font for total immersion baptisms, with traces of 5th-century frescos.

The cupola dates from the 19th century: its predecessor, possibly the original, was dismantled prior to that, probably in error.

The interior of the Baptistry, with the remains of a font at its centre

ISOLA GALLINARA

Riserva Naturale Regionale dell'Isola Gallinara *Tel 0182 541 351 (comune di Albenga).* **www**.parks.it

This island lies just off the coast between Albenga and Alassio. Its name derives from the hundreds of wild hens *(galline)* that used to be resident here. It was also once inhabited by hermit monks: St Martin of Tours found refuge here in the 4th century and Benedictine monks later founded an abbey, which was destroyed in the late 15th century; its ruins are still visible. At the top of the island stands the Torre di Vedetta, a tower built by the Republic of Genoa in the 16th century. Isola Gallinara is now a nature reserve and cannot be visited. Boat trips (including for diving) leave from Alassio.

🔒 Palazzo Vescovile

Piazza San Michele.
Museo Diocesano d'Arte Sacra
Tel 0182 502 88. ☐ *10am–noon, 3–6pm Tue–Sun.* 📷
This palazzo, whose principal façade faces the Baptistry, is an assembly of medieval buildings, rebuilt in the 16th century. The oldest wing, to the far right, dates from around 1000, while a 12th-century tower rises from the left-hand corner. On Via Ricci, typically Genoese black and white striped decoration, dating from the 15th century, is still visible.

The Palazzo Vescovile is now home to the **Museo Diocesano d'Arte Sacra**, where visitors can admire precious church furnishings, illuminated manuscripts, Flemish tapestries, silverware and some fine works of art, including *Martyrdom of St Catherine* by Guido Reni, a *Last Supper* by Domenico Piola and an *Annunciation* by Domenico Fiasella, all painted in the 17th century.

Environs

A short distance south of Albenga, interesting archaeological ruins of the Roman town of *Albingaunum* can be seen, including an amphitheatre, aqueduct, various other buildings and a funerary monument known as "il Pilone"; there are also traces of Roman road, thought to have been part of the Via Julia Augusta *(see p144)*.

Around 10 km (6 miles) west of the city, **Villanova d'Albenga** (close to the international airport) is well worth a visit. This fortified settlement, laid out in the 13th century to provide extra protection for Albenga, has a polygonal layout and outer walls reinforced with square towers. The alleys through the town are full of atmosphere and the scent of the abundant flowers that the locals use to adorn their windows and doorways.

The famous "Muretto" of Alassio, in front of Caffè Roma

Alassio 15

Savona. **Road Map** B4. [img] 11,300.
[FS] [bus] Piazza della Libertà 5,
0182 647 027. [img] Election of "Miss
Muretto" (late Aug); Premio Alassio
Centolibri, a literature prize (summer).
www.comune.alassio.sv.it

A beach of beautifully fine
sand, which extends for
some 4 km (over 2 miles) and
slopes almost imperceptibly
down to the sea, makes
Alassio the undisputed queen
of the Riviera delle Palme. In
the 19th century, it became a
favourite holiday destination
among the English, who came
here and built splendid villas
with gardens. Many of these,
including some Art Nouveau
gems, have since been turned
into hotels.

Local legend has it that the
town's name derives from
Adelasia, daughter of Holy
Roman Emperor Otto I of
Saxony, who came here
in the 10th century.
(Alassio is still very
popular with German
visitors). Originally a
fishing village, in the
Middle Ages it became
the property of Albenga
and, later, of Genoa. The
Roman road Via Aurelia
still passes through it.
The typically Ligurian
character of Alassio can
be seen in the long
carruggio (narrow street)
that runs parallel with
the sea, hemmed in by
16th–17th-century houses
and modern shops; this is
Via XX Settembre, known

as the "Budello", and the heart
of the town's commercial life.
From here, narrow streets
known locally as *esci* fan out,
leading to the seafront.

At the corner of Via Dante
and Via Cavour, **Caffè Roma**
has been a popular meeting
place since the 1930s. In the
1950s, the café's owner had
the idea of making ceramic
tiles out of the autographs of
famous visitors to Caffè Roma,
to hang on the wall of the
garden opposite. The **Muretto**
now bears the signatures of
many famous personalities,
including Ernest Hemingway,
Jean Cocteau and Dario Fo.

Alassio's most significant
monument is the parish
church of **Sant'Ambrogio**.
Founded in the 1400s, it has a
19th-century façade, an early
16th-century bell tower and
a Baroque interior.

Environs
From Alassio, you can
go on a lovely (but
steep) panoramic walk
along the route
of an old Roman
road, the start of an
archaeological walk
that runs all the way to
Albenga. In 45 minutes
you can reach Capo
Santa Croce, where a small
13th-century church of the
same name overlooks the sea.
At the southern end of the
bay of Alassio lies **Laigueglia**,
a civilized seaside resort
with a well-preserved and
picturesque old centre. Of
Roman origin, it became an
important centre for coral

The round tower in Laigueglia

fishing in the 16th century.
A round tower, known as the
Torrione circolare (1564), the
only bastion remaining of
three which once protected
Laigueglia from pirates, is the
oldest building in the village.
The church of **San Matteo**
has two bell towers with
bright, majolica-covered
cupolas, a delightful example
of Ligurian Baroque.

On the ridge between
Laigueglia and Andora is **Colla
Micheri**, a hamlet whose
houses were restored and
made into a home by Thor
Heyerdahl, the Norwegian
navigator and ethnologist
famous for his epic journey
by raft from Peru to Polynesia
in 1958; he died here in 2002.

Santi Giacomo e Filippo church, Andora

Andora 16

Savona. **Road Map** B4.
[img] 6,500. [FS] [bus] [img] Via Aurelia
122/a, Villa Laura, 0182 681 004.
[img] Estate Musicale Andorese,
festival of classical music in church of
Santi Giacomo e Filippo (Jul & Aug).
www.comune.andora.sv.it

The last coastal town at the
western end of the Riviera
delle Palme, Andora groups
together several communities,
including Marina di Andora
on the coast. Founded
perhaps by the Phocaeans,
from Asia Minor, several
centuries BC, Andora later
belonged to the Romans, who
built a bridge over the River
Merula. The ten-arched Ponte
Romano visible today dates,
in fact, from the Middle Ages.
The old Roman road goes
up to the ruins of **Andora
Castello**, in a lovely spot at
the top of the hill. Built by
the Marchesi di Clavesana in
around 1000, this fortified

Cervo ⑦

Imperia. Road Map B5.
👥 1,300. 🚉 FS 🚌 ℹ️ AT, Piazza Santa Caterina 2, Tel 0183 408 197. 🎵 Festival Internazionale di Musica da Camera, chamber music festival (nine evenings Jul & Aug). www.rivieradeifiori.org and

This village, perched on a hill between Capo Cervo and the mouth of the River Cervo, signals the beginning of the province of Imperia. Once the property of the Del Carretto and then the Doria families, from the 14th century Cervo came under Genoese domination and followed that city's fortunes. Nowadays, Cervo is an extremely pretty resort, with houses painted in white and pale shades of yellow overlooking a shingle beach. Dominating the village is a 12th-century **castello**, which belonged to the Marchesi di Clavesana and was a control point along the Via Aurelia in the Middle Ages. The site is now occupied by the **Museo Etnografico del Ponente Ligure**, which features reconstructions of life at sea and on land, together with original rooms from a local house.

Facing the sea is the attractive parish church of **San Giovanni Battista**, with its distinctive concave, stucco-embellished façade that

Museo Etnografico, Cervo

features a stag (*cervo* in Italian). Begun in 1686, it is a fine example of Ligurian Baroque. The bell tower and the interior, which is decorated with frescoes and stuccoes, both date from the 18th century. The latter contains a *St John the Baptist*, a 17th-century work in multicoloured wood by Poggio, and an 18th-century *Crucifixion* attributed to Maragliano. Also in the town there are several interesting 17th- and 18th-century palazzi. These include **Palazzo Morchio**, now the town hall, and **Palazzo Viale**, which has 18th-century porticoes.

complex must have been impressive in its heyday. Through the castle gate is the lovely church of **Santi Giacomo e Filippo**, founded in around 1100 and once part of the castle's defences. Entirely built out of stone from nearby Capo Mele, the church façade is adorned with Gothic cornices and arches. Inside, there are great round columns and octagonal pilasters of bare stone. Another church within the castle, San Nicolò, is of proto-Romanesque origins.

ⅲ Museo Etnografico del Ponente Ligure
Piazza Santa Caterina 2, Tel 0183 408 197. ⏰ 9am–12:30pm, 3–7pm daily (Jul & Aug, 4:30–10pm).

Pieve di Teco ⑱

Imperia. Road Map B4.
👥 1,450. FS Imperia Oneglia. ℹ️ Piazza Brunengo 1, 0183 364 53. 🛍 Mercatino dell'Antiquariato e dell'Artigianato, antiques and craft market (last Sun of month).

Heading inland, almost as far as the border with Piemonte, you reach the busy market town of Pieve di Teco. Founded in 1293, the town belonged, like many others in the area, to the Marchesi di Clavesana and subsequently (from the late 14th century) to Genoa. The town is known for its handmade

walking boots, as well as its small but excellent antiques market held on the last Sunday of the month. Two squares mark either end of the arcaded and typically medieval **Corso Ponzoni**, the heart of the town. On either side, craft workshops alternate with the

palazzi of well-to-do families. The oldest part of Pieve di Teco is focused around the 15th-century church of **Santa Maria della Ripa**. Also of interest is the late 18th-century collegiate church of **San Giovanni Battista**, which contains several important paintings, including a *St Francis de Paul* attributed to Luca Cambiaso (16th century), and a *Last Supper* by Domenico Piola (17th century). The 15th-century **Convento degli Agostiniani** has the largest cloister (which is also one of the prettiest) in the whole region. Not far from the town, a lovely medieval humpbacked bridge straddles the River Arroscia.

The porticoes on Corso Ponzoni

The medieval bridge over the Arroscia, close to Pieve di Teco

Imperia ⓳ - Oneglia

Coat of arms of the Museo dell'Olivo, Imperia

One of four provincial capitals in Liguria, Imperia lies at the centre of the coastal strip known as the Riviera dei Fiori. It consists of the two centres of Oneglia and Porto Maurizio, united in 1923 by Mussolini. People like to say that he chose the name Imperia out of arrogance, but it derives from the River Impero, which divides the two centres. Historically rivals, the two cities seem to share as little as possible (there are two harbours, two railway stations, even two dialects). Imperia is fascinating because of its split personality.

The name Oneglia probably derives from a plantation of elms (*olmi*), on which the town was originally built. Oneglia was recorded in documents as far back as 935, when it was destroyed by the Saracens. From the 11th century it was owned by the bishops of Albenga, but they sold it to the Doria family in 1298. (The great admiral, Andrea Doria, was born here in 1466.) The House of Savoy claimed ownership for a time, but Oneglia, along with Porto Maurizio, passed into the hands of the Genoese republic in 1746. The House of Savoy returned in 1814, and made Oneglia the provincial capital. In 1887, an earthquake caused severe damage to the town.

The Port

East of the mouth of the River Impero, the port of Oneglia (Porto di Levante) is dedicated largely to commercial trade, in particular the trade in olive oil (the town has a museum devoted to olive oil); there is

also a vast pasta factory on the seafront. The port, whose appearance dates mainly from the Savoy period, is the centre of activity in Oneglia. In the summer (from mid-June to mid-September), look out for boats offering to take guests out to sea to watch whales and dolphins – a great experience.

🏛 Calata Giovan Battista Cuneo

This characteristic quay building faces the harbour, its traditional arcades perfectly designed to shelter fishmongers, trattorias and fishermen's houses. When the boats of Oneglia's fishing fleet return from their trips out on the open sea, an auction of fresh fish is held here, usually around the middle of the afternoon. The fish trade is vital to the local economy. The local bars and restaurants are always entertaining places to while away the time.

🔒 Collegiata di San Giovanni Battista

Piazza San Giovanni.
Tel 0183 292 671. 🕐 *8am–noon, 3–7pm daily.*

This church stands in the piazza of the same name, right at the heart of Oneglia's shopping district. It was built from 1739–62 in late Baroque style, though the façade was finished only in 1838. The fresco decoration inside also dates from the 19th century.

Look out for the marble tabernacle (to the left of the presbytery), which dates from 1516 and is attributed to the Gagini school; various saints are represented here and, in the lunette, *Christ arising from the Tomb.* Also of interest are the wooden choir stalls; the lovely *Madonna del Rosario* (in the first chapel in the left-hand aisle), attributed to the school of the 18th-century sculptor Maragliano; and *St Clare drives out the Saracens* (1681), a moving work painted by Gregorio De Ferrari, a native of Porto Maurizio, though he spent much of his time in Genoa.

The Madonna del Rosario

🏛 Chiesa di San Biagio

Piazza Ulisse Calvi.
Tel 0183 292 747.
🕐 *7–11:30am, 4–6pm daily.*

This church, dated 1740, has a sober façade and a Baroque bell tower. The spacious, light-filled interior is shaped, curiously, in an oval and ends in a choir.

The church contains various works of art, among them a *Gloria di San Biagio* (Glory of St Blaise) by Bocciardo, visible in the apse, and a wooden *Crucifixion* by the school of Maragliano on the right-hand altar.

🏛 Via Bonfante

From Piazza San Giovanni, the pedestrian street of Via San Giovanni leads north to Via Bonfante, Oneglia's main shopping street. This is a wonderful place for a stroll, and for soaking up the atmosphere of the town.

The multicoloured, arcaded houses of Calata Giovan Battista Cuneo

Piazza Dante, at the heart of Oneglia

VISITORS' CHECKLIST

Road Map B5. 🚊 *40,400.* 🚉
🚌 ℹ️ *Porto Maurizio, Viale Matteotti 37, 0183 660 140.* 🚤 *Infiorata del Corpus Domini, Raduno Internazionale di Vele d'Epoca, a gathering of historic boats (Sep, even years only).* **www**.visitrivieradeifiore.it

Beneath Via Bonfante's 19th-century arcades visitors can find all manner of art galleries and shops (including several designer boutiques), as well as cafés that manage to tempt even the hardiest passers-by inside.

🚱 Piazza Dante

At the end of Via Bonfante is the central Piazza Dante. This is the real heart of Oneglia, also known locally as the "Piazza della Fontana" (square of the fountain).

A busy crossroads, the piazza is surrounded by neo-medieval palazzi: among the most interesting of these is the ex-**Palazzo Comunale**, at no. 4, built in the 1890s in an eclectic mix of styles.

🏛 Museo dell'Olivo

Via Garessio 11. **Tel** *0183 295 762.* ◯ *9am–12:30pm, 3–6pm Mon–Sat.* 🎫 ♿
www.museodellolivo.com
Housed in an old olive oil mill, the Museo dell'Olivo was opened by the Fratelli Carli, owners of just one of the many local producers of olive oil that compete for market share in the region.

One part of the museum traces the history of olive cultivation, starting with the Roman period, when the oil was used more for medical and cosmetic purposes than as a food; little bottles, used to store oil as perfume or medicine, are on display. There is also a reconstruction of the hold of a Roman ship,

which shows how amphorae full of olive oil were stacked ready for transportation.

The main section, complete with audiovisual aids, is dedicated to explaining the production of olive oil: on display are all sorts of mills, presses, machines for filtering oil, and containers for storing and for transporting it.

The visit concludes with a visit to an oil mill that is still being used by the Fratelli Carli company.

Reconstruction of the hold in a Roman ship with its cargo of oil

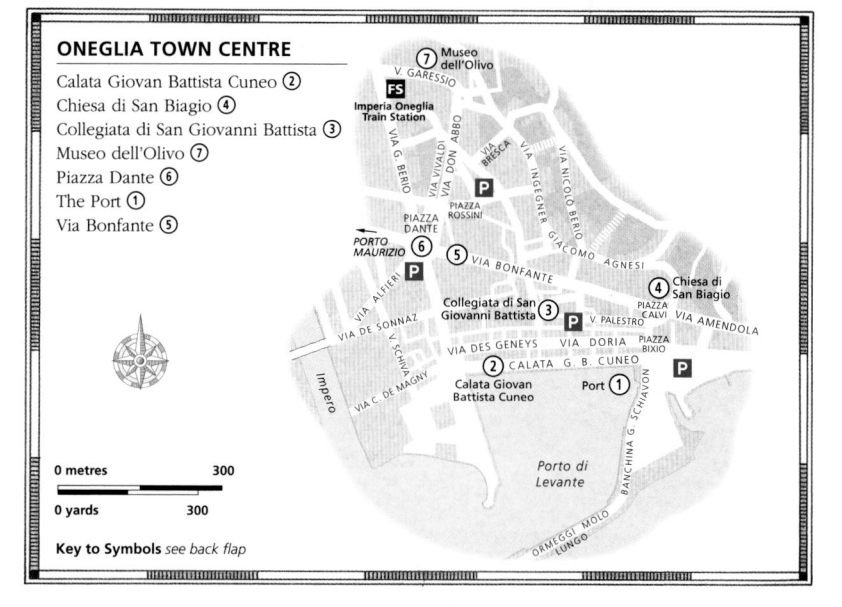

ONEGLIA TOWN CENTRE

0 metres 300
0 yards 300

Key to Symbols *see back flap*

Imperia - Porto Maurizio

Plaque dedicated to San Maurizio

While Onegia represents the more modern, commercial side of Imperia, Porto Maurizio is its old heart, with its long porticoes, 16th-century bastions and Baroque churches.

The quarter of Parasio, the medieval part of town with narrow alleys in typically Ligurian style, is focused around the cathedral. The two most important museums in Imperia are also found here. Porto Maurizio has two coastal districts, known as Borgo Foce and Borgo Marino.

The second town forming the city of Imperia has a history that is very similar to, and yet different from, that of Onegia. Porto Maurizio, on the west side of the mouth of the River Impero, has kept more traces of its earlier history than Onegia, which developed primarily in the 18th and 19th centuries. Indeed, its Centro Storico, largely a monument to the Genoese golden age, remains almost intact. Porto Maurizio fell into Genoese hands in 1797, and in 1805 was annexed, along with Genoa, to France during the Napoleonic era. Restored to the Ligurian Republic in 1814, it was united for the first time with Onegia as part of the Kingdom of Sardinia, and in 1860 was absorbed into the Kingdom of Piemonte, under whose rule it remained until union with Onegia in 1923.

The Port

Also known as the Porto di Ponente (to distinguish it from Onegia's Porto di Levante), the port is protected by two piers. With its floating landing stages, the harbour is reserved for holiday yachts and contrasts sharply with Onegia's commercial port.

⛪ Duomo
Piazza del Duomo.
Tel 0183 61901. 🕐 *7:35-11:45am, 2:45-6:45pm daily.*

As you take in the majestic bulk of the Duomo di San Maurizio, it should come as no surprise that this is the largest church in Liguria. It was built between 1781 and 1838 by Gaetano Cantoni in Neo-Classical style to replace the old parish church of San Maurizio, which had been demolished.

The impressive façade features eight Doric columns, culminating in a drum flanked by two solid bell towers, which form a portico. A lantern crowns the great cupola.

Beneath the portico are statues that once belonged to the old parish church. The impressive interior, built on a Greek cross plan, contains a rich array of 19th-century canvases and Neo-Classical-style frescoes, the work of painters mostly from Liguria and Piemonte. Highlights among these include a *Predica di San Francesco Saverio,* attributed to De Ferrari. In the third chapel on the left, there is a fine wooden cross by the school of Maragliano, while the second chapel on the right contains a statue of the *Madonna della Misericordia* (1618), which also came from the demolished San Maurizio.

The interior of Porto Maurizio's Duomo

🏛 Museo Navale Internazionale del Ponente Ligure
Piazza del Duomo 11. *Tel 0183 651 541.* 🕐 *summer: 9am-11pm Wed & Sat; winter: 3:30-7:30pm Wed, 4:30-7:30pm Sat.*

Imperia's naval museum is one of the most interesting institutions in the city, unmissable for anyone with an interest in seafaring, though the exhibition space is somewhat cramped. The museum is subdivided into various sections and includes dioramas and models of ships. Most visitors enjoy the section that deals with life on board ship the most. There are also displays of various documents and other mementoes relating to the seafaring tradition along the Riviera di Ponente.

Model of a diving suit, Museo Navale

🏛 Parasio
The old palace of the Genoese governor was known in the local dialect as "Paraxu" (the Ligurian for Palatium, as in Palatine Hill).

🏛 Pinacoteca Civica
Piazza del Duomo. *Tel 0183 60847.* 🕐 *4-7pm Wed & Sat (also 9-11pm in Jul & Aug).*

Also on Piazza del Duomo is the entrance to the Pinacoteca Civica, the municipal art gallery. On display here are collections derived from legacies and various donations, but exhibitions of local work are held here, too. Works by Barabino, Rayper, Fraschieri and Semino, among others, form part of the Rebaudi collection, which includes 19th-century Ligurian and Genoese works.

Parasio, the old city, set above Porto Maurizio

in Rome); translated into Italian, this became Parasio, the name now given to Porto Maurizio's medieval district. The governor's palace was built on the top of the hill, in Piazza Chiesa Vecchia, now at the heart of the medieval district and only a short walk from the Piazza del Duomo, along Via Acquarone.

After a long period of real neglect and decline, Parasio has in recent years been the subject of an ambitious restoration project, financed mainly by foreign investors. Visitors cannot truly claim to have seen Imperia unless they have strolled around and climbed these charming and steep streets, lined with handsome palaces and churches, including the

convent of Santa Chiara and the Oratorio di San Leonardo. In Via Acquarone, look out for striking **Palazzo Pagliari** (1300–1400), with an entrance portico with ogival arches.

Oratorio di San Leonardo

Via Santa Caterina.
Tel 018362783. ◯ 9am–noon, 3–7pm. ◉ first Mon of the month.
In the southern part of Parasio, looking out towards the sea, this oratory (1600) is dedicated to Imperia's official patron saint. Inside is a lovely work, *Our Lady of Sorrows and souls in Purgatory*, by Gregorio De Ferrari (1647–1726).

St Leonard (1676–1751) was born in the house standing next to the oratory.

Convento di Santa Chiara

Via Santa Chiara 9. **Tel** 0183 62762.
Church ◯ 7am–noon, 3:30–7pm Mon–Sat (from 9am Sun & hols).
The principal reason to visit these buildings, which date from 1300 (modified in the 18th century), is to see the splendid arcade behind the convent, from which there is a fantastic view of the sea, and which is used to stage classical concerts in summer.

Inside the church are two lovely works of art: a *San Domenico Soriano and Madonna*, the work of Domenico Fiasella, and a *Madonna with Child and Santa Caterina da Bologna* by Sebastiano Conca.

Chiesa di San Pietro

Salita San Pietro. **Tel** 0183 60356.
◯ 6pm Sat for mass.
This Parasio church stands on the same level as a loggia overlooking the sea. Founded in 1100, it was built on the ruins of the old town walls. A medieval lookout tower forms the base of the round bell tower.

The façade, dating from 1789, is lively, with paired columns supporting three arches. Inside, a pictorial cycle on the *Life of St Peter* is attributed to Tommaso and Maurizio Carrega (late 1700s).

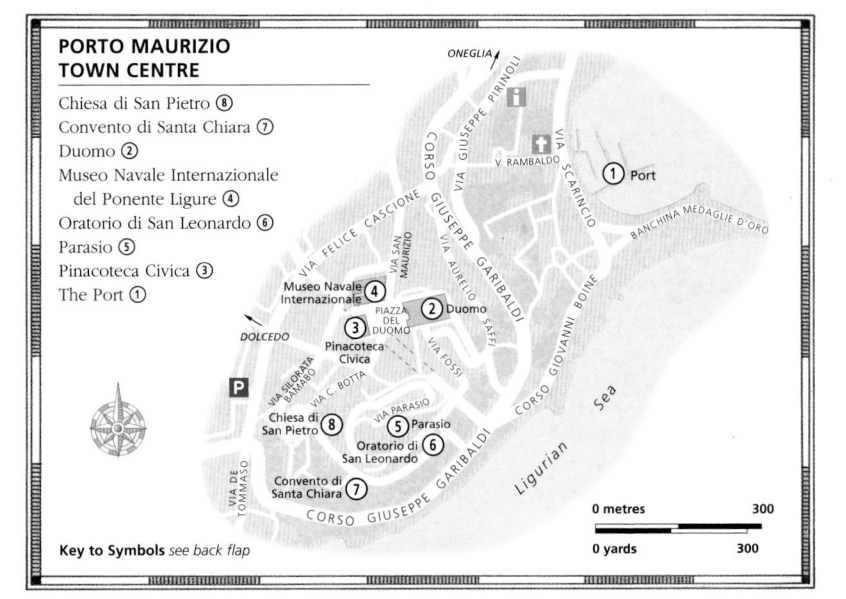

PORTO MAURIZIO TOWN CENTRE

Chiesa di San Pietro ⑧
Convento di Santa Chiara ⑦
Duomo ②
Museo Navale Internazionale del Ponente Ligure ④
Oratorio di San Leonardo ⑥
Parasio ⑤
Pinacoteca Civica ③
The Port ①

Key to Symbols *see back flap*

The church of the Assunta, Triora

Dolcedo ⑳

Imperia. **Road Map** B4–5. ⚊ 1,200. ⊞ Imperia. ⊞ *Comune, 0183 280 004.* ⚉ *La Mongolfiera, traditional country festival (1st Sun, Sep), organic market (3rd Sun of month).*

Situated in the hinterland behind Porto Maurizio, in the Prino valley, is Dolcedo a mountain village with paved mule tracks and watermills along the banks of the river, evidence of an olive oil tradition dating back to the 1100s, the local olive groves are among the most famous in the region.

There are no less than five bridges across the river. The oldest, known as **Ponte Grande**, was built in 1292 by the Knights of St John. The parish church of **San Tommaso** overlooks a small piazza, paved in the Ligurian style in black and white pebbles. This Baroque jewel was built in 1738.

Triora ㉑

Imperia. **Road Map** A4. ⚊ 500. ⊞ San Remo. ⊞ *Pro Loco, Corso Italia 7, 0184 944 77.* ⚉ *Processione del Monte (2nd Sun after Easter); Festa della Madonna della Misericordia (1st Sun in Jul).* **www**.comune.triora.im.it

The old medieval village of Triora, an outpost of the Republic of Genoa, lies near the head of the Valle Argentina. With the Ligurian Alps rising up behind, this is a truly enchanting place.

Also known as the "paese delle streghe" (village of witches), Triora is famous above all for the witchcraft trials, held here between 1587 and 1589. The unique and popular **Museo Etnografico e della Stregoneria** is devoted to the story of these trials. The centre of Triora still preserves much evidence of the village's medieval origins, with little alleys, narrow streets and houses huddled together around small squares. Of seven original gates, the only survivor is **Porta Soprana**, with a rounded arch. Nearby is the **Fontana Soprana**, the oldest fountain in the town. The one sight not to miss is the collegiate church of the **Assunta**. It was originally Romanesque-Gothic and still retains the old bell tower and main door, though the façade is Neo-Classical. Inside (reduced to a single aisle in 1770) there are several notable works of art, including several by Luca Cambiaso; but chief among them is an exquisite painting *Baptism of Christ* (1397), by the Sienese artist Taddeo di Bartolo. It is the oldest known painting of its type in the Riviera di Ponente.

There is also a delightful church, of **San Bernardino**, just outside Triora, its interior is virtually smothered in 15th-century frescoes.

🏛 **Museo Etnografico e della Stregoneria**
Corso Italia 1. **Tel** *0184 944 77.* ◷ *winter 2:30–6pm daily (from 10:30am–noon Sat & Sun); summer 10:30am–noon, 3–6:30 pm daily.* 🎥

Environs

About 10 km (6 miles) beyond Triora, just a stone's throw from the French border, is the tiny village of **Realdo**. It is set in a stunning position, teetering on a rocky cliff at 1,065 m (3,500 ft) above sea level, with some of Liguria's highest peaks as a backdrop. The houses have a distinctly Alpine look and the few inhabitants speak in old Provençal.

Taggia ㉒

Imperia. **Road Map** A5. ⚊ 14,000. ⊞ **P** *Via Boselli, Arma di Taggia, 0184 437 33.* ⚉ *Corteo Storico dei Rioni (4th Sun in Feb); Festa della Maddalena (3rd Sun in Jul); antiques market (last weekend of month).* **www**.rivieradeifiori.org and **www**.taggia.it

Lying close to the mouth of the Valle Argentina is Taggia, whose 16th-century walls conceal a fascinating medieval village. One of the most impressive sights is the **medieval bridge** across the Argentina, with 16 arches of which two are Romanesque. **Via Soleri**, the heart of the old centre, is flanked by porticoes with black stone arches and many fine old buildings. The Baroque parish church of **Santi Giacomo e Filippo** is certainly lovely, but Taggia's most important monument is the **Convento di San Domenico**. Built between 1460 and 1490, it is considered to have the best collection of works by the Liguria-Nice school. Its masterpieces include five works by the French artist Ludovico Brea. It is worth popping down to Arma di Taggia, the small resort a 10-minute drive along the coast. It has a lovely beach, as well as several hotels and restaurants.

🏛 **Convento di San Domenico**
Piazza Beato Cristoforo. **Tel** *0184 476 254.* ◷ *9am–noon, 3–6pm Mon–Sat.* 🎥

The arcaded Via Soleri in Taggia, with its black stone arches

Ludovico Brea

Of the many foreign artists working in Liguria, and in particular on the Riviera di Ponente, between the mid-15th century and the mid-16th century, Ludovico Brea (1443–c.1523) is the best documented. Born in Nice, Brea became a painter in his native city and was probably influenced by the artistic trends emanating from Avignon. Cultural exchange, encouraged by trade between Liguria and the South of France – a depot for goods from northern Europe – was lively at that time, and it was not unusual for Flemish paintings, or the artists themselves, to find themselves in the Ligurian area. Thus, Ludovico Brea was able to learn from and be influenced by works from different

schools of painting and absorb a variety of cultural elements. Of northern European styles, he was particularly interested in Flemish art, but was also fascinated by the miniatures found in medieval manuscripts. Brea was extremely adept at understanding the taste of his Ligurian patrons, a skill that enabled him to work in Italy for many years.

After producing some early work in his native city, Brea transferred to Liguria. Traces of his various moves and of his life in general at that time are scant, and generalizations about his artistic influences are usually made by looking at his later work. While in Liguria, you may also come across the work of Ludovico's brother, Antonio, and his son, Francesco.

The polyptych dedicated to *Santa Caterina da Siena* (1488), has an astonishing gold background, against which the figures emerge in an almost surreal fashion.

The Baptism of Christ (1495) *is a polyptych in San Domenico, in Taggia, in the chapel on the left of the presbytery, and is the only work complete with its frame and predella.*

The Madonna del Rosario, *which dates from 1513 and is also in San Domenico in Taggia, features a landscape background of some depth. A lightening sky looms in the background.*

Pietà by Ludovico Brea, in Taggia

THE ARTIST AT WORK

Ludovico Brea did most of his work in three Ligurian cities: in Genoa, where his works can be seen in the gallery of Palazzo Bianco (a *St Peter* and *Crucifixion*) and in the church of Santa Maria di Castello (*Conversion of St Paul and Coronation of the Virgin*); in Savona, where there are works in the oratory of Nostra Signora di Castello (*Madonna and Saints*), in the Cathedral treasury (*Madonna and Saints*), detail shown left) and in the Pinacoteca Civica (*Christ on the Cross between the Madonna and St John the Evangelist*); and in Taggia, with works in the Convento di San Domenico and the adjacent museum. All three paintings illustrated below can be seen in Taggia.

Tour of the Armea and Crosia Valleys ㉓

One of the colourful murals in Apricale

This itinerary follows a route which can be covered easily in a day. It takes the visitor to some of the most picturesque villages in the far west of the Riviera del Ponente, on the slopes of the hinterland behind the strip between San Remo and Bordighera. Interesting though the coastal towns are, this part of the Ligurian interior also has a great deal to offer visitors. Here you will find ancient towns and villages which grew up along the old salt routes, often very close to the border with France. Set among green hills which rise rapidly to become mountains, many of these ancient centres have managed to preserve their old appearance and atmosphere, despite the passing of time.

Apricale ③

At the heart of this medieval village, set in a panoramic position, is Piazza Vittorio Emanuele, with the parish church of the Purificazione di Maria, the Oratory of San Bartolomeo and some castle ruins. Apricale (from *apricus*, which means "facing towards the sun") is also known as the "artists' village", because of the modern murals painted on the façades of the old houses.

Perinaldo ④

At the top of Val Crosia, this village was the birthplace of Italy's greatest astronomer, Gian Domenico Cassini (1625–1712), discoverer of asteroids and moons and famous for his work for Louis XIV; a museum in the Palazzo del Comune is dedicated to him. The parish church of San Nicolò dates from 1495.

Vallecrosia Alta ⑤

Set among fields of flowers and vineyards which produce Rossese, one of Liguria's most prized wines, this town is the older twin of the modern seaside village of Vallecrosia, just west of Bordighera. In the medieval quarter is the church of San Rocco. Nearby, at Garibbe, there is an unexpected Museum of Song and Sound Reproduction.

PIGNA

R. Bonda

Isolabonana •

③

④

T. Nervia

T. di Vallecrosia

⑤

NICE

• *Ventimiglia*

Bordighera

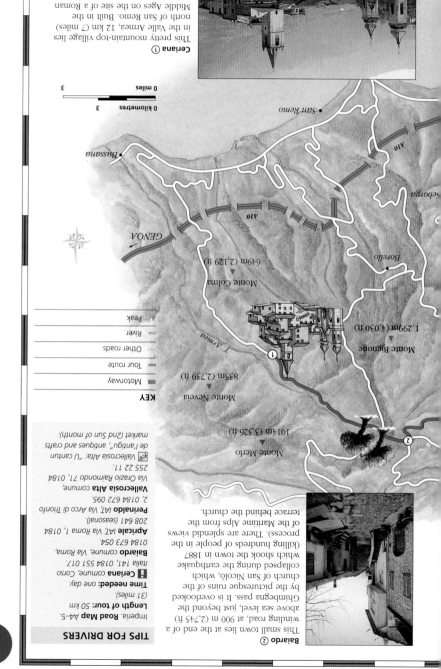

Ceriana ①

This pretty mountain-top village lies in the Valle Armea, 12 km (7 miles) north of San Remo. Built in the Middle Ages on the site of a Roman villa, Ceriana's old centre is still encircled by perfectly preserved walls. Walking around the narrow streets and alleys, you can enjoy unexpected glimpses of the surrounding countryside.

Bajardo ②

This small town lies at the end of a winding road, at 900 m (2,745 ft) above sea level, just beyond the Ghimbegna pass. It is overlooked by the picturesque ruins of the church of San Nicolò, which collapsed during the earthquake which shook the town in 1887 (killing hundreds of people in the process). There are splendid views of the Maritime Alps from the terrace behind the church.

TIPS FOR DRIVERS

Imperia. **Road Map** A4–5.
Length of tour: 50 km
(31 miles).
Time needed: one day.
🛈 **Ceriana** comune, Corso Italia 141, 0184 551 017.
Bajardo comune, Via Roma, 0184 673 054.
Apricale (AT, Via Roma 1, 0184 208 641 (seasonal).
Perinaldo (AT, Via Arco di Trionfo 2, 0184 672 095.
Vallecrosia Alta comune.
Via Orazio Raimondo 71, 0184 255 22 11.
🛒 Vallecrosia Alta: "U cantun de l'antigu", antiques and crafts market (2nd Sun of month).

KEY

— Motorway
— Tour route
— Other roads
= River
▲ Peak

Monte Nevia 835m (2,739 ft)
Monte Colma 649m (2,129 ft)
Monte Bignone 1,299m (4,030 ft)
Monte Merlo 1014m (3,326 ft)

t. Armea

GENOA

• Bussana
• San Remo
Seborga
Borello

0 kilometres 3
0 miles 3

For hotels and restaurants in this region see pp181–3 and pp195–7

San Remo ❷

Imperia. Road Map A5. 🚗 59,000. 🚉 🚌 **i** IAT Riviera dei Fiori, Largo Nuvoloni 1, 0184 590 59. 🎭 Festival della Canzone Italiana (late Feb or early Mar); Milano–San Remo cycle race (Sat following 19 Mar); Rally di San Remo (early Oct). www.rivieradeifiori.org and www.comunedisanremo.it

Defined, in the eyes of many Italians, by its thriving flower industry and its Festival of Italian Song, San Remo is also one of the Italian Riviera's best-known and most atmospheric resorts. The city is divided into three distinct areas: Corso Matteotti and around (the heart of the shopping district), La Pigna (the old town), and the west end of the seafront, which was the heart of the resort during its heyday. Tourism, mainly English, boomed in San Remo from the mid-1800s to the early 1900s, a period of great expansion when all manner of grand hotels and villas were built, including various Art Nouveau palazzi. There is no better Belle Epoque monument than the splendid and still-thriving **Casino Municipale**, built by Eugenio Ferret in 1904–06.

Another unmistakable San Remo landmark, with its onion domes, is the **Russian Orthodox Church**, built in the 1920s. The Russians were almost as passionate about

The harbour at San Remo

▷ *The little church of Sant'Ampelio, in Bordighera*

the top of the hill. The main monuments, including the cathedral and the Oratorio dell'Immacolata Concezione (1563), are found in the central Piazza San Siro. The **Cathedral of San Siro**, founded in the 12th century, has two fine side doors featuring bas-reliefs in the lunette: the one on the left, which dates from the 12th century, represents the *Agnello pasquale*, or paschal lamb. Inside, there are three aisles and three apses, extended in 1600. There are good works of art including a 15th-century *Crucifixion*.

San Remo as the English, and the seafront **Corso Imperatrice** was named in honour of Maria Alexandrovna, wife of Czar Alexander II and a frequent visitor to San Remo. This seafront boulevard is a favourite place to stroll, and provides a wonderful taste of the old aristocratic resort.

Beyond **Lungomare Vittorio Emanuele II** and **Lungomare Italo Calvino,** where the streets are broken up by lawns, the road continues to the modern marina, Portosole, and the old, or town, port. At the end of Corso Trento e Trieste, beyond the **Giardini Ormond**, stands **Villa Nobel**, where the famous Swedish scientist lived and where he also died in 1896.

The other part of San Remo that no one should miss is medieval "città vecchia", fortified in the 11th century in order to keep out the Saracens. The area is known as **La Pigna**, or pine cone, because of its layout: the steps, arches and covered walkways spread out in concentric circles from

Statue of Spring, on the San Remo seafront

At the top of La Pigna is the sumptuous **Santuario di Nostra Signora della Costa,** remodelled in the 1630s. There is a fine pebble mosaic outside and four statues by Maragliano on the high altar. As well as shops, there are some interesting palazzi on Corso Matteotti. One of these is Palazzo Borea d'Olmo, a curious mix of Mannerism and Baroque. As the **Museo Civico,** it houses a mix of archaeological finds, Garibaldian relics and 18th- and 19th-century paintings.

Finally, for an insight into the local flower trade, visit San Remo's famous wholesale flower market, which lies just east of the city centre in the Armea valley.

🏛 Museo Civico
Corso Matteotti 143.
Tel 0184 531 942.
🕐 9am–noon, 3–6pm Tue–Sat.

Environs

About 10 km (6 miles) east of San Remo is the suburb of **Bussana Nuova** and, beyond, **Bussana Vecchia,** one of the most charming spots on the Riviera di Ponente. Destroyed by the 1887 earthquake, which left only the bell tower of the Baroque church of **Sacro Cuore** intact, Bussana Vecchia was partially restored in the 1960s, when an artists' colony moved in. They opened up studios and crafts workshops, but took care to change the original appearance of the village as little as possible.

San Remo's famous casino

Pigna ㉕

Imperia. **Road Map** A4.
🏠 1,015. **FS** Ventimiglia. 🚌
🛈 *Comune, Piazza Umberto 1,
0184 241 016.*

Situated in the foothills of the Maritime Alps in the Alta Val Nervia, some 40 km (25 miles) north of San Remo, Pigna is a fascinating place; its form is reminiscent of the eponymous district in San Remo. Strolling around the narrow streets, known as *cbibi*, you can understand how the medieval town was built, with the houses grouped defensively on concentric streets.

Among a number of fine churches, the most important is the church of **San Michele**, founded in 1450. A splendid white marble rose window, perhaps the work of Giovanni Gagini from the early 1500s, adorns the façade. Inside, the *Polyptych of St Michael* is a monumental work by the Piemontese artist Canavesio (1500s), in which the influence of the Brea brothers (*see p159*) is evident. Also by Canavesio are the frescoes portraying *The Passion of Christ* housed in the small church of **San Bernardo**, within the cemetery. Other places of interest are the ruins of the church of **San Tommaso**, and **Piazza Castello**, with lovely views over the village of Castel Vittorio.

The rose window at San Michele, Pigna

Dolceacqua ㉖

See pp166-7.

Bordighera ㉗

Imperia. **Road Map** A5. 🏠 11,300.
FS 🚌 🛈 *Via Vittorio Emanuele II
172-174, 0184 262 322.*
📅 *Bordighera* Città dell'Umorismo, *a festival of humour (late Apr-early May).* www.rivieradeifiori.org

A famous painting by Monet called *A View of Bordighera* is evidence of the historic fame of this sunny and lively resort. As was the case elsewhere on the Riviera, Bordighera was particularly popular with the British. Here, too, you find Art Nouveau palazzi (many converted into hotels or apartments), and a popular seafront boulevard – the **Lungomare Argentina**, with Capo Sant'Ampelio at the far end. The beach is good and often busy, and there are palm trees wherever you look.

The **Biblioteca Museo Clarence Bickenell** was founded by one of Bordighera's many British visitors, a vicar, botanist and archaeologist. Bickenell's library-cum-museum houses Roman funerary objects and, more interestingly, casts of rock drawings and a vast photographic archive of ancient graffiti from the nearby Vallée des Merveilles in France.

There is a handful of sights of historic interest. By the sea, on Capo Sant'Ampelio, is the Romanesque church of **Sant'Ampelio**, with an 11th-century crypt; it stands on the spot where Ampelio (a hermit who later became a saint), once lived. More centrally, look out for the 17th-century church of **Santa Maria Maddalena**, with a fine early 16th-century marble sculpture on the high altar, attributed to the workshop of Domenico Parodi. In nearby Piazza De Amicis there is a marble fountain (1783) featuring a statue of Magiargè, a slave to the Spanish Moors who died in Bordighera.

For a quiet but interesting interlude, go to the **Giardino Esotico Pallanca**, which has more than 3,000 species of cacti and succulents.

🏛 **Biblioteca Museo Clarence Bickenell**
Via Bickenell 3. **Tel** 0184 263 694.
⏰ 9:30am-1pm, 1:30-4:45pm
Mon-Fri. 🚫 *public hols.*

🌵 **Giardino Esotico Pallanca**
Via Madonna della Ruota 1.
Tel 0184 266 347. ⏰ winter:
9am-5pm daily; summer:
9am-12:30pm, 2:30-7pm daily,
Mon-Fri. 🚫 *public hols.*
🌐 www.pallanca.it

Environs
In a lofty position about 12 km (7 miles) north of Bordighera is the ancient village of **Seborga**, which, along with its 350 inhabitants, enjoys the unexpected title of "principality". Thanks to an historical anomaly, the town was able to elect its own sovereign, Giorgio I, in 1963, and pass a constitution, which was renewed in 1995. They have their own currency, the *luigino* (Seborga's first mint was set up by Benedictine monks in 1660), and print their own stamps, and cars carry SB on their licence plates.

Cactus in the tropical garden of Pallanca at Bordighera

Benvenuti · Bienvenue · Willkommen · Welcome
nell'antico Principato di Seborga

Plaque welcoming people to Seborga, near Bordighera

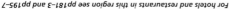

Dolceacqua ㉖

Inscription with the words of Monet

By a quirk of fate, this delightful medieval village is, despite its name (which means "fresh water"), home to one of the most prized and famous red wines in Italy, Rossese, a favourite with Napoleon and Pope Julius III. Overlooked by the imposing but not overbearing mass of the ruined Castello dei Doria, the village spreads out on the slopes of the mountain and is reminiscent of one of Liguria's traditional *presepi* (nativity scenes) when seen from above. The River Nervia divides Dolceacqua into two. On one side is the older part, known as Borgo, while the newer district on the right is called Terra. The artist Claude Monet, who loved this area, painted the castle and described the old bridge which links the two quarters as a "jewel of lightness".

View of Dolceacqua
The picturesque medieval village has narrow alleyways and tall houses.

STAR SIGHTS

★ Castello dei Doria

★ Ponte Vecchio

★ Ponte Vecchio
This light and elegant bridge has a single ogee arch with an impressive span of 33 m (110 ft). Built in the 15th century, the bridge links the two quarters of Terra and Borgo, separated by the River Nervia.

Monument to the "Gombo"
This modern work is dedicated to Pier Vicenzo Mela, a local man who was the first to use an olive press (gombo) to extract oil, in the 1700s.

★ Castello dei Doria
Built to defend the town in 1100 and bought by the Doria in 1270, this castle gradually acquired the look of a noble palazzo. It was damaged in 1754 but was dealt its final blow by the earthquake in 1887.

VISITORS' CHECKLIST

Imperia. **Road Map** A5.
2,000.
FS *Ventimiglia.*
Via Barberis Colomba 3, 0184 206 666.
Procession of San Sebastiano (Sun closest to 20 Jan); Festa Patronale dell'Assunta (15 Aug); Festa della "Michetta" (16 Aug).
www.dolceacqua.it

Palazzo Doria is where the Doria family settled in the 18th century after their castle became uninhabitable. An old passageway still links the palazzo to the church of Sant'Antonio, a route that was reserved for the Doria family alone.

The bell tower of Sant'Antonio Abate forms part of the village's encircling walls.

Church of San Giorgio
Across the river from the old village (at the end of the bridge south of this illustration), the 13th-century church of San Giorgio has the remains of a Romanesque bell tower, and a ceiling with interesting painted beams. In the crypt is a Doria family tomb.

The church of Sant'Antonio Abate
Dolceacqua's parish church has in front of it a broad square paved with pebbles, in the Ligurian tradition. The church dates from 1400, but was altered in the Baroque era. Inside there is a lovely polyptych painted by Ludovico Brea.

Ventimiglia ㉘

Imperia. **Road Map** A5.
🚶 *26,000.* 🚆 🚌
ℹ *Via Cavour 61, 0184 351 183.*
🎭 *Corteo Storico, historical procession (1st or 2nd Sun in Aug, odd years); Battaglia di Fiori (summer).*
www.rivieradeifiori.org and
www.ventimiglia.it

Ventimiglia is the last major town on the Riviera di Ponente before the French border. It is a perfect synthesis of the characteristics of towns along this part of the coast, and, more generally, of all coastal towns in the region: a place where past and present seem to co-exist quite happily, where Roman ruins rub shoulders with the latest tourist facilities.

A frontier town par excellence (its history is studded with numerous disputes with nearby France over the national border lines), Ventimiglia straddles the Roia and the Nervia valleys, among the most beautiful in the Ligurian Alps. Nearby are marvels of nature such as the Grotte dei Balzi Rossi and the Hanbury Botanical Gardens (*see pp170–71*).

The River Roia divides Ventimiglia into two: the medieval part on a hill to the west, and the modern town on the coastal plain to the east. Traces of the era of Roman domination, which followed rule by the Liguri Intemelii people, can be seen at **Albintimilium**, on the eastern periphery of the new town. Clearly visible from the flyover on the Via Aurelia, the ruins consist of a stretch of the *decumanus maximus* (or

View of the apse of the Cattedrale dell'Assunta, Ventimiglia

main street), a few houses and the great baths (the source of the lovely Mosaico di Arione, now in front of the hospital). More important than any of these, however, is the small **Theatre**, the most significant Roman monument in Liguria. Dating from the early 3rd century BC, the theatre could seat more than 5,000 spectators. Ten levels of steps in the lower section, made from Turbia stone, are still well preserved, while the western entrance gate is practically intact. Various finds discovered at the site are on display in the nearby **Museo Archeologico Gerolamo Rossi**, in the Forte dell'Annunziata in town.

Via Garibaldi (also known as "la piazza") is the main street through the cobbled and charming *centro storico*. There are some fine palazzi here, some with hanging gardens to the back opening onto the upper floors, in the 16th-century tradition. Among the most important buildings are the Palazzo Pubblico,

the Loggia del Magistrato dell'Abbondanza, and the Neo-Classical former Teatro Civico. This houses the **Civica Biblioteca Aprosiana**, the oldest public library in Liguria (founded in 1648) with a fine collection of rare books and manuscripts.

At the heart of Via Garibaldi is the imposing bulk of the **Cattedrale dell'Assunta**. This was built in place of an 8th-century Carolingian chuch in the 11th and 12th centuries, and has been modified at intervals since: the façade is Romanesque, for example, while the portico, added in 1222, is Gothic. The bell tower, constructed on a 12th-century base, was rebuilt in the Baroque era and remodelled once again in the 19th century.

Marble cover of a funerary urn, 1st century AD

Inside, there is not much to see, though in the crypt you can see parts of the old medieval church, as well as some pre-Roman sculptures.

Adjoining the Assunta is the octagonal **Baptistry** (11th century); this contains a wonderful font dating from the 12th–13th centuries.

Continuing along Via Garibaldi, past another couple of churches, you eventually reach Porta Nizza. From here, following Via della Torre and Via Appio, you reach Piazza Colletta and the lovely Romanesque church of **San Michele**. The unimpressive façade is 19th-century, but the main body of the church, of which only the central nave survives, dates from the 11th century; the bell tower, apse and vault are from the 12th century. Inside is an interesting 11th-century

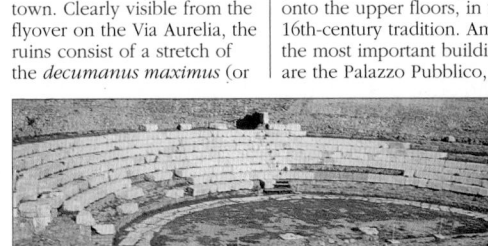

The Roman theatre in Ventimiglia, dating from the 3rd century AD

Overlooking the town of Ventimiglia

crypt, incorporating various Roman materials, including columns used in the high altar.

From Porta Nizza, you can also climb up west of the old city to the ruins of three medieval forts, a reminder of the battles once fought over Ventimiglia. One of these, the **Castel d'Appio**, built by the Genoese in the 13th century, occupies the site not only of a Roman military camp *(castrum)* but also of an early Ligurian defence post. There are marvellous views of the Riviera from here.

The modern, eastern part of Ventimiglia, complete with seaside promenades, is a shopping mecca and is very popular with the French. The streets are busy at weekends and on Fridays, when people from the surrounding area flood in for the weekly market.

🏛 **Albintimilium**
Corso Genova. **Tel** 0184 252 320.
⏲ 3–6pm Sat, Sun.

🏛 **Museo Archeologico Gerolamo Rossi**
Via Verdi 41. **Tel** 0184 351 181.
⏲ 9am–12:30pm, 3–5pm Tue–Sat; 10am–12:30pm Sun. 🎟 📷

Balzi Rossi ㉙

Grimaldi di Ventimiglia (Imperia). **Road Map** A5.

This prehistoric site, one of the most famous in the western Mediterranean, lies about 10 km (6 miles) west of Ventimiglia, below the village of Grimaldi and just a stone's throw from the Italy-France frontier. It consists of nine caves, which have been explored at various times since the 19th century. The name of Balzi Rossi (meaning "red rocks") derives from the reddish colour of the precipitous limestone cliffs.

This atmospheric place has yielded fascinating evidence of human settlement in this part of Liguria, going back as far as the Paleolithic age. The area was probably chosen because of the favourable natural conditions, including the warm climate and the proximity of the sea. There is a walkway connecting some of the caves, some of which you are also allowed to enter.

Numerous stone and bone instruments, fossil remains of animals, and various ornamental and artistic

Necklace found in the Triple Tomb

objects have been discovered in the caves, in particular in the Grotta del Principe, slightly removed from the other caves and also the largest. Of greatest interest are the many tombs, which provide a few tangible snippets of information about the people who lived here some 240,000 years ago. They were undoubtedly among the most sophisticated of any people then living in Europe.

The most famous of these tombs, known as the **Triple Tomb**, was discovered in Barma Grande cave in 1892. Today, it is on display in the **Museo Preistorico dei Balzi Rossi**, founded by the Englishman Sir Thomas Hanbury *(see p170)* in 1898. To the sides are two male individuals, a boy on the left and a man over 2 m (6 ft) tall on the right.

At the centre is a girl of around 16 years old. Funerary objects, such as sea shells, pendants of worked bone, deer teeth and necklaces fashioned out of fish vertebrae, traditionally accompanied the deceased.

The museum also has on display a reproduction of the only figure engraved in a naturalistic style to be discovered at Balzi Rossi. Found in the Grotta del Caviglione, it is the profile of a shortish, stocky horse, 40 cm (16 in) long and 20 cm (8 in) high. It is known as the **Przewalskii Horse**; a few rare examples of the breed survive in Mongolia.

Also on display are stone instruments, animal skeletons and small statues.

🏛 **Grotte e Museo Preistorico dei Balzi Rossi**
Ponte San Ludovico, Via Balzi Rossi 9. **Tel** 0184 381 13. ⏲ Museum: 8:30am–7:30pm Tue–Sun; Grotte: 8:30am–1 hour before sunset. 🎟 hourly. 📷

One of the nine Balzi Rossi caves

Hanbury Botanical Gardens ㉚

This splendid botanical garden was founded in 1867 by Sir Thomas Hanbury, a rich English businessman, and his brother Daniel, a botanist, with the help of the eminent German botanist Ludovico Winter. Sir Thomas was passionate about Liguria, and saw the opportunity that its warm climate provided: the exotic plants that he brought back from his travels, particularly those from hot, dry areas such as Southern Africa and Mexico, he was able to acclimatize to co-exist with the local flora. By 1898, the garden included more than 7,000 plant species. The gardens were left to decay during much of the 20th century but are now being coaxed back to their former glory by the University of Genoa.

Oriental bronze bell

Agave
Aloes and agaves, particular favourites of Sir Thomas, are planted among the rocks to re-create the desert habitat they come from.

★ Dragon Fountain
Encircled by papyruses, warm-climate plants which have acclimatized well here, this fountain has an ancient and rather mysterious air. Sitting on the rim is a dragon, an echo of Sir Thomas's beloved Far East.

Temple of the Four Seasons
This is one of many temples that Sir Thomas had built around the gardens, in line with late 19th-century taste. Its classical style is evocative of an Italian Renaissance garden.

STAR SIGHTS

★ Dragon Fountain

★ The Villa

For hotels and restaurants in this region see pp181–3 and pp195–7

The Terraces
In this part of the garden the plants are grouped so as to form "themed gardens". There are wonderful views from the Pavilion.

VISITORS' CHECKLIST

Corso Montecarlo 43, La Mortola Inferiore (Imperia). **Road Map** A5. *Tel* 0184 229 507. FS Ventimiglia. Mar–mid-Jun & mid-Sep–mid-Oct: 9:30am–5pm daily; mid-Jun–mid-Sep: 9:30am–6pm daily; mid-Oct–Feb: 9:30am–4pm. **www**.parks.it and **www**.coop-omnia.it

The Viale dei Cipressi (avenue of cypresses) is one of the most charming parts of the garden, with its lines of tall trees, a familiar sight in the Italian countryside.

★ The Villa
The original palazzo was built in the 14th century and extended in the 17th. In the 1930s, Mussolini held a notorious meeting with General Franco here. The villa now houses offices and is not open to the public, but you can enjoy the lovely views over the gardens and down to the sea from the villa's loggia.

TRAVELLERS' NEEDS

WHERE TO STAY

Liguria has long been popular with holiday-makers and therefore has a long tradition of providing a wide range of accommodation, particularly on the coast. Along both the Riviera di Levante and the Riviera di Ponente, with their collection of renowned resorts, visitors will find an almost uninterrupted string of sumptuous hotels and family-run *pensioni*, which are open virtually all year round. Genoa, sandwiched

between the two rivieras, has accommodation to suit all tastes and budgets both in the Centro Storico and in the immediate vicinity.

In general, visitors tend to stay on the coast and make day trips inland. If you want to try out the increasingly popular option of *agriturismo*, which means staying on a farm, you should head into the Ligurian hinterland. Camping is another option, which you can do either inland or along the coast.

Logo of the Grand Hotel Diana in Alassio

HOTEL CATEGORIES AND PRICES

In Liguria, hotels are classified according to the Italian national system. The categories go from one up to five stars, that is, from budget accommodation to luxury hotels. In general, you can expect services to be of a good standard, but the best value for money is generally found in the three-star category. Note that hotels in the lower categories may not accept credit cards.

Prices vary according to the season, rising in the (admittedly long) high season and during major festivals and cultural events.

BOOKING

In a popular region like Liguria the low season tends to be limited to relatively short periods, such as mid-

winter. High season, obviously, is the summer, when Liguria's long coastline and beaches attract big crowds. Anyone planning to visit the region in the summer is strongly advised to book accommodation well in advance. In most cases a fax or an e-mail will suffice to confirm a booking.

HOTELS

A region that depends to a large extent on tourism for its economy, Liguria has a well-developed network of hotels, with generally good facilities. The one exception on the coast is the Cinque Terre, where accommodation tends to be fairly simple.

Most of the coastal resorts can offer hotels in all the five categories. A list of hotels, including family-run *pensioni*, with prices, can be obtained from the regional tourist (IAT)

offices *(see opposite)* or from the local offices in the larger resorts *(see p207)*.

AGRITURISMO AND BED & BREAKFAST

Agriturismo (or farm holidays) have become a popular alternative form of accommodation, particularly for people who love the outdoors or who want to choose from activities such as fishing or horse riding. Staying in a rural farm also provides a chance to escape from the hubbub of the coast. The *agriturismo* formula, which can be found in other regions of Italy, is simple: working farms offer rooms (including self-catering options) and authentic home-made food, as well as other facilities, ranging from a

Comfortable public rooms at the Royal Hotel in San Remo

▷ Colourful houses, typical of coastal Liguria, and beach huts

Holidaymakers on the beach at Monterosso

The seafront at Bordighera, lined with hotels

children's play area to a swimming pool. The options range from the small family-owned farm, able to accommodate just a handful of people, to the grander, less traditional places that offer greater comfort and a wider range of facilities.

At all of the farms, however, you can expect genuinely good food, based on local ingredients, in many cases grown or made by the owners themselves, whether in the form of fruit and vegetables, home-reared meat or home-made cheese. It is usually possible to buy the farm produce, too.

Bed & breakfast accommodation, also available in Liguria, is generally comfortable and inexpensive. This type of lodging is found mainly in the larger cities and in the principal coastal resorts – rarely in the interior. Unlike on farms geared to *agriturismo*, meals are not provided.

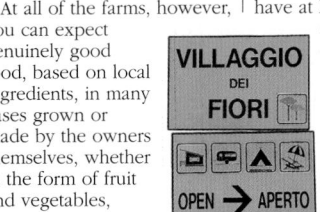

Tourist signs

CAMPING

Camping in Italy does not have as big a following as in some other European countries, so you may have to search quite hard for a camp site to suit your needs. Even so, most of the Riviera resorts have at least one site that can accommodate tents, camper vans or caravans. Many camp sites are situated close to the sea, some with private beaches reserved for camp residents. Sites are usually clean and well-cared for and in reasonably natural surroundings. Coastal sites are often particularly busy in August, so be sure to book in advance. And, since camping is not necessarily a cheap option in Italy, always check the rates.

Note that there are strict regulations as to where camper vans can be parked. A list of camp sites can be obtained from any regional tourist (IAT) office.

SELF-CATERING

Besides the option of self-catering on an *agriturismo* farm or camp site, there are also self-catering apartments available for rent. These can be found primarily in the largest seaside resorts along the riviera, and may well suit families with young children

A Casa di Roby, a bed & breakfast in Moneglia

DIRECTORY

Agenzia Regionale per la Promozione Turistica "In Liguria"
Piazza de Ferrari 1,
Genova.
Tel 010 548 51.
Fax 010 548 87 42.
www.turismoinligura.it

APT Genova
Palazzo delle Torrette
Via Garibaldi 12r, Genova.
Tel 010 557 29 03.
Fax 010 557 24 14.
www.apt.genova.it

IAT Riviera dei Fiori
Largo Nuvoloni 1,
San Remo.
Tel 0184 590 59.
Fax 0184 507 649.
www.rivieradeifiori.org

IAT Tigullio
Via XXV Aprile 4,
Santa Margherita Ligure.
Tel 0185 287 485.
Fax 0185 283 034.
www.provincia.genova.it

Provincia La Spezia Sezione Turismo
Viale Mazzini 45,
La Spezia.
Tel 0187 770 900.
Fax 0187 770 908.

UIT Riviera Ligure delle Palme
Via Sormano 12,
Alassio.
Tel 019 831 33 26.
Fax 019 831 32 69.
www.turismo.provincia.savona.it

better than a hotel. Again, the accommodation listings provided by the many tourist (IAT) offices should provide the names, addresses and phone numbers of the various agencies which deal with short-term lets. In addition, the tourist literature should also include details and phone numbers of private individuals who offer apartments for rent.

Choosing a Hotel

Hotels have been selected across a wide price range for facilities, good value and location. All rooms have private bath, TV and are wheelchair accessible unless otherwise indicated. Most have Internet access, and in some cases, fitness facilities may be offsite. The hotels are listed by area. For map references, *see pp94–9* and the back endpaper.

PRICE CATEGORIES
The following price ranges are for a double room per night, including breakfast, tax and service.
€ Under €85
€€ €85–€150
€€€ €150–€250
€€€€ €250–€350
€€€€€ Over €350

GENOA

IL CENTRO STORICO Acquario
€€

Vico San Pancrazio 9, 16124 **Tel** 010 246 1742 **Fax** 010 246 1456 **Rooms** 30 ● Map 5 B2

Clean and friendly, the Acquario is right in the heart of Genoa, up a little alleyway. It is not the easiest hotel to find, but the central location more than makes up for the initial difficulty. Blue features in the decor, but the aquarium theme of the hotel's name is not overdone in the design. There is also a cosy bar. **www.acquariohotelgenova.it**

IL CENTRO STORICO Bel Soggiorno
€€

Via XX Settembre 19, 16121 **Tel** 010 542 880 **Fax** 010 581 418 **Rooms** 19 ● Map 3 A3

Located on one of Genoa's main arteries, the Bel Soggiorno ("lovely stay") suits visitors on a budget who still want a central position. The hotel is located near Brignole railway station, the exhibition centre and the aquarium. Simple pastel decor, mosaic floors and friendly, helpful staff complete the experience. **www.belsoggiornohotel.com**

IL CENTRO STORICO Colombo
€€

Via Porta Soprana 27, 16123 **Tel & Fax** 010 251 3643 **Rooms** 15 ● Map 2 F4

Housed in an old building, the Colombo is within walking distance of all the major attractions of the city. Each room is different, but all are clean, with old furniture, warm colours and a touch of style. The hotel also boasts a lovely terrace with tables and chairs for relaxing while enjoying great views down to the port. **www.hotelcolombo.it**

IL CENTRO STORICO Veronese
€€

Vico Cicala 3, 16124 **Tel** 010 251 0771 **Fax** 010 251 0639 **Rooms** 19 ● Map 5 B2

This friendly, good-value hotel is ideally located for exploring the aquarium, the old shipyard and the Children's City, not to mention the many museums, churches and *palazzi* that Genoa has to offer. The rooms are quiet, clean and well appointed, and you can dine on the fresh seafood on offer in the restaurants at the port. **www.hotelveronese.com**

IL CENTRO STORICO Bristol Palace
€€€

Via XX Settembre 35, 16121 **Tel** 010 592 541 **Fax** 010 561 756 **Rooms** 133 ● Map 6 E4

The Bristol Palace is a grand dame of a hotel near Brignole station. Housed in a 19th-century palazzo, the decor is sumptuous, with a grand sweeping staircase, elegant rooms, spacious public rooms and a bar. Rooms contain period furniture and are soundproofed and air conditioned. Some baths have whirlpools. **www.hotelbristolpalace.com**

IL CENTRO STORICO Palazzo Cicala
€€€

Piazza San Lorenzo 16, 16123 **Tel** 010 251 8824 **Fax** 010 246 7414 **Rooms** 10 ● Map 5 C3

This chic hotel is located in a 16th-century palazzo. The faded grandeur has been revived by stylish decor and simple, minimalist furniture that doesn't detract from the original stucco ceilings and window details. A lounge overlooks the cathedral square. Rooms have Internet, fax and DVD. Six apartments are available to rent. **www.palazzocicala.it**

IL CENTRO STORICO Jolly Hotel Marina
€€€€

Molo Ponte Calvi 5, 16124 **Tel** 010 25 391 **Fax** 010 251 1320 **Rooms** 140 ● Map 2 E3

Right on the old port, in the marina complex designed by renowned architect Renzo Piano, the Jolly Hotel Marina faces the aquarium. The hotel has a contemporary, clean and fresh feel, and it features a bar, a restaurant, meeting rooms and a private garage. Check the website for weekend deals. **www.jolly-hotels.it**

LE STRADE NUOVE Acquaverde
€€

Via Balbi 29/6, 16126 **Tel** 010 265 427 **Fax** 010 246 4839 **Rooms** 30 ● Map 2 E2

The Acquaverde occupies the top three floors of a 17th-century building that used to belong to a noble merchant family. Ask for a room with Baroque frescoed ceilings. The hotel has a restaurant and breakfast room, but four of the rooms also have kitchenette facilities. Easy access to the old port and ferry terminal. **www.hotelacquaverde.it**

LE STRADE NUOVE Agnello d'Oro
€€

Vico delle Monachette 6, 16126 **Tel** 010 246 2084 **Fax** 010 246 2327 **Rooms** 20 ● Map 2 D2

The Agnello d'Oro is situated in a building dating back to 1580 that was formerly the convent of the Teresiane Scalze. The original convent windows still remain. Fully refurbished, though not fancy, this hotel is quiet, charming and close to the best palaces. Check out the lovely roof garden. **www.hotelagnellodoro.it**

Key to Symbols see back cover flap

LE STRADE NUOVE Balbi

Via Balbi 21, 16126 **Tel** 010 247 2112 **Fax** 010 252 362 **Rooms** 13   **Map 2 D2**

This family hotel is set in a historic building with decorative frescoes on the ceilings and original parquet floors. The Balbi is in the city centre, near Stazione Principe, the port terminal and the aquarium. Full of character and charm, the hotel also has a bar and an Internet point. American Express cards are not accepted. www.hotelbalbigenova.it

LE STRADE NUOVE Best Western Metropoli

Piazza Fontane Marose, 16123 **Tel** 010 246 8888 **Fax** 010 246 8686 **Rooms** 48   **Map 6 D2**

Located in one of the prettiest piazzas in the heart of the city, this hotel is close to museums, the Palazzo Ducale, the opera house and the aquarium. Bus and metro stops are nearby. The rooms are decorated in a modern style and provide comfort with basic facilities. www.bestwestern.it/metropoli_ge

LE STRADE NUOVE Hotel Cairoli

Via Cairoli 14/4, 16124 **Tel** 010 246 1454 **Fax** 010 246 7512 **Rooms** 12   **Map 2 F3**

Housed in a 16th-century palazzo, the two-star Cairoli offers excellent facilities for its price category, with a reading room and bar, plus fitness room and reiki massage treatments. www.hotelcairoligenova.com

LE STRADE NUOVE Vittoria & Orlandini

Via Balbi 33, 16126 **Tel** 010 261 923 **Fax** 010 246 2656 **Rooms** 41   **Map 2 E2**

This welcoming, family-run hotel located in an elegant building in the heart of the city is within easy walking distance of the old part of Genoa and close to the main sights, including the Palazzo Ducale, the aquarium and the Naval Museum. The hotel offers only basic amenities and services. www.vittoriaorlandini.com

LE STRADE NUOVE Astoria

Piazza Brignole 4, 16122 **Tel** 010 873 316 **Fax** 010 831 7326 **Rooms** 69   **Map 2 E3**

Dating back to 1860, the building housing the Astoria was the former home of an aristocratic family. It retains some floral Liberty-style details, classical elegance and frescoed ceilings. In a good location to visit Genoa's sights, the hotel also offers Internet access in the rooms and Wi-Fi in the lobby. www.hotelastoriagenova.com

LE STRADE NUOVE Europa

Vico delle Monachette 8, 16126 **Tel** 010 256 955 **Fax** 010 261 047 **Rooms** 37   **Map 2 D2**

Make the most of the views of the port and the city from the lovely roof terrace at this hotel. The Europa is close to Stazione Principe, the main station, which means it is well situated as a base for short train trips along the coast, as well as being central for Genoa's sights. It also has a bar and Wi-Fi in all rooms. www.hoteleuropa-genova.com

LE STRADE NUOVE Soglia

Via Balbi 38, 16128 **Tel** 010 246 0991 **Fax** 010 246 2942 **Rooms** 97   **Map 2 E2**

A pleasant hotel located within walking distance of the main sights. The style is minimal and modern, featuring fresh natural wood. In addition to a sauna, gym and small snack bar/restaurant, the hotel has good views from the top floor. It also has split-level deluxe rooms and an apartment. www.sogliahotels.com

LE STRADE NUOVE Best Western City

Via S Sebastiano 6, 16123 **Tel** 010 584 707 **Fax** 010 586 301 **Rooms** 66   **Map 3 A2**

A welcoming hotel for both individual travellers and tour groups. Superb facilities include Wi-Fi, high-speed Internet and hypo-allergenic pillows. Packages with reductions to the city's sights are available. Good Ligurian cuisine is on the menu at the hotel's own restaurant, Le Rune, which is also popular with non-guests. www.bwcityhotel-ge.it

LE STRADE NUOVE Savoia Genova

Via Arsenale di Terra 5, 16126 **Tel** 010 261 641 **Fax** 010 261 883 **Rooms** 44   **Map 2 D2**

The charm and elegance of the five-star Savoia Genova are apparent in details such as the 19th-century palazzo's pretty façade and its fin-de-siècle lift. Rooms are elegant and well appointed, and there is also a cosy bar and reading room where you can relax between outings. All rooms have Wi-Fi. www.hotelsavoiagenova.it

FURTHER AFIELD (CENTRAL GENOA) Bellevue

Salita della Providenza 1, 16134 **Tel** 010 246 2400 **Fax** 010 265 932 **Rooms** 36   **Map 2 D1**

Centrally located, close to the station and harbour, the Bellevue represents a typical Genoese two-star hotel. The décor is simple and basic, but perfectly adequate. There is a lift, porter service, a large roof terrace and a garage nearby for an extra fee. Rooms are clean and fairly quiet. www.hotelbellevuegenoa.com

FURTHER AFIELD (CENTRAL GENOA) Le Tre Stazioni

Via San Benedetto 25r, 16152 **Tel** 010 246 3601 **Fax** 010 265 991 **Rooms** 19   **Map 1 C2**

This little hotel takes its name from its location, nestled between the main railway station, the harbour ferry terminals and the metro station. Although somewhat spartan, the rooms are well designed and offer all the basics. A good choice for low-budget travellers, the hotel also has a bar. Parking is available nearby. www.hotellerestazioni.it

FURTHER AFIELD (CENTRAL GENOA) Assarotti

Via Assarotti 40C, 16122 **Tel** 010 885 822 **Fax** 010 839 1207 **Rooms** 25   **Map 6 E2**

Assarotti offers comfortable B&B-style accommodation in a convenient central location with standard facilities. In the lobby, guests can browse papers and magazines or check emails at the free Internet point. The rooms are simply decorated and furnished, but unfailingly pleasant and clean. Garage parking is available. www.hotelassarotti.it

FURTHER AFIELD (CENTRAL GENOA) Hermitage €€€

Via Alberto Liri 29, 16145 **Tel & Fax** 010 311 605 **Rooms** 38   **Map 4** E5

The Hermitage features contemporary rooms, facilities and services. The clean, fresh, modern rooms boast an attractive decor and subtle design, not to mention views of the mountains or the sea. Guests can use the lounge and bar in the hotel, as well as the tennis court. **www.hermitagehotel.ge.it**

FURTHER AFIELD (CENTRAL GENOA) Starhotel President €€€

Via Corte Lambruschini 4, 16129 **Tel** 010 553 5227 **Rooms** 192   **Map** 3 C3

Overlooking the gardens of Piazza Verdi, this hotel has a rather stately feel to it. It offers comfort, luxury, function and space, as well as the gourmet restaurant La Corte, which serves international and local cuisine. Hotel services include Wi-Fi Internet access, a complimentary newspaper, parking and a fitness room. **www.starhotels.it**

FURTHER AFIELD (CENTRAL GENOA) Moderno Verdi (Golden Tulip) €€€€

Piazza Giuseppe Verdi 5, 16121 **Tel** 010 553 2104 **Fax** 010 581 562 **Rooms** 87   **Map** 3 C3

Located near Brignole station, and handy for the Palazzo Ducale and the aquarium, this hotel within a Liberty-style building features shiny wood panelling throughout. In addition to a bar and restaurant, there is also a library that guests can take advantage of. Rates increase during trade fairs and exhibitions. **www.modernoverdi.it**

FURTHER AFIELD (OUTER GENOA) Serafino €

Via Verona 8, 16152 **Tel** 010 650 7261 **Fax** 010 601 1731 **Rooms** 43   **Road Map** D3

A little out of the centre, the Serafino offers affordable simple rooms. Ideal for those on a tight budget or those arriving by car (it is close to a motorway exit), this family-run hotel has a bar and restaurant. Some rooms have air conditioning, and most have a private bathroom. Easy bus access to the port. **www.hotelserafino.it**

FURTHER AFIELD (OUTER GENOA) AC Hotel €€

Corso Europa 1075, Quarto, 16148 **Tel** 010 307 1180 **Fax** 010 307 1275 **Rooms** 139   **Road Map** D3

The AC Hotel is a good base from which to take trips out of the city to Nervi, Boccadasse and Sturla. Its sleek design is stylish and comfortable, using soft fabrics, warm tones and dark wood. The contemporary restaurant serves up Italian and international food. Other facilities include Wi-Fi Internet, a sauna and a gym. **www.hotelacgenova.com**

FURTHER AFIELD (OUTER GENOA) La Capannina €€

Via Tito Speri 7, 16146 **Tel** 010 317 131 **Fax** 010 362 2692 **Rooms** 32   **Road Map** D3

La Capannina is a family-run hotel near picturesque Boccadasse and its many seafood restaurants. Public transport to the centre of Genoa and the main sights is easy from here. Rooms on the top floor have great views of the sea from the private terraces. Weekend rates may be cheaper. Room service available. **www.lacapanninagenova.it**

FURTHER AFIELD (OUTER GENOA) Mediterranée €€

Lungomare di Pegli 69, 16155 **Tel** 010 697 3850 **Fax** 010 696 9850 **Rooms** 88   **Road Map** D3

The family-run Mediterranée is smart and classic in appearance. It also offers an extensive garden, plus a bar and a private parking area. The rooms are neat and compact. The hotel's restaurant, Torre Antica, serves regional and national dishes. This hotel is located on the seafront with good sea views. **www.hotel-mediterranee.it**

FURTHER AFIELD (OUTER GENOA) Torre Cambiaso €€€

Via Scarpanto 49, 16157 **Tel** 010 698 0636 **Fax** 010 697 3022 **Rooms** 45   **Road Map** D3

This unique noble villa has a romantic tower, orchards, formal gardens and a tree-lined avenue leading up to the entrance. Rooms with swathes of fabric and period furniture are located in the villa or in elegantly restored stables. Guests can enjoy the hotel's heated outdoor pool and the restaurant's Ligurian cuisine. **www.antichedimore.com**

FURTHER AFIELD (OUTER GENOA) Sheraton €€€€

Via Pionieri e Aviatori d'Italia 44, 16154 **Tel** 010 65 491 **Fax** 010 654 9055 **Rooms** 284   **Road Map** D3

The Sheraton is conveniently located near the airport, with good public-transport links and a regular shuttle bus to central Genoa. Its exterior has a very modern glass-and-steel look. The on-site Il Portico restaurant has a typical local vaulted gallery structure (*portici*) and serves Mediterranean and Ligurian specials. **www.sheratongenova.com**

NERVI Hotel Romantik Villa Pagoda €€€

Via Capolungo 15, 16167 **Tel** 010 372 6161 **Fax** 010 321 218 **Rooms** 17   **Road Map** D3

A very romantic hotel, once the villa of an 18th-century merchant who chose to decorate it in the Oriental style after falling in love with a Chinese girl. Marbled floors, chandeliers, antique screens, palms and terraces on different levels are some of the delightful touches. Closed Nov–Mar. **www.villapagoda.it**

THE RIVIERA DI LEVANTE

AMEGLIA Locanda dell'Angelo €€

Viale XXV Aprile 60, Ca' di Scabello, 19031 **Tel** 0187 64 391/392 **Fax** 0187 64 393 **Rooms** 36   **Road Map** F5

A lovely, sleek little hotel set in the countryside but still near the coast. It has some nice gardens, plus a good restaurant and a swimming pool. The decor is colourful and tasteful, with modern art in the lobby and halls. Facilities nearby include tennis, golf and riding. Some rooms have balconies. The suites have sea or mountain views. **www.paracucchilocanda.it**

Key to Price Guide see p176   **Key to Symbols** see back cover flap

BONASSOLA Villa Belvedere

Via Ammiraglio Serra 33, 19011 **Tel** 0187 813 622 **Fax** 0187 813 709 **Rooms** 16   *Road Map E4*

Located between the sea and the hills, this hotel has a charming, picturesque setting, boasting superb panoramic views. In addition to free parking, the hotel also offers a garden with a large shady terrace, a bar and a restaurant. The comfortable rooms have a romantic feel to them. Closed mid-Oct–Mar. **www.bonassolahotelvillabelvedere.com**

CAMOGLI La Camogliese

Via Garibaldi 55, 16032 **Tel** 0185 771 402 **Fax** 0185 774 024 **Rooms** 21   *Road Map D4*

Located close to the train and bus stations in the centre of Camogli, La Camogliese is a typical family-run inn with a welcoming feel. Some of the bright, spacious rooms boast sea views. Enjoy a carefully prepared buffet breakfast in the restaurant, which overlooks the pretty little harbour. **www.lacamogliese.it**

CAMOGLI Cenobio dei Dogi

Via Cuneo 34, 16032 **Tel** 0185 72 41 **Fax** 0185 772 796 **Rooms** 103   *Road Map D4*

On the shores of the fishing village, the villa of the Dogi was frequented by priests and cardinals in the 17th century; now it is a vast luxury hotel. It has gorgeous sun terraces with views over the town and out to sea, palms and Mediterranean pines around the pool and comfortable rooms decorated in sea-blue tones. **www.cenobio.it**

CAMOGLI Hotel Portofino Kulm

Viale Bernardo Gaggini 23, 16030 **Tel** 0185 73 61 **Fax** 0185 776 622 **Rooms** 77   *Road Map D4*

This Art Nouveau jewel nestles in a verdant park on Mount Portofino, between Camogli and Santa Margherita. The elegant Regency dining room has an outdoor terrace offering splendid sunset views over the bay. Facilities include Jacuzzis, beauty treatments and tennis courts. **www.portofinokulm.it**

CAMOGLI Villa Rosmarino

Via Figari 38, 16032 **Tel** 0185 771 580 **Rooms** 6   *Road Map D4*

Located in the verdant hills above the charming seaside village of Camogli is this 200-year-old palazzo, painted in shades of rose and with green shutters. Rooms are small, but well equipped, with state-of-the-art bathrooms. The well-manicured lawns and lovely pool area add to the appeal. **www.villarosmarino.com**

CHIAVARI Santa Maria

Viale Tito Groppo 29, 16043 **Tel** 0185 363 321 **Fax** 0185 323 508 **Rooms** 36   *Road Map E4*

The Santa Maria looks out on to the Gulf of Tigullio and is a short walk from the centre of Chiavari. It has a pleasant garden, bikes for guests to use, a bar and a fine restaurant, Le Caravelle, with alfresco dining in summer. The hotel also offers free Internet. American Express and Diners cards are not accepted. **www.santamaria-hotel.com**

FIASCHERINO/TELLARO Il Nido

Via Fiascherino 75, 19030 **Tel** 0187 967 286 **Fax** 0187 964 617 **Rooms** 34   *Road Map F5*

This yellow-coloured hotel has a nice garden of olive trees and umbrella pines, plus its own beach. Rooms are comfortable, light and unfussy, subtly decorated with cream tones. Ask for a room with a balcony, facing the sea for great panoramic views of the bay. Closed Nov–Feb. **www.hotelnido.com**

ISOLA PALMARIA Locanda Lorena

Via Cavour 4, 19025 **Tel** 0187 792 370 **Fax** 0187 766 077 **Rooms** 7   *Road Map F5*

This small beach hotel is situated on Palmaria, the island facing Portovenere. Stylish motorboats shuttle guests to and from the mainland. The sunny rooms have a simple, fresh style, bright colours and sea views. Watch the fishermen bring in the daily catch before it is served up for lunch. Closed Dec–mid-Feb. **www.locandalorena.com**

LA SPEZIA Corallo

Via Crispi 32, 19124 **Tel** 0187 731 366 **Fax** 0187 754 490 **Rooms** 35   *Road Map F4*

The Corallo serves as a good base for boat trips along the coast of the Golfo dei Poeti, since it is close to the seafront. It is unpretentious and reliable, located close to the shopping centre and many good restaurants. The light-filled rooms have a classic Italian feel. American Express cards are not accepted. **www.hotelcorallospezia.com**

LA SPEZIA Firenze e Continentale

Via Palecapa 7, 19122 **Tel** 0187 713 210 **Fax** 0187 714 930 **Rooms** 68   *Road Map F4*

A good base for exploring the Cinque Terre by train, this hotel is located in the central station square. There are several restaurants to choose from in the area. Chintzy-style rooms and wood panelling in the public rooms give the Firenze e Continentale a classic atmosphere. Parking is available on request. **www.hotelfirenzecontinentale.it**

LAVAGNA Fieschi

Via Rezza 12, 16033 **Tel** 0185 304 400 **Fax** 0185 313 809 **Rooms** 13   *Road Map E4*

Housed in an elegant 19th-century villa that once belonged to a patrician family, this hotel is set in its own grounds, and offers a period atmosphere with good facilities. Find a spot in the garden to unwind, or relax in the shade of the ancient trees. Closed Oct–Mar. **www.hotelvillafieschi.it**

LERICI Florida

Lungomare Biaggini 35, 19032 **Tel** 0187 967 332 **Fax** 0187 967 344 **Rooms** 40   *Road Map F5*

An attractive family-run hotel on the seafront. Rooms are airy and flooded with sunlight; those with balconies offer lovely sea views. The hotel has Wi-Fi Internet access and a fifth-floor terrace looking down over the beach. A comfortable, friendly base from which to explore the Golfo dei Poeti. Closed Nov–mid-Mar. **www.hotelflorida.it**

LEVANTO Nazionale

Via Jacopo da Levanto 20, 19015 **Tel** *0187 808 102* **Fax** *0187 800 901* **Rooms** *38*   **Road Map** *E4*

This classic seaside hotel has welcomed generations of visitors. It still retains its flair and Art Deco-inspired façade, as well as palm trees in its lovely Mediterranean garden. Enjoy the multicoloured array of gardenias, jasmine, hortensias and fuchsias. There is a roof terrace with parasols. Closed Nov–Mar. **www.nazionale.it**

LEVANTO Stella Maris

Via Marconi 4, 19015 **Tel** *0187 808 258* **Fax** *0187 807 351* **Rooms** *15*   **Road Map** *E4*

The Stella Maris is housed within Palazzo Vannoni, in the heart of Levanto. With its fine period furniture, paintings, stucco, frescoed ceilings, flowers and pretty garden, it takes you back in time to an elegant past. Free Internet access is provided, as well as bikes and beach towels. Compulsory half-board. **www.hotelstellamaris.it**

MANAROLA Ca' d'Andrean

Via Discovolo 101, 19010 **Tel** *0187 920 040* **Fax** *0187 920 452* **Rooms** *10*   **Road Map** *E4*

This small family-run hotel has a great setting high up in Manarola, in the stunning Cinque Terre. Pick one of the bright, airy rooms with a terrace. Ca' d'Andrean is a clean, modern, functional hotel offering a bar and a garden courtyard for breakfast and relaxing throughout the day. Closed mid-Nov–mid-Dec. **www.cadandrean.it**

MONEGLIA B&B A Casa di Roby

Strada San Lorenzo 7a, 16030 **Tel & Fax** *0185 49 642* **Rooms** *3*   **Road Map** *E4*

This peaceful and upmarket B&B has a stunning location in an old mill among olive groves. It is set back from the coast but still only a short distance from the beach, and with great views over Moneglia Bay. A country-house environment, with great breakfasts and plenty of scope for good walks, plus a pool to relax by. **www.acasadiroby.it**

MONTEROSSO AL MARE Il Giardino Incantato

Via Mazzini 18, 19016 **Tel** *0187 818 315* **Fax** *0187 818 315* **Rooms** *4*   **Road Map** *E4*

There are only three rooms and one suite at this charming B&B in Monterosso's historic centre, so be sure to book in advance. The owner, Maria Pia, does her best to make you feel at home. There's a lovely garden where breakfast is served, and the rooms all have a safe and refrigerator. **www.ilgiardinoincantato.net**

MONTEROSSO AL MARE Porto Roca

Via Corone 1, 19016 **Tel** *0187 817 502* **Fax** *0187 817 692* **Rooms** *43*   **Road Map** *E4*

Set amid the famed natural beauty of the area, this medium-sized hotel perches on a cliff just outside of the fishing village Monterosso al Mare, with magnificent views. It offers an oasis of calm, a lovely garden terrace and its own beach, with parasols and sun loungers in summer months. Closed Nov–end Mar. **www.portoroca.it**

PORTOFINO La Torretta

Via Votto 20, Manarola 19017 **Tel** *0187 920 327* **Rooms** *9*   **Road Map** *E4*

This lovely retreat overlooks the Mediterranean sea and is a cut above most other guesthouses in Le Cinque Terre. Almost all of the comfortable, clean and tastefully decorated rooms have spectacular sea views. There are nice extras, such as a free aperitivo during happy hour and iPod docking stations. **www.torrettas.com**

PORTOFINO Splendido

Salita Baratta 16, 16034 **Tel** *0185 267 801* **Fax** *0185 267 806* **Rooms** *64*   **Road Map** *D4*

Positioned on a series of terraces and housed in a former monastery overlooking Italy's luxurious fishing-village resort of Portofino, this is a truly magnificent place to stay. Service is impeccable, and the views from all the rooms are unforgettable. Closed mid-Nov–Mar. **www.hotelsplendido.com**

PORTOVENERE Genio

Piazza Bastreri 8, 19025 **Tel & Fax** *0187 790 611* **Rooms** *7*   **Road Map** *F5*

A simple hotel near the old ramparts and the church of St Peter. The family-run Genio is built into the ivy-clad wall of an ancient castle. It is on several levels, with little terraces and sea views. A hotel since 1813, it has plenty of character. American Express and Diners cards are not accepted. Closed mid-Jan–mid-Feb. **www.hotelgenioportovenere.it**

PORTOVENERE Royal Sporting

Via dell'Olivo 345, 19025 **Tel** *0187 790 326* **Fax** *0187 777 707* **Rooms** *60*   **Road Map** *F5*

The Royal Sporting is a sprawling hotel built around its swimming pool, with panoramic views across the Golfo dei Poeti. Facilities and amenities include a pool with purified sea water, garden, bar, tennis courts (racquets can be hired) and a garage. The hotel's Ristorante dei Poeti serves some good local cuisine. **www.royalsporting.com**

RAPALLO Hotel Italia e Lido

Lungomare Castello 1, 16035 **Tel** *0185 50 492* **Fax** *0185 50 494* **Rooms** *50*   **Road Map** *E4*

A perfect spot between Portofino and the Cinque Terre, this hotel overlooks the promenade, Rapallo's old medieval castle and the Gulf of Tigullio. The rooms are small, bright and compact; be sure to book one with a sea view. Bask in the sun on the rocky stepped terrace at the water's edge. Closed Nov–Christmas. **www.italiaelido.com**

RAPALLO Rosa Bianca

Lungomare V Veneto 42, 16035 **Tel** *0185 50 390* **Fax** *0185 65 035* **Rooms** *18*   **Road Map** *E4*

A pleasant and comfortable hotel on Rapallo's palm-fringed seafront, Rosa Bianca is located close to the town's amenities. Some of the simple, rooms have a little balcony. The cream Italianate building still holds a classic Riviera charm. **www.hotelrosabianca.it**

RAPALLO Excelsior Palace

Via San Michele di Pagana 8, 16035 **Tel** *0185 230 666* **Fax** *0185 230 214* **Rooms** *131*   **Road Map E4**

Overlooking the bay, the Excelsior Palace is a classic hotel on the coast, which has attracted some illustrious guests in the past – the Duke of Windsor and Wallis Simpson stayed here, among others. It offers pure luxury, with sumptuous decor and exclusive service. Arches set into the cliffs offer a private bathing spot. www.excelsiorpalace.thi.it

SAN FRUTTUOSO Da Giovanni

Via San Fruttuoso 10, 16032 **Tel & Fax** *0185 770 047* **Rooms** *7*   **Road Map D4**

If you are on a budget but still want to stay in the beautiful area around Portofino, try Da Giovanni. The rooms here are spartan, but adequate. The hotel is located close to the sea and the famous abbey. Make the most of the great seafood restaurant below. Compulsory half-board. www.dagiovanniristorante.com

SANTA MARGHERITA LIGURE Hotel Jolanda

Via Luisito Costa 6, 16035 **Tel** *0185 287 512* **Fax** *0185 284 763* **Rooms** *50*   **Road Map E4**

Although there is no sea view, the Jolanda offers comfort and many amenities at a much more reasonable price than any of the seafront hotels. Spacious, stylish and modern rooms have a refrigerator and safe, and the facilities include a gym, Turkish bath and Jacuzzi. www.hoteljolanda.it

SANTA MARGHERITA LIGURE Grand Hotel Miramare

Lungomare Milite Ignoto 30, 16038 **Tel** *0185 287 013* **Fax** *0185 284 651* **Rooms** *75*   **Road Map E4**

The Grand Hotel Miramare is a Riviera resort hotel with a history to match. It was originally a private villa that drew the chicest of international stars. The heated outdoor sea-water pool is surrounded by a wonderful garden. The whole property has wireless LAN Web access, even beside the pool. www.grandhotelmiramare.it

SANTA MARGHERITA LIGURE Imperiale

Via Pagana 19, 16038 **Tel** *0185 288 991* **Fax** *0185 284 223* **Rooms** *89*   **Road Map E4**

A real institution in Santa Margherita Ligure, the Imperiale dominates the bay. This classic traditional hotel is full of Belle Epoque glamour and sophisticated elegance. Sweeping stone steps, chandeliers, ornate frescoes and sumptuous furnishings set the tone for the high level of service and facilities. Closed Nov–Easter. www.hotelimperiale.com

SESTRI LEVANTE Grand Hotel Villa Balbi

Viale Rimembranza 1, 16039 **Tel** *0185 429 41* **Fax** *0185 482 459* **Rooms** *85*   **Road Map E4**

This grand aristocratic four-star hotel has palm trees, terraces, rooms boasting lovely sea views and elegant decor, refined ancient touches (frescoes, marble, parquet), extensive gardens and a fine restaurant. The Villa Balbi also offers a pool and a private beach. Surfing, sailing and trekking facilities are available nearby. Closed mid-Oct–4 Apr. www.villabalbi.it

SESTRI LEVANTE Grand Hotel dei Castelli

Via Penisola 26, 16039 **Tel** *0185 487 220* **Fax** *0185 44 767* **Rooms** *50*   **Road Map E4**

A truly beautiful hotel lovingly converted from an old castle. The old-style rooms have modern decor and furniture, Moorish-style mosaics, marble and pillars. Set in a park overlooking the bay, the Grand Hotel dei Castelli has winding staircases, a private beach and a sun terrace on the roof. Closed mid-Oct–Mar. www.hoteldeicastelli.com

THE RIVIERA DI PONENTE

ALASSIO Al Saraceno Hotel

Corso Europa 64, 17021 **Tel** *0182 643.957* **Fax** *0182 645 972* **Rooms** *47*   **Road Map B4**

Alassio provides a pleasant environment combining both seaside and hillside. Al Saraceno is a nice, modern and centrally located hotel from which to enjoy the best of both. Even its restaurant serves a menu that embraces the surf-and-turf ethos. The rooms are spacious, contemporary and filled with light. www.alsaracenogroup.it

ALASSIO Beau Rivage

Via Roma 82, 17021 **Tel** *0182 640 585* **Fax** *0182 640 426* **Rooms** *20*   **Road Map B4**

This charming and comfortable hotel has a small Ligurian restaurant with a good wine selection and a terrace for alfresco dining. Some of the simple and pleasant rooms have frescoed or cask-shaped ceilings. The Beau Rivage is located just across the road from a lovely beach. Closed mid-Oct–26 Dec. www.hotelbeaurivage.it

ALASSIO Grand Hotel Diana

Via Garibaldi 110, 17021 **Tel** *0182 642 701* **Fax** *0182 640 304* **Rooms** *54*   **Road Map B4**

This hotel is indeed grand in nature. It boasts its own beach, a pool and lovely grounds, as well as a health spa with sauna, gym and solarium. Choose between several restaurant options within the hotel, either in or out, formal or less so. The palm-filled garden offers a relaxing spot to unwind. Closed Nov, 7 Jan–mid-Feb. www.dianagh.it

ALBENGA Marisa

Via Pisa 28, 17031 **Tel** *0182 50 241* **Fax** *0182 555 122* **Rooms** *31*   **Road Map B4**

The period furniture and decor are reminiscent of a classic hotel from the 1930s; however, the facilities are up to date. There are antiques and paintings throughout, as well as an old piano. The Marisa is situated close to the lungomare (seafront), as well as to the shops and historic centre of Albenga. www.marisahotel.com

ALBISSOLA MARINA Hotel Garden

Viale Faraggiana 6, 17012 **Tel** 019 485 253 **Fax** 019 485 255 **Rooms** 54   **Road Map** C4

This hotel faces Albissola Marina's wide beach. The rooms are comfortable and airy, with a Jacuzzi in the bathroom and sea views. There are also apartments to let. After a day on the beach or by the pool, you can enjoy the fresh catch of seafood in the hotel's restaurant. Also offers sauna, gym and bar. www.hotelgardenalbissola.com

APRICALE Locanda dei Carugi

Via Roma 12, 18030 **Tel** 0184 209 010 **Fax** 0184 209 942 **Rooms** 6   **Road Map** A4

Housed in an old stone building in the heart of the medieval village of Apricale, this charming little hotel boasts a great location at the foot of the castle in a square with views across the valley. It offers a warm welcome and a refined change from the busy seafront hotels. Diners card is not accepted. www.locandadeicarugi.it

BORDIGHERA Villa Elisa

Via Romana 70, 18011 **Tel** 0184 261 313 **Fax** 0184 261 942 **Rooms** 35   **Road Map** A5

Classic elegance abounds in this Victorian villa set in a pretty garden full of lemon and orange trees. Rooms are fresh and bright, some come with a balcony and garden view. Public rooms still hold an air of Riviera grandeur, while interior services meet modern needs. The restaurant follows a Slow Food ethos, serving locally sourced food. www.villaelisa.com

BORDIGHERA Grand Hotel del Mare

Via Portico della Punta 34, 18012 **Tel** 0184 262 201 **Fax** 0184 262 394 **Rooms** 107   **Road Map** A5

Grand by name and by nature, this hotel boasts a sumptuous elegance full of antiques, sculptures, gilt and marble, though the building itself is modern. Rooms have sea views and balconies overlooking palm trees. The hotel's Thalasso Spa offers relaxing treatments and a nice indoor pool. Closed Oct–22 Dec. www.grandhoteldelmare.it

BORGIO VEREZZI Villa delle Rose

Via Nazario Sauro 1, 17022 **Tel & Fax** 019 610 461 **Rooms** 46   **Road Map** C4

Rooms at the top offer more comfort and small terraces with views of the coast. Air conditioning is provided at an extra cost, except in the top rooms at the height of summer. The hotel has a pub/restaurant and piano bar with music and dancing in summer, plus a large terrace. Minimum stay of three days; compulsory half-board. www.villarose.it

CERVO Miracervo

Via Aurelia 53, 18010 **Tel & Fax** 0183 400 263 **Rooms** 13   **Road Map** B5

The Miracervo is only a short distance from the seaside, located in the area of Cervo just below the castle. It has a bar and a restaurant serving traditional Ligurian food as well as pizza. This family-run two-star hotel has its own parking spaces for guests and good public-transport links. Rooms have terraces overlooking the Old Town.

FINALE LIGURE Punta Est

Via Aurelia 1, 17024 **Tel** 019 600 612 **Fax** 019 600 611 **Rooms** 40   **Road Map** C4

An 18th-century villa houses this elegant hotel, which maintains the period charm in its furniture and exposed beams. Set among palms, pines and olives, it has majestic views across the bay, as well as a great pool. Paths, steps and shady terraces lead down to the sea. Closed Nov–Mar. www.puntaest.com

GARLENDA La Meridiana

Via ai Castelli, 17033 **Tel** 0182 580 271 **Fax** 0182 580 150 **Rooms** 28   **Road Map** C4

In the heart of the Ligurian countryside, 4 km (2.5 miles) from the sea, this relaxing country house with wonderful gardens is perfect for walking holidays and outdoor activities, such as golf. The rooms and restaurant are elegantly decorated, and the service and facilities are excellent. Closed end Oct–Mar. www.lameridiana.eu

IMPERIA Hotel Kristina

Spianata Borgo Peri 8, 18100 **Tel** 0183 293 564 **Fax** 0183 293 565 **Rooms** 34   **Road Map** B5

One of Imperia's smart seafront hotels, the Kristina has its own private beach reserved for guests, as well as a light-filled restaurant serving good fish and meat dishes for dinner. The rooms are simple and classic in style, with views across the bay from the balcony. The hotel is just a short walk to the city centre. www.hotelkristina.com

IMPERIA Grand Hotel Diana Majestic

Via degli Oleandri 15, 18013, Diano Marina **Tel** 0183 402 727 **Fax** 0183 403 040 **Rooms** 75   **Road Map** B5

This hotel sits in Diano Marina, on the edge of Imperia, and features some grand touches. Each room has a large terrace, and the bathrooms are in Carrara marble. Enjoy great sea views and high-quality Ligurian fare in the restaurant. There are two pools, one of which boasts a nice terrace, and there is a private beach. www.dianamajestic.com

LOANO Villa Beatrice

Via Sant'Erasmo 1, 17025 **Tel & Fax** 019 668 244 **Rooms** 30   **Road Map** B4

The Villa Beatrice is located outside the centre of Loano, opposite the yacht marina. It is ideal for families who want to stay by the pool or enjoy its numerous fitness facilities. A lovely garden is also on offer. Try the home-grown produce cooked in the restaurant. Closed Oct–20 Dec. www.panozzohotels.it

LOANO Grand Hotel Garden Lido

Lungomare Nazario Sauro 9, 17025 **Tel** 019 669 666 **Fax** 019 668 552 **Rooms** 77   **Road Map** B4

This hotel provides a modern lido complex on the beachfront. You can go straight from the pool down on to the beach, and the airy rooms have sea views from their balconies. There are fitness facilities, a piano bar and plenty for kids to do, plus a sun terrace, two good restaurants, billiards and bikes. Closed Oct–20 Dec. www.gardenlido.com

Key to Price Guide see p176 Key to Symbols see back cover flap

NOLI Miramare

Corso Italia 2, 17026 **Tel** 019 748 926 **Fax** 019 748 927 **Rooms** 28

📧 | **Road Map** C4 | ⓔⓔ

The Miramare is centrally located, facing the sea and the palm-fringed seafront. It also forms part of Noli's medieval fortifications, which gives it a refined air of history. Rooms come in varying sizes with either garden or sea views. There is also a small bar. **www.hotelmiramarenoli.it**

PIETRA LIGURE Hotel Ca' Ligure

Via Concezione 10, Ranzi, 17027 **Tel** & **Fax** 019 625 181 **Rooms** 16

📧 🅿 | **Road Map** B4 | ⓔ

A comfortable hotel with a friendly atmosphere, the Ca' Ligure is situated on a hillside overlooking the sea 3 km (2 miles) away. All rooms have a private bathroom and a balcony with sea view. Relax in the garden by the pool or on the sun terrace. A lovely cosy feel, away from the bustle. Great for families or those with a car. **www.caligure.it**

SAN REMO Nyala Suite

Via Solaro 134, 18038 **Tel** 0184 667 668 **Fax** 0184 666 059 **Rooms** 81

📧 ⓟ ⓟ ⓟ ⓟ ⓟ | **Road Map** A5 | ⓔⓔ

Surrounded by tropical vegetation, this large hotel is well suited for families. There is an elegant bar and pool terrace, children's playground, swimming pools, a kids' club and a good restaurant. The Nyala Suite also offers special services for cyclists, as well as non-smoking rooms and rooms for people with disabilities. **www.nyalahotel.com**

SAN REMO Castellaro Golf Resort

Strada per I Piani, Castellaro, 18011 **Tel** 0184 479 085 **Fax** 0184 054 150 **Rooms** 64

📧 ⓟ ⓟ ⓟ ⓟ ⓟ | **Road Map** A5 | ⓔⓔ

This four-star resort is a highly modern affair, and perfect for golf enthusiasts who also want to enjoy the coast and sea views. As well as excellent golf facilities, a club house and two fine restaurants, the complex also offers great health and beauty treatments, a pool and fitness facilities. **www.castellarogolf.it**

SAN REMO Paradiso

Via Roccasterone 12, 18038 **Tel** 0184 571 211 **Fax** 0184 578 176 **Rooms** 41

📧 ⓟ ⓟ ⓟ ⓟ ⓟ | **Road Map** A5 | ⓔⓔⓔ

A pleasant hotel in the hands of the same family since 1926, the Paradiso boasts a peaceful location in a leafy part of town away from the busy seafront, but overlooking both the sea and Marsaglia Park. Rooms are comfortable and clean. As well as a lovely verandah restaurant, there is a pool and a garden. **www.paradisohotel.it**

SAN REMO Royal Hotel

Corso Imperatrice 80, 18038 **Tel** 0184 53 91 **Fax** 0184 661 445 **Rooms** 127

📧 ⓟ ⓟ ⓟ ⓟ ⓟ ⓟ ⓟ | **Road Map** A5 | ⓔⓔⓔⓔ

This grand dame of a hotel on the seafront in flower-filled San Remo is renowned for its gardens and exceptional restaurant. It offers wonderful service and facilities, including Internet access, an outdoor swimming pool, sunbeds at the lido, reading rooms, tennis courts, a hairstylist and much more. **www.royalhotelsanremo.com**

SAVONA Riviera Suisse

Via Paleocapa 24, 17100 **Tel** 019 850 853 **Fax** 019 853 435 **Rooms** 80

📧 ⓟ ⓟ ⓟ ⓟ | **Road Map** C4 | ⓔⓔ

Staying at this hotel in a fine 19th-century palazzo complete with ancient arcades, you will be able to soak up the history and culture of the area, while being centrally located on Savona's main street. The Riviera Suisse has a welcoming feel, having been run by the same family for decades. **www.rivierasuissehotel.it**

SPOTORNO Delle Palme

Via Aurelia 39, 17028 **Tel** 019 745 161 **Fax** 019 745 180 **Rooms** 32

📧 ⓟ | **Road Map** C4 | ⓔⓔ

The Delle Palme occupies a spot right on the beachfront in the centre of Spotorno. It offers a fairly modern hotel with TV lounge, reading room and bar. The rooms have balconies and look out over the beach, where you can reserve your lounger and parasol. Try the hotel's air-conditioned restaurant Pinna Rossa for dinner. **www.hoteldellepalme.it**

SPOTORNO Best Western Acqua Novella

Via Acqua Novella 1, 17028 **Tel** 019 741 665 **Fax** 019 7416 6155 **Rooms** 50

📧 ⓟ ⓟ ⓟ ⓟ ⓟ | **Road Map** C4 | ⓔⓔⓔ

This modern hotel boasts a fine view across the bay. The lobby is full of local Vietri ceramic tiles, and the rooms are decorated in a modern elegant style. You can take the lift down to the beach, enjoy great seafood in the hotel's restaurant, or take in fantastic views out across the gulf from the pool. Closed Nov–Feb. **www.acquanovella.it**

VARAZZE Best Western El Chico

Strada Romana 63, 17019 **Tel** 019 931 388 **Fax** 019 932 423 **Rooms** 38

📧 ⓟ ⓟ ⓟ ⓟ ⓟ | **Road Map** C3 | ⓔⓔ

Housed in a Mediterranean villa-type complex in the midst of parkland full of ancient olive, pine and oak trees, this hotel offers guests bright, airy rooms with balconies. The public areas are spacious, and there are terraces with views, as well as a pool surrounded by trees. Closed 24 Dec–Jan. **www.elchico.eu**

VENTIMIGLIA Kaly Residence Hotel

Lungomare Trento e Trieste 67, 18039 **Tel** 0184 295 218 **Fax** 0184 295 118 **Rooms** 26

📧 ⓟ | **Road Map** A5 | ⓔⓔ

Modern apartments can be rented on a weekly basis here. The location is right by the sea in a quiet residential area of town. The suites provide guests with kitchen facilities; some even have a small garden. All overlook the sea on one side. The decor is modern if a little plain. Ideal as a base for exploring the area. **www.hotelkaly.it**

VENTIMIGLIA Sole Mare

Passeggiata Marconi 22, 18039 **Tel** 0184 351 854 **Fax** 0184 230 988 **Rooms** 28

📧 ⓟ | **Road Map** A5 | ⓔⓔ

Sole Mare's bright sunny rooms are well equipped and comfortable, and they all come with sea views. The hotel boasts a private beach and parking for its guests, as well as a TV lounge and reading room. The restaurant serves a good variety of pasta dishes, typical local seafood and home-made desserts. **www.hotelsolemare.it**

WHERE TO EAT

M eat does feature on menus in the region of Liguria, but anyone that doesn't eat fish is likely to feel that they are missing out: Ligurian cooking revolves around seafood, particularly on the coast. This is a land of strong flavours and long-standing traditions, where many cooks follow recipes that have not changed for many generations: a fact celebrated in many of the region's restaurants and trattorias. Liguria has

some excellent upmarket restaurants, but more pleasure can often be derived from discovering a family-run trattoria by chance while strolling around the historic district of a resort or one of the hilltowns of the interior. A good opportunity to try the local specialities is during the many gastronomic festivals that take place in every season. *Agriturismo*, or farm holidays, also give visitors the chance to taste real home cooking.

Summer tables at a Ligurian restaurant, placed in the characteristic carruggi

OPENING HOURS AND PRICES

Restaurants and trattorias in Liguria operate similar opening hours to those in other northern regions of Italy. Lunch is usually served from midday to 2:30–3pm, while dinner is served from 7pm until late in the evening, the latest hours being kept in the big resorts with an active nightlife. Closing days depend both on the season and on the type of establishment; in general, restaurants and trattorias stay open most of the year, particularly in the towns along the coast.

Prices can obviously vary. In many restaurants the bill can easily exceed 50 euros a head, excluding wine, particularly if the meal includes fresh fish; in a more everyday trattoria, on the other hand, the bill is likely to come to around 25–30 euros.

In terms of tipping, it is usual to leave around 5 per cent of the total bill in a trattoria, and 10 per cent in a restaurant.

LOCAL PRODUCE

Ligurian cooking is inspired by an ancient tradition born out of the superb fruits of the land and the sea. The fact that meat and cheese are of relatively small significance in Liguria leaves fish and vegetables to rule the roost. The variety of seafood on local menus is huge: bream (*orata*), red mullet (*triglia*) and sea bass (*branzino*) are all popular, alongside staple shellfish such as prawns and mussels. Many restaurants offer fish soups and stews, a choice of grilled or roasted fish, or a mix of

fried fish. Fancier fish dishes include *cappon magro*, a salad of fish, greens and hard-boiled eggs in a garlicky sauce. Dried cod (*stoccafisso*) is also popular.

That the Ligurian diet is considered to be so healthy is due in part to the fact that fruit and vegetables (grown in abundance on the plain of Albenga) are central to the local diet. Any menu will show that chefs make good use of the local produce. As well as being combined with fish or meat, vegetables are also the focus of many dishes. Stuffed (*ripieni* or *farciti*) vegetables are very popular.

The olives that are the source of the region's rightly sought-after olive oil are also used in cooking. Olives known as *taggiasca*, meaning from the area around Taggia, are particularly renowned. Basil, thyme, rosemary and marjoram, all grown in the mountain valleys, are the classic Ligurian herbs.

Fresh fish, abundant in the seas along the Riviera

FARINATA

Sign for a shop selling Ligurian specialities

A traditional trattoria offering authentic Ligurian cuisine

Supreme among these is basil (*basilico*), the basis for the region's world-famous pesto. This is served with the region's fantastic array of local pastas, with intriguing names such as *fidelini*, *jazzoletti* and *stracci*. The best-known pastas are *trofie* (twists from Genoa) and *trenette* (flat cousins of spaghetti). The most popular stuffed pastas are *pansòti* (see p186) and ravioli.

LIGURIAN TRATTORIAS

Typical Ligurian trattorias may provide more modest decor and simpler menus than the average restaurant, but they often cook excellent meals. Unfortunately, tourist development along the coast has brought with it a proliferation of fast food joints and pizza parlours, which means that it can be hard to find a good trattoria along the coast. Your best chance of finding one is in the hinterland. Wherever you are, to find the best and most authentic trattorias just ask the local residents. An alternative, if you want to eat genuine local food, is to visit an *agriturismo* farm, one that offers rooms and home-cooked meals to visitors (see p174).

BARS AND CAFÉS

A typical day in Liguria starts with a visit to a café or bar for breakfast. It's a daily ritual to sit at a table or counter, inside or out, reading the newspaper or just watching the world go by. Furthermore, drinking coffee in a bar or café can often provide good opportunities to get to know some of the local people. The best cafés offer cakes and pastries, as well as often delicious home-made ice creams. Note that in Liguria's most historic cafés and those in the fashionable resorts, prices can be high. See pages 202–203 for details of some of the region's grandest cafés.

Vegetable tart and focaccia, typical produce

FOOD FESTIVALS

In common with the rest of Italy, food and village festivals in Liguria provide great opportunities for trying the local food. Among the region's main food festivals, highlights include: the Sagra delle Focacette (focaccia festival) at Recco, at the Festa dell'Olio (olive oil) in Bajardo, near San Remo, and the Festa del Basilico (basil) in Diano Marina, both in May; and the famous Sagra del Pesce (fish) in Camogli, in mid-May. During the Festa del Limone (lemon festival), which is held in Monterosso al Mare, one of the towns on the pretty Cinque Terre, at the end of May, the heaviest lemon wins a prize. On the last Sunday in June, the Sagra dell'Acciuga (anchovy festival) takes place in Lavagna, while from 4–8 July Sestri Levante hosts the Sagra del Totano (squid). At Riva Trigoso, the popular Sagra del Bagnun (a local dish made with anchovies) is held on 15 July; on the same day, in Diano Borganzo, everyone turns out for the Sagra delle Trenette al Pesto (trenette pasta). Lastly, at Badalucco, in mid-September, around 500 kg (1,100 lb) of stockfish (dried cod) is cooked and distributed annually at the Sagra del Stoccafisso.

Relaxing at one of Liguria's many seaside bars

DISABLED ACCESS

Restaurants in Liguria are improving facilities for the disabled. Even so, in old-fashioned restaurants the disabled may still have difficulty moving around.

SMOKING

It has been illegal to smoke in any bar, café or restaurant since 2005. Some establishments do have properly ventilated rooms for smokers, and the no-smoking restrictions do not apply to outdoor tables.

The Flavours of the Italian Riviera

The quintessentially Mediterranean cuisine of the Italian Riviera can be sampled in sophisticated upmarket restaurants, but it is best enjoyed in simple local *trattorias* using age-old recipes. The hallmark flavours are the exceptionally delicate local olive oil and herbs like marjoram, oregano, rosemary and sage that grow wild, perfuming the inland hills. Symbolic of Liguria is the bright green aromatic basil that is pounded in a mortar with garlic, olive oil, pine nuts and pecorino cheese to produce pesto, a local speciality. Fish, either fresh, dried or preserved in oil, is another of the region's many culinary assets.

Fresh basil

FOOD FROM THE LAND

Liguria's narrow belt of steeply terraced land, sandwiched between the sea and the mountains, has always been a challenge to farmers. This is not cattle-grazing country; lamb and goat are much better suited to this terrain. Menus feature lamb, kid, hare and rabbit either stewed or roasted, and cheeses are made from ewe's and goat's milk. Poultry is also raised for meat and eggs.

Olive and citrus trees, and even vines, manage to thrive on almost vertical terraces carved centuries ago into the hillsides. The mild winter climate and year-round sunshine are the perfect growing conditions for the commercial production of fresh produce in the greenhouses that flank the coastline. More than meat, or even fish, Ligurian cooking is dependent on a wide range of fresh vegetables, including artichokes, pumpkins (squash) and courgettes (zucchini). Wild mushrooms and herbs are picked and dried to provide distinctive flavours through the year, while local almonds, walnuts, chestnuts and hazelnuts are used in pasta sauces, casseroles, and in cake-making.

Delicious *focaccia* bread made with Ligurian olive oil

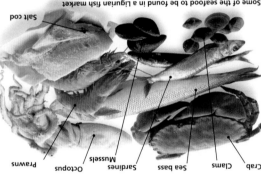

Some of the seafood to be found in a Ligurian fish market

Salt cod

Prawns

Octopus

Mussels

Sardines

Sea bass

Clams

Crab

LIGURIAN DISHES AND SPECIALITIES

Pansoti is a type of ravioli, stuffed with spinach, ricotta or offal and often served with a creamy walnut sauce (*salsa di noci*). Meat and fish courses include chicken or rabbit *alla cacciatore* (with olives, wine and herbs) and red mullet is braised with olives too. Vegetables are given the grand treatment in *torta pasqualina* (Easter pie) filled with layers of different vegetables and sometimes egg or cheese. Many foods are cooked in local olive oil: *gattafin* is fried vegetable-filled ravioli. *Friggitorie* (from *friggere*, to fry) sell flaky pastry pies stuffed with cheese and vegetables. *Farinata* is a pancake made from chickpea (garbanzo) flour, crispy outside and moist inside. Cooked in a wood-fired oven and topped with onions, cheese and herbs, it is eaten by the slice as a snack.

Olives and olive oil

Cuppin, *from Sestri Levante, is a puréed soup made from fish and shellfish, tomatoes, parsley, wine and garlic.*

Trenette con pesto, a Genoese speciality, is flat noodles with a sauce of basil, garlic, pine nuts and olive oil.

La Cima is poached veal stuffed with meat, cheese, egg and vegetables, usually eaten cold in thin slices.

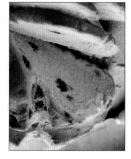

Pandolce is a cross between cake and bread, with raisins, candied fruit, fennel seeds, pine nuts and orange water.

with the shape of a cross. Aristocrats and merchants would later modify the design to include their family crests, using wooden stamps made in nearby Chiavari. Sailors returning from long voyages at sea would crave the taste of fresh food. The flavourful vegetable soup *minestrone alla genovese* was a particular favourite, with its all-important dollop of pesto, which was reputedly invented to help sailors avoid scurvy. The city has also given its name to *fagiolini alla genovese* (green beans with anchovies and herbs) and *focaccia alla genovese*, the famous flat bread made with olive oil.

GENOESE FOOD

As a major port, Genoa has always been a gateway for delicacies from around the world. The dish *corzetti*, which means "little crosses", was created for Genoese crusaders; the coin-sized discs of pasta were stamped

Fresh artichokes on a market stall on the Italian Riviera

FOOD FROM THE SEA

Fish and seafood from the Mediterranean have always been part of the local diet. Recently it has become more common for restaurants to import some of the fish they use, however mullet (*cefalo*), bream (*dorata*) and sea bass (*spigola*) are usually local. Many traditional dishes rely on the "poor" fish that are so plentiful – such as sardines (*sarde*), octopus (*polpo*), squid (*calamari*), cuttlefish (*seppia*), mussels (*cozze*) and clams (*vongole*). Cooked with olive oil, vegetables and herbs, they are made into soups, stews and sauces for pasta. Anchovies (*acciughe*) are a staple, used fresh or preserved in salt or oil. The Ligurian passion for dried salt cod (*baccalà*) dates back to the Viking traders. It is often served gently braised.

Boxes of fresh fish are unloaded onto a Ligurian quayside

WHAT TO DRINK

Liguria's steep terrain is not ideal for vines, but eight DOC wines are produced. Among the most highly regarded are:

Pigato A light, perfumed white wine that goes well with seafood or *farinata*.

Cinque Terra Light, dry white wines from the terraces of the region of the same name.

Sciacchetrà A delicious sweet white of Cinque Terra wine with an intense, flowery scent.

Rossese A light but full-flavoured red wine, often known as Dolceacqua.

Ormeasco di Pornassio A rich red with a red berry perfume.

Choosing a Restaurant

The restaurants in this guide have been selected from across a wide price range for their good value for money, quality of food, atmosphere and interesting location. They are listed by area, starting with Genoa, and in ascending order price-wise within each area. For map references, *see pp94–9* and the back endpaper.

PRICE CATEGORIES
The following price ranges are for a three-course meal for one, including a half-bottle of house wine, cover charge, tax and service.
€ Under €25
€€ €25–€35
€€€ €35–€4
€€€€ €45–€55
€€€€€ Over €55

GENOA

IL CENTRO STORICO Café Klainguti

Piazza Soziglia 98, 16123 **Tel** *010 247 552*

Map 5 C3

This renowned little coffee shop and *pasticceria* is where Giuseppe Verdi used to hang out in the 1840s (his original note of appreciation is framed and displayed on the wall). Located in the historic Old Town, Klainguti is famous for the "Zena", a zabaglione-filled pastry speciality, and for a delicious hazelnut croissant named "Falstaff".

IL CENTRO STORICO Caffè degli Specchi

Salita Pollaioli 43r, 16123 **Tel** *010 246 8193*

Map 5 C4

This traditional bar and café serves light meals and attracts a young crowd, particularly at *aperitivo* hour. The restaurant on the first floor is also open for lunch, with a daily changing menu. These days Caffè degli Specchi has an upmarket, modern feel, but in the 1920s it was the haunt of artists and intellectuals. Closed Sun.

IL CENTRO STORICO Nabil

Vico Falamonica 21r, 16123 **Tel** *010 247 6114*

Map 5 C3

For something a little different, head to Nabil for some Middle Eastern cuisine. Arabic tiles and furniture make up the decor. The restaurant is located in a narrow alleyway in the Old Town, which is reminiscent of an Arab souq. Sample the cous cous or *mansaf*, a typical dish from Jordan with lamb, almonds, pine nuts, rice and yogurt. Closed Sun.

IL CENTRO STORICO Ristorante Yuan

Via Ettore Vernazza 8, 16121 **Tel** *010 570 2327*

Map 6 D4

Yuan provides the Oriental touch not found elsewhere in Genoa. On the menu are the cuisines of several Far Eastern countries, from Thailand to Japan and China. Expect to find sushi, tempura, prawn ravioli, chicken with chestnuts cooked in a terracotta pot and Thai rice. The decor also nods subtly to the Orient. Closed Mon.

IL CENTRO STORICO Sa' Pesta

Via Giustiniani 16r, 16100 **Tel** *010 246 8336*

Map 5 C4

If you are looking for a simple, traditional Genoese eaterie with good service, basic prices and good food, look no further than Sa' Pesta. This restaurant serves up a good mix of savoury tarts and pasta dishes with pesto, it is located in one of the narrow alleyways that form the heart of old Genoa. Bookings only in the evening. Closed Sun.

IL CENTRO STORICO Sul Fronte del Porto

Calata Cattaneo, Palazzina Millo, third floor, 16129 **Tel** *010 251 8384*

Map 5 B3

Sul Fronte del Porto is a brasserie and sushi bar, plus a club and cocktail bar. Located in the old port, it allows you to dine while enjoying good views over the harbour. The sushi restaurant on the third floor offers a mix of low Japanese tables and western tables. The tone of the decor is simple and Zen, with warm berry-red walls.

IL CENTRO STORICO Cantine Squarciafico

Piazza Invrea 3, 16123 **Tel** *010 247 0823*

Map 5 C3

Located just behind the cathedral, in a former villa with frescoes on the façade and ancient pillars inside, this is a traditional Ligurian wine bar serving local specialities including *stracci*, a kind of lasagne, and a delicious chocolate tart. Wine bottles line the walls of the vaulted dining room. Booking is compulsory. Closed last week Jul, first week Aug.

IL CENTRO STORICO Da Rina

Mura delle Grazie 3r, 16128 **Tel** *010 246 6475*

Map 2 F5

Da Rina is more expensive than most other *trattorias*, but it is worth the money. Founded in 1946, this family-run restaurant serving predominantly fish is a typical simple *trattoria* with pink tablecloths in an old vaulted dining room. A house special is fish served with anchovies, mushrooms and vegetables. Closed Mon.

IL CENTRO STORICO In Vino Veritas

Vico delle Vele 27r, 16128 **Tel** *010 247 2293*

Map 5 A4

Right next to the old port, this is a small, informal and intimate restaurant with vaulted brick ceilings, a pale-yellow colour scheme on the walls, and plenty of wine bottles on display. Start with a risotto, followed by a meat dish, all accompanied by a fine choice of wines. The atmosphere is both refined and informal at the same time. Closed lunch.

Key to Symbols *see back cover flap*

IL CENTRO STORICO Tristano & Isotta

€€ Map 5 C3

Vico del Freno 33r, 16123 **Tel** 010 247 4301

This is a pleasant, modern pizzeria and restaurant serving Genoese cuisine, as well as a variety of national dishes. Located off one of the narrow alleyways in the old part of town, it is spacious and popular, with a homely atmosphere. Try the house mixed antipasti and wood-oven-cooked pizzas with names like Tristan and Isolde or Centro Storico. Closed Mon.

IL CENTRO STORICO Da Genio

€€€ Map 6 E5

Salita San Leonardo 61r, 16128 **Tel** 010 588 463

Situated in the old quarter, this is one of Genoa's best-loved trattorias, with a loyal clientele. The menu includes well-prepared fish dishes, such as fresh swordfish stuffed with anchovies and capers, but the star of the show is arguably their famous starter of trenette al pesto (pasta with pesto sauce). Closed Sun; 3 weeks Aug.

IL CENTRO STORICO Maxelà

€€€ Map 5 C2

Vico Inferiore del Ferro 9r, 16123 **Tel** 010 247 4209

This is partly a butcher's, partly a casual trattoria which specializes in beef dishes and is popular with Genoese businessmen and locals. The building dates from 1790 and is cavernous, with wood-beamed ceilings and tables made from slabs of marble with wooden benches alongside them. Dishes are simple but flavourful.

IL CENTRO STORICO Panson

€€€ Map 5 C4

Piazza delle Erbe 5r, 16123 **Tel** 010 246 8903

Panson offers diners typical local cuisine combining fresh Ligurian fish and herbs. The ambience is full of classic, understated elegance in a vaulted dining room. Some of the typical regional dishes to try are basil gnocchi in a prawn sauce, trofiette pasta twists in a pesto sauce, or pansoti (ravioli-style pasta) in a nut sauce. Closed Sun dinner.

IL CENTRO STORICO Vegia Zena

€€€ Map 5 B2

Vico del Serriglio 15r, 16124 **Tel** 010 251 3332

Hidden in the old alleyways, Vegia Zena ("Old Genoa" in the local dialect) offers some of the best pesto dishes in town. Close to the old port, this is a lively, white-walled and wood-panelled restaurant with an excellent menu full of Genoese food. Busy and popular, sharing with other guests at long tables is the norm. Closed Sun dinner; Mon.

IL CENTRO STORICO Soho Restaurant and Fish Work

€€€ Map 2 F4

Via al Ponte Calvi 20r, 16123 **Tel** 010 869 2548

Choose your lunch from the daily catch displayed in the restaurant's fish counter, and enjoy a delicious meal in the super-chic dining room or on the outside patio. Specialties include velluta di porri con gamberi (thick leek soup with fresh shrimp) and guazzetto ai frutti di mare (clams and mussels in broth).

IL CENTRO STORICO Da Toto

€€€€€ Map 5 A2

Molo Ponte Morosini Sud 19-20, 16100 **Tel** 010 254 3879

An airy, modern restaurant set in a large lobster-coloured building with wide arched windows overlooking the old port. Diners can enjoy views of the private yachts below. The elegant restaurant is run by chef Antonio "Toto" Fratea, who serves great Genoese food, especially seafood. The wine cellar holds over 200 Italian and international wines.

IL CENTRO STORICO Zefferino

€€€€€ Map 6 D/E4

Via XX Settembre 20, 16121 **Tel** 010 570 5939

Pink tablecloths and starched linen set the tone in this upmarket establishment, a Genoese institution that has been serving high-class cuisine since 1939. All kinds of seafood can be found on the menu, including lobster. Leave room for the Ligurian delights on the sweet and cheese trolleys. Famous guests have included Frank Sinatra and Pavarotti.

LE STRADE NUOVE Da Maria

€ Map 6 D3

Vico Testadoro 14, 16100 **Tel** 010 581 080

Da Maria is a laid-back and low-key affair. Focaccias, soups and filling pasta dishes are on the menu: try the trenette pasta with pesto. The place has a very simple feel, with checked tablecloths and a canteen atmosphere. The place to visit for a bit of local flavour (many workers stop here for a bite to eat) and a very affordable menu. Closed Sun.

LE STRADE NUOVE Antica Cantina i Tre Merli

€€€ Map 5 C2

Vico dietro il Coro della Maddalena 26r, 16124 **Tel** 010 247 4095

A traditional Genoese osteria where the locals come for simple, homely food, good wine and a hearty laugh. Located in the former stables of the listed Palazzo Campanila, i Tre Merli now includes a wine bar with more than 300 wines, a refined restaurant and a wine shop. The creative menu offers several good fish dishes. Closed Sat lunch; Sun.

LE STRADE NUOVE Europa

€€€ Map 6 D3

Galleria G Mazzini 33r, 16121 **Tel** 010 581 259

The food at Europa takes centre stage over the decor, which has a rather dated feel. The restaurant is set in la Galleria Mazzini, a colonnaded arcade in the city centre. Specials are the pesto sauce made with local basil and olive oil, the home-made ravioli and the daily catch. The restaurant has been going for over 40 years. Closed Sun.

LE STRADE NUOVE Le Mamme del Clan

€€€ Map 6 D3

Salita Pallavicini 25r, 16123 **Tel** 010 252 882

Housed in the palazzo in front of the club Il Clan, this restaurant features arched vaulted ceilings, soft lighting and a sophisticated decor, not to mention a menu rich in home-made ancient local dishes. It is popular for its themed evenings, which transform the venue – even the waiters take part in the show. Closed Mon.

LE STRADE NUOVE Le Rune
Vico Domoculta 14r, 16123 **Tel** *010 594 951* **Map 6 D3**

Tucked away in a small street just off Via XXV Aprile, this restaurant is located within the Best Western City hotel. The menu offers a great variety of traditional fish dishes, good wines, cheeses and desserts. A set menu is also available. Refined cuisine, relaxed surroundings and a fresh, modern interior. Closed Sat, Sun lunch.

LE STRADE NUOVE Saint Cyr
Piazza Marsala 4, 16122 **Tel** *010 888 897* **Map 3 A1**

A reputable family-run restaurant with a menu leaning towards meat dishes, with Piedmontese influences and good wines. Located in the heart of the city, Saint Cyr has two connecting dining rooms decorated in walnut wood. Try the high-quality organic dishes such as the lamb, quail or duck, or the courgette quiche. Closed Sat lunch, Sun.

FURTHER AFIELD (CENTRAL GENOA) Enoteca Sola
Via Carlo Barabino 120r, 16129 **Tel** *010 594 513* **Map 3 C4**

This central *enoteca* is decked out in a maritime style and serves a varied Ligurian menu of meat and fish. The ambience is classical and elegant but still retains a relaxed bistro-style decor. The homely food is complemented by excellent wines. Sola is a popular spot for dinner, so it is best to book ahead. Closed Sun; Aug.

FURTHER AFIELD (CENTRAL GENOA) Gran Gotto
Viale Brigata Bisagno 69r, 16129 **Tel** *010 564 344* **Map 3 C4**

A traditional Genoese restaurant with a reputation for good food and an elegant atmosphere. Contemporary art hangs on the walls, and the style of the interior is modern. The restaurant makes the most of the great fish on offer, and house specials include pasta filled with borage in a creamy pine-nut sauce. Closed Sun; Aug.

FURTHER AFIELD (CENTRAL GENOA) La Bitta nella Pergola
Via Casaregis 52r, 16129 **Tel** *010 588 543* **Map 4 D4**

Run by a Neapolitan family, La Bitta nella Pergola is small and close to the Fiera exhibition grounds. On the menu are excellent fish dishes and wonderful home-made deserts and pastries. The menu represents a blend of rustic tradition alongside old Genoese recipes. Seasonal ingredients dictate the mainly seafood-based menu. Closed Mon, Sun.

FURTHER AFIELD (CENTRAL GENOA) Le Perlage
Via Mascherpa 4r, 16129 **Tel** *010 588 551* **Map 3 C5**

This elegant restaurant is tastefully decorated, though not particularly modern. The cuisine, however, is inventive and contemporary, with a very good wine list. The chef uses fresh fish from the daily catch, transforming it into delightful dishes that draw influences from the past. The atmosphere is warm and welcoming. Closed Sun.

FURTHER AFIELD (CENTRAL GENOA) Leo Passami l'Olio
Via Rimassa 150r, 16129 **Tel** *010 561 753* **Map 3 C5**

This restaurant offers a high level of regional and international cuisine. It is located close to the Fiera di Genova and specializes in fish, seafood and meat dishes. Excellent sushi, paella and truffles (in season) are available if you book ahead. It consists of two smart dining rooms, lined with some of the 300 wines served here. Closed Sat lunch, Sun.

FURTHER AFIELD (OUTER GENOA) Osteria dell'Acquasanta
Via Acquasanta 281, Mele, 16100 **Tel** *010 638 035* **Road Map D3**

This *osteria* in a suburb of Genoa can be tricky to find, but well worth the effort. Some of the Slow Food specials are *carciofi in umido ripieni* (stuffed artichokes), *tagliolini con sugo di funghi* (pasta in mushroom jus), pesto lasagne or ravioli Genoese-style. The cheese and wine selection is worthy of a more upmarket restaurant. Closed Mon.

FURTHER AFIELD (OUTER GENOA) Chiara
Via Padre Garré 14, Località Besolagno Savignone, 16010 **Tel** *010 967 7040* **Road Map D3**

A popular place to come for good wood-oven pizzas. It is located some way out of Genoa, in the Parco Naturale dell'Antola, surrounded by natural beauty, which can be enjoyed on the garden terrace. In addition to pizzas, there are grilled meats and regional dishes. A fish menu is available if booked in advance. Closed Tue lunch & Mon (low season).

FURTHER AFIELD (OUTER GENOA) Da O'Colla
Via alla Chiesa di Murta 10, Località Bolzaneto, 16162 **Tel** *010 740 8579* **Road Map D3**

Simple but excellent home-cooked Ligurian cuisine is on offer here. Typical fare includes *minestrone genovese* (vegetable soup) served with pasta or rice and pesto) and focaccia bread served with local olive oil. This *trattoria* is located some distance outside the city, but it is definitely worth the trip. Closed Mon, Sun; 3 weeks Jan, Aug.

FURTHER AFIELD (OUTER GENOA) Pintori
Via San Bernardo 68r, 16123 **Tel** *010 275 7507* **Road Map D3**

A family-run *trattoria* with great wines and a Sardinian bent to the menu. Pintori is loved by locals for its affordable cuisine and sleek, stylish ambience. Specialities include vegetarian dishes such as *torta di verdura* (vegetable flan) and *maialino sardo* (Sardinian pig) on request. The fish dishes, desserts and cheeses are also fine. Closed Mon, Sun.

FURTHER AFIELD (OUTER GENOA) Astor
Via delle Palme 16–18, Nervi, 16167 **Tel** *010 329 011* **Road Map D3**

This bright and unpretentious hotel/restaurant is equidistant from the seaside promenade in Nervi and the wonderful parkland. It offers fine Ligurian cuisine and good wines in a simple, elegant setting. A house special is *pansotti al sugo di noci* (fresh pasta filled with ricotta cheese, herbs and lemon rind, served in a walnut sauce).

FURTHER AFIELD (OUTER GENOA) Baldin
€€€

Piazza Tazzoli 20r, Sestri Ponente, 16154 **Tel** *010 653 1400* **Road Map** D3

Baldin is well known for excellent dishes incorporating fish, wild mushrooms and truffles. The home-made desserts are also delicious. The interior decor is minimal but pleasant, and the menu offers an interesting blend of traditional regional cuisine with a creative contemporary touch. Be sure to book in advance. Closed Mon, Sun.

FURTHER AFIELD (OUTER GENOA) Bruxaboschi
€€€

Via F Mignone 8, San Desiderio, 16133 **Tel** *010 345 0302* **Road Map** D3

Opened in 1862, Bruxaboschi has been in the same family for five generations. You can sit outside in the lovely garden or in the warm, relaxed ambience of the dining room and enjoy an array of inland Ligurian specialities. Home-made pasta and mushrooms are among the most popular dishes. Closed Sun dinner, Mon.

FURTHER AFIELD (OUTER GENOA) Edilio
€€€

Corso A de Stefanis 104r, 16139 **Tel** *010 811 260* **Road Map** D3

This classic restaurant offers a pleasant mix of Ligurian and Piedmontese food. Service is attentive, and the atmosphere is elegant. Some of the house specials include *funghi e tartufi* (mushrooms and truffles), filled anchovies, green gnocchi in a velvety lobster sauce, or the sea bass in a potato crust. The desserts are also superb.

FURTHER AFIELD (OUTER GENOA) La Pineta
€€€

Via Gualco 82, Struppa, 16165 **Tel** *010 802 772* **Road Map** D3

Set in a peaceful area at the edge of a pine forest, this *trattoria* specializes in grilled meat, game, wild mushrooms and other dishes typical of the hills around Genoa. All the home-made pastas and desserts are excellent. A rustic atmosphere with a vast fireplace makes this place worth the trek out of the city centre. Closed Sun dinner, Mon.

FURTHER AFIELD (OUTER GENOA) Osvaldo Antica Trattoria
€€€

Via della Casa 2r, Boccadasse, 16100 **Tel** *010 377 1881* **Road Map** D3

This small, family-run restaurant located on a small square in Boccadasse is simple but expensive. Book ahead, since both the superb food and the pretty location make it a popular option. The fish, seafood and pasta dishes are simple, minimal, but always full of flavour, such as the *frittura mista* (plate of mixed fried fish). Closed Mon, Aug.

FURTHER AFIELD (OUTER GENOA) Santa Chiara
€€€

Via al Capo di Santa Chiara 69, Boccadasse, 16146 **Tel** *010 377 0081* **Road Map** D3

Santa Chiara is an excellent little restaurant, perfect for a romantic dinner à deux, in the lovely little fishing village of Boccadasse. It has a wonderful terrace overlooking the water and serves typical Ligurian cuisine, mainly from the sea, but also from the surrounding countryside. Booking is advisable. Closed Sun.

FURTHER AFIELD (OUTER GENOA) Toe Drue
€€€

Via C Corsi 44r, Sestri Ponente, 16154 **Tel** *010 650 0100* **Road Map** D3

There is a modern-rustic feel to Toe Drue ("hard table"), which serves traditional recipes with a contemporary Ligurian and Trieste twist. The strawberry cheesecake and caramelised pears are a delight. The Cantina del Toe next door offers great cheeses, salamis and wines for those on a budget. Closed Sat lunch, Sun.

FURTHER AFIELD (OUTER GENOA) Antica Osteria del Bai
€€€€

Via Quarto 12, Quarto dei Mille, 16148 **Tel** *010 387 478* **Road Map** D3

This ancient *osteria* serves up an array of fresh fish and seafood worked into good old Ligurian-style dishes. It is located close to the sea and provides a lovely little romantic place to eat in the evenings, when candlelight adds to the cosy atmosphere. It has a classic, elegant feel and a good wine list. Closed Mon, 2 weeks in Jan, Aug.

FURTHER AFIELD (OUTER GENOA) Da Giacomo
€€€€€

Corso Italia 1r, 16129 **Tel** *010 311 041* **Road Map** D3

Although Da Giacomo is rather expensive, you certainly get value for money here, since the quality is unfailingly high, and you are guaranteed fine, elegant dining. The restaurant lies near the Fiera and has a car park for guests. The seafood and fish dishes are highly recommended, as are the wines. The service is courteous and efficient.

THE RIVIERA DI LEVANTE

AMEGLIA Locanda dei Poeti
€

Piazza della Liberta 4, 19030 **Tel** *0187 608 068* **Road Map** F5

This restaurant has a romantic setting to match its name, "The Poets' Inn". Set in a lovely medieval hilltop village, it offers good food, as well as great views. Opt for a pizza or local meat and fish dishes; owner Donato can recommend good Tuscan wines to accompany your choice. Open all summer. Parking is available in a square nearby. Closed Tue.

AMEGLIA Locanda delle Tamerici
€€€€€

Via Litoranea 106, Fiumaretta di Ameglia, 19031 **Tel** *0187 64262* **Road Map** F5

A Michelin-starred hotel restaurant in Fiumaretta, on the border of Liguria and Tuscany, this lovely venue serves a reinvented traditional menu of regional seafood and vegetables. The dining room, with its old furniture, is warm and welcoming, and in summer it opens on to a nice garden where you can enjoy the sea breeze. Reservations required.

AMEGLIA Paracucchi
€€€€€

Viale XXV Aprile 60, 19031 **Tel** *0187 64391*

Road Map F5

Paracucchi is a stylish affair located at the Locanda dell'Angelo hotel *(see p178)*. The unusual mix of ingredients gives a bold take on fresh seasonal and local produce. Chef Matteo Cargioli also runs cookery courses for hotel guests. Try the scampi and aubergine rolls, sea bass on a bed of lentils, or the chestnut mousse. Closed Mon low season.

BOGLIASCO Il Tipico
€€€€

Via Poggia Favoro 20, 16031 **Tel** *010 347 0754*

Road Map D4

A traditional Ligurian fish restaurant with views from its hilltop position overlooking Golfo Paradiso. The building is an old maritime fortress with a medieval feel and a cosy interior. Try the antipasti, followed by basil fettuccine with a prawn sauce, or chestnuts with potatoes, all accompanied by excellent wines. Closed Mon; 20 days in Jan.

CAMOGLI La Cucina di Nonna Nina
€€

Via Molfino 126, San Rocco di Camogli, 16032 **Tel** *0185 773 835*

Road Map D4

Located on the other side of the Portofino promontory, in the quiet village of San Rocco, this restaurant occupies two rooms in a rustic villa with stunning views. It serves delicious Ligurian dishes using the great seafood and herbs of the region. Try the stuffed cuttlefish or the pasta cooked with nettles and pesto. Closed Wed; last 2 weeks Feb, Nov.

CAMOGLI Rosa
€€€€€

Largo Casabona 11, 16032 **Tel** *0185 773 411*

Road Map D4

Housed in an Art Nouveau-style villa, this restaurant has a winter garden verandah and a summer terrace with great views across the bay and the old fishing harbour of Camogli. Typical seafood and pasta specials include tuna in a sweet and sour sauce, pasta in red mullet sauce, and stewed cuttlefish. Closed Wed lunch; Tue, Jan, last 2 weeks Nov.

CASTELNUOVO DI MAGRA Da Armanda
€€€

Piazza Garibaldi 6, 19030 **Tel** *0187 674 410*

Road Map F5

Armanda is a typical Ligurian restaurant offering predominantly fish-based regional fare. It boasts unforgettable panoramic views, great antipasti, a warm welcome and simple decor. Local meat and vegetable dishes, such as rabbit with fennel and olives, also appear on the handwritten menu. Closed lunch Mon–Fri in summer; Wed.

CHIAVARI Lord Nelson
€€€€€

Corso Valparaiso 27, 16043 **Tel** *0185 302 595*

Road Map E4

This welcoming restaurant is actually a pub with rooms. Over the years it has developed a reputation for serving some of the best food in town. There is also a bar, summer terrace and *cantina* (wine store) with a good wine selection. The Lord Nelson is decorated in dark wood offset by crisp white-linen tablecloths. Closed Wed; 20 days Nov.

LA SPEZIA La Pia
€

Via Magenta 12, 19124 **Tel** *0187 739 999*

Road Map F4

For more than 125 years La Pia has been serving arguably the best *farinata* (chickpea pancake cooked in a pizza oven) in Liguria. Expect a line out the door during the lunch hour as it's considered an institution amongst locals. La Pia is housed in an old building; the decor is not the main attraction here.

LA SPEZIA All'Incontro
€€€

Via Sapri 10, 19121 **Tel** *0187 241 16*

Road Map F4

All'Incontro offers a Ligurian menu of seasonal fish and meat in arched vaulted brick-walled rooms. Try deliciously uncomplicated dishes such as linguine with scampi and lemon, or smoked swordfish with rocket and small tomatoes. Risotto and pasta dishes are consistently good. There is also a menu based on bison meat. Closed Sun.

LAVAGNA La Brinca
€€€€

58 Località Campo di Ne, Ne in Valgraveglia, 16040 **Tel** *0185 337 480*

Road Map E4

Head to La Brinca for a taste of fine peasant cooking. It is a traditional restaurant passed down the generations in a family-run inn with a shop, mill and oil press. Ingredients are sourced locally and combined with seasonal produce and home-grown herbs. A special is *noix de veal*, served with a pine-nut sauce. Closed Mon.

LAVAGNA Raieu
€€€€

Via Milite Ignoto 25, Cavi di Lavagna, 16033 **Tel** *0185 390 145*

Road Map E4

Raieu boasts an authentic maritime feel. It serves a traditional but simple menu of seafood and pasta dishes. It also offers good wines and parking for its diners. The fish served in the restaurant is all caught by the owners in their own fishing boat. Try the *pansoti* (stuffed pasta) in nut sauce or the pesto lasagne.

LERICI Bonta Nascoste
€€

Via Cavour 52, 19032 **Tel** *0187 965 500*

Road Map F5

This small but charming restaurant serves some of the best pizza and *farinata* (chickpea pancakes) in the area. Other notable dishes include pasta and beef fillet in a pepper sauce. The restaurant is located in the historic centre of Lerici, in a pedestrian-only alleyway. Seating is limited, so make sure to reserve in advance.

LERICI Il Frantoio
€€€

Via Cavour 19, 19032 **Tel** *0187 964 174*

Road Map F5

Housed in a former olive factory with stone walls and floors dating back 200 years, this restaurant serves fine cuisine; specialties include abundant *antipasti del Mare* (such as *carpaccio* of swordfish and marinated anchovies), pasta with pesto and a mixed grilled fish plate.

Key to Price Guide see p188 Key to Symbols see back cover flap

LERICI Due Corone
Calata Mazzini 14, 19032 **Tel** *0187 967 417*　　　　　　　　　　　　　　**Road Map** *F5*

Renowned as the best restaurant in Lerici, the Michelin-starred Due Corone serves a creative take on traditional Ligurian coastal dishes. The tone of the dining room is elegant, with wine bottles on display, and the small windows look out on to the seafront. The wine selection is also excellent. Closed Tue; 10 days Nov, 8 Jan–8 Feb.

LEVANTO Cavour
Piazza Cavour 1, 19015 **Tel** *0187 808 497*　　　　　　　　　　　　　　**Road Map** *E4*

Located between the station and the seafront, this typical *trattoria* with local cuisine specializes in fish and seafood. The original restaurant dates back to 1800. Dishes on the menu include *gattafin* (large fried ravioli filled with herbs, eggs, onion and cheese), anchovies in lemon and *trofiette* pasta with pesto sauce. Closed Mon; Dec–mid-Jan.

LEVANTO Tumelin
Via Grillo 32, 19015 **Tel** *0187 808 379*　　　　　　　　　　　　　　**Road Map** *E4*

This restaurant's plentiful seafood antipasti are a renowned speciality. Select from dishes such as octopus salad, shrimp with white beans, stuffed sardines, smoked swordfish *carpaccio* (raw, thin slices) and fresh anchovies with lemon. Hand-pick your fish for the main course, and end with the *pannacotta* dessert. Closed Thu (winter); Jan.

MANAROLA Marina Piccola
Via Lo Scalo 16, 19010 **Tel** *0187 920 923*　　　　　　　　　　　　　　**Road Map** *F4*

This wonderful little restaurant has great views – both of the colourful mosaic of houses in this Cinque Terre village and also down the rocks to the sea. The menu offers the local catch fresh from the sea in the form of fish soup, excellent regional seafood dishes, various antipasti and grilled mixed fish. Closed Tue; Nov.

MONEGLIA La Ruota
Via Lemeglio 6, 16030 **Tel** *0185 49565*　　　　　　　　　　　　　　**Road Map** *E4*

Set up on a hill overlooking the bay, La Ruota offers a set menu of seafood, pasta, vegetables and starters such as squid with mushrooms. The seafood risotto is excellent, as is their special *piatto mediterraneo* (baby squid, tomatoes, potatoes, parsley and olive oil), and the crêpes suzettes. Closed Wed; Nov.

MONTEROSSO AL MARE Miky
Via Fegina 104, 16030 **Tel** *0187 817 608*　　　　　　　　　　　　　　**Road Map** *E4*

It's all about the sea at Monterosso's top restaurant, which is located across from the beach in the new part of town, known as Fegina. Try the delicious linguine with lobster or the tender grilled calamari, finished off with cake for dessert, and ask to sit in the lovely back garden among the jasmine and wisteria.

PORTOFINO El Portico
Via Roma 21, 16034 **Tel** *0185 269 239*　　　　　　　　　　　　　　**Road Map** *D4*

Located on the cobbled street leading down to the harbour, El Portico serves great pizzas right in the heart of this pretty fishing village. The pizzas are baked in traditional old tins, while wooden chairs sit at tables covered in red-checked tablecloths. Pesto accompanies most dishes. Closed Mon; Jan–mid-Feb.

PORTOFINO Chuflay, Splendido Mare
Via Roma 2, 16034 **Tel** *0185 267 802*　　　　　　　　　　　　　　**Road Map** *D4*

The Chuflay Restaurant at the Splendido Mare hotel *(see p180)* has a prime spot at the top of the harbour square. It offers great quality local dishes such as home-made pasta with traditional Genovese pesto sauce, and fresh clam soup with pine nuts, black olives and marjoram. Good wines and great service complete the picture.

PORTOFINO Da Puny
Piazza Martiri dell'Olivetta 5, 16034 **Tel** *0185 269 037*　　　　　　　　　　　　　　**Road Map** *D4*

One of the best restaurants lining Portofino's tiny harbour square. The proprietor is a gregarious character, happy to recount anecdotes and flatter his guests. Fresh fish, *pasta in pesto corto* (with a rich basil, cheese and pine-nut sauce lifted by a dash of tomato) and house antipasti are excellent. Closed Thu; mid-Dec–mid-Feb.

PORTOVENERE Da Iseo
Calata Doria 9, 19025 **Tel** *0187 790 610*　　　　　　　　　　　　　　**Road Map** *F5*

A lovely little panoramic *trattoria* run by the Locanda Lorena hotel *(see p179)* on the island of Palmaria and located on the waterfront, with views over the pretty harbour and the Golfo dei Poeti. Typical dishes include Ligurian mussels stuffed with meat, anchovies in lemon sauce and a glorious seafood antipasti. Closed Wed; Nov.

PORTOVENERE La Chiglia
Via dell'Olivo 317, 19025 **Tel** *0187 792 179*　　　　　　　　　　　　　　**Road Map** *F5*

The views from this little *trattoria* stretch across to the island of Palmaria. The menu consists of reinvented traditional Ligurian dishes, mainly fish and seafood combined with great local herbs. A popular place under vast umbrella pines, La Chiglia also offers good wines. Open for lunch and dinner.

PORTOVENERE Le Bocche
Calata Doria 102, 19025 **Tel** *0187 790 622*　　　　　　　　　　　　　　**Road Map** *F5*

Perched on the promontory overlooking Portovenere, this restaurant is located below the church of St Peter, with great views. The minimalist design and wonderful shaded tables outdoors create the ideal background for the delicate flavours of the Ligurian fish dishes on offer. There is a fine wine list too. Closed Tue; Nov–Dec.

RAPALLO Elite

Via Mille Ignoto 19, 16035 **Tel** *0185 50551*　**Road Map** *E4*

The simple, refined dishes on the menu at Elite are based on the local daily catch – look out for mussels, swordfish, scallops, sole, bass and lobster, as well as, basil risotto, *pansoti* (stuffed pasta) and black ravioli filled with fish, rocket and large prawns. Italian regional wines complete the picture. Closed Wed, Nov.

RAPALLO Roccabruna

Via Sotto la Croce 6, Località Savagna, 16035 **Tel** *0185 261 400*　**Road Map** *E4*

High above Rapallo, in a splendid villa in Savagna, is Roccabruna, a warm, welcoming place with a large open terrace and great views. Expect high-level cuisine with a regularly changing menu that includes dishes such as swordfish *carpaccio* (raw, thin slices) in scampi jus, and black pasta with shellfish. Closed lunch; Mon.

RAPALLO U Giancu

Via San Massimo 78, 16035 **Tel** *0185 260 505*　**Road Map** *E4*

U Giancu is a restaurant in the countryside offering an informal and friendly atmosphere, and excellent home-made pasta, meat, fish and mushroom dishes. Decorated with framed cartoon drawings and comic strips on the walls, this simple, welcoming little restaurant has a leafy verandah in summer; it also offers fun cooking lessons. Closed Wed.

RAPALLO Luca

Via Langano 32, Porto Turistico Carlo Riva, 16035 **Tel** *0185 60323*　**Road Map** *E4*

Although Luca is located at the entrance to the harbour, the views are not great. The restaurant, however, offers elegant dining with comfortable chairs and cream linen on the tables. This is a good place for seafood specialities such as peppered mussels, lemon anchovies, black dumplings with shrimps and sour scampi with lemon. Closed Tue.

RIOMAGGIORE Cappun Magru

Via Volastra 19, Località Groppo, 19017 **Tel** *0187 920 563*　**Road Map** *F5*

Maurizio Bordoni, the chef at Cappun Magru (the name of a local fish salad) offers a good wine list and a daily changing menu according to what comes in from the local farmers and fishermen. The restaurant is open only in the evenings, but the wine shop, where you can sample wines with salami and cheeses, is open all day. Closed Mon, Tue.

SANTA MARGHERITA LIGURE Cinzia e Mario

Via XXV Aprile 13, 16038 **Tel** *0185 287 505*　**Road Map** *E4*

In the central pedestrianized zone near the shops, this restaurant is handy for the port. It welcomes children, who can entertain themselves in the large play area. There are two terraces and pink decor throughout, and the menu offers a variety of pasta and pizza dishes, with local specialities such as *penne alla Portofino* (with pesto).

SANTA MARGHERITA LIGURE Trattoria dei Pescatori

Via Bottaro 43–45, 16038 **Tel** *0185 286 747*　**Road Map** *E4*

This fishermen's *trattoria* is located in former fishing-net workshops facing the harbour in the centre of Santa Margherita Ligure. It is a good place to try the local *pansoti* (stuffed pasta in a nut sauce) or the catch of the day fresh from the boats. Enjoy the simple menu amid antique furniture, retro finds and old-fashioned decor. Closed Tue.

SANTA MARGHERITA LIGURE Oca Bianca

Via XXV Aprile 21, 16038 **Tel** *0185 288 411*　**Road Map** *E4*

Oca Bianca is a restaurant dedicated mainly to various types of meat, but it also offers some excellent vegetable and cheese dishes – all of which makes a nice change from the ever-present seafood-based menus. The antipasti are particularly memorable, as are the pasta parcels with gorgonzola. Book ahead.

SARZANA Taverna Napoleone

Via Bonaparte 16, 19068 **Tel** *0187 627 974*　**Road Map** *F5*

Expect to find a friendly, cosy atmosphere at Taverna Napoleone. The menu offers a variety of meat, vegetable, mushroom and truffle dishes, all with a traditional local spin. Specials include pasta with pesto sauce, and bean and veal soup. Closed Wed.

SESTRI LEVANTE Polpo Mario

Via XXV Aprile 163, 16039 **Tel** *0185 480 203*　**Road Map** *E4*

Set in a former papal summer residence dating back to the 16th century, Polpo Mario now features a marine-themed decor, with old photos of the restaurant and its illustrious guests. The proprietors' own boat brings in the daily catch of prawns, scampi, mullet, octopus and other fish. Smart and chic, with a summer terrace and a good wine list. Closed Mon.

TELLARO Locanda Miranda

Via Fiascherino 92, 19030 **Tel** *0187 968 130*　**Road Map** *F5*

The warm, inviting dining rooms at Locanda Miranda boast a lovely view of the Golfo dei Poeti. The creative menu consists of seafood specialities and delicious fish dishes. An old-fashioned place with a warm welcome and good straightforward food made using excellent ingredients. It also has a B&B with a few rooms and a rustic charm. Closed Mon; Nov, Jan.

VERNAZZA Gambero Rosso

Piazza Marconi 7, 19018 **Tel** *0187 812 265*　**Road Map** *E4*

Creative modern interpretations of Ligurian seafood dishes are what Gambero Rosso is all about. Prawns feature heavily on the menu of this little terrace restaurant directly on the harbour. The fish ravioli and lemon risotto are unforgettably delicious, as are the original desserts. Opt for a tasting menu or eat à la carte. Closed Mon; Dec-Feb.

Key to Price Guide *see p188* **Key to Symbols** *see back cover flap*

ALASSIO Palma

€€€€

Via Cavour 5, 17021 **Tel** *0182 640 314* **Road Map** *B4*

Located in an 18th-century palazzo, this elegant Michelin-star restaurant seats up to 30 people. It is a family-run affair, with the owner's wife as the chef and their son as the sommelier. House specialities include tuna seared with goat's cheese and red wine sauce, or buffalo mozzarella flan with orange, tomato and red-pepper sauce. Closed Wed.

ALBENGA Lo Scoglio

€€€€ 🖼️ 🚗

Viale Che Guevara 40, 17031 **Tel** *0182 541 893* **Road Map** *B4*

This simple, unpretentious little restaurant is built on a small pier a short walk from the seafront, on the small coastal road to Cerale. Lo Scoglio has no written menu – simply walk in and ask Paolo for his daily specials. The fish is excellent, as are the antipasti and deserts. Closed Mon.

ALBENGA Babette

€€€€ 📖 🚗

Viale Pontelungo 26, 17031 **Tel** *0182 544 556* **Road Map** *B4*

Good, innovative Ligurian cuisine is on the menu at this predominantly fish restaurant, where quality, style and presentation play a big role. Try the Mediterranean fish fantasy, drizzled with olive oil and marjoram. Good wines and friendly hospitality are also staples at this smart restaurant located near the historic centre. Parking is nearby.

ALBENGA Il Pernambucco

€€€€€ 🖼️

Viale Italia 35, 17031 **Tel** *0182 53458* **Road Map** *B4*

Despite its location in a sports complex close to the sea, Il Permambucco offers a refined atmosphere. The restaurant takes its name from a type of Brazilian tree; while the atmosphere is Brazilian, the menu takes a contemporary look at Ligurian flavours and traditional dishes. Stewed fish or fish in the pan are typical specialities. Closed Wed.

ALBISOLA SUPERIORE Au Fundegu

€€€€€ 🖼️ 🚗

Via Spotorno 87, 17013 **Tel** *019 480 341* **Road Map** *C3*

Located in the former summer residence of the aristocratic Della Rovere family of Savona, Au Fundegu has smart, subtle decor and crisp white table linen. The old vaulted rooms feature exposed brick and are decorated with the coat of arms of the previous palazzo owners and a range of wine bottles. Excellent wine list. Dinner only.

ALBISSOLA MARINA Ai Cacciatori da Mario

€€€ 🚗 🖼️

Corso Bigliat 70, 17012 **Tel** *019 481 640* **Road Map** *C4*

Stuffed red chairs and paintings on the walls lend an elaborate, elegant air to this smartly decorated little family restaurant. It is close to the sea and has a lovely terrace with views and palms wafting in the sea breezes. Expect the local catch on the menu, from stuffed anchovies to squid, seafood salad and home-made pasta dishes.

ALTARE Quintilio

€€ 📖

Via Gramsci 23, 17041 **Tel** *019 58000* **Road Map** *C3*

The menu on offer here is a blend of Ligurian and Piedmontese cuisine. Some 250 wines accompany dishes such as stuffed peppers, artichoke tart, and pansoti (stuffed pasta) or gnocchi with black truffle. This restaurant has a historic feel, and at dinner the modern dining room is bathed in candlelight. Good wine list. Closed Sun dinner; Mon.

ANDORA Casa del Priore

€€€€ 🖼️ 🚗 🍴 🍷

Via Castello 34, 17051 **Tel** *0182 684 377* **Road Map** *B4*

This is the kind of place where the stunning hilltop location rather overrides the food, although the standard is still high. Casa del Priore is off the beaten track, in a 15th-century Benedictine parsonage. There is a restaurant, brasserie and bar. Guests dine in a fine room with fabulous views over the bay. Open until 2am. Closed lunch; Mon.

ARENZANO L'Agueta du Sciria

€€ 🖼️ 🚗

Via Pecorara 18, 16011 **Tel** *010 911 9762* **Road Map** *C4*

Set in the natural park of Beigua and surrounded by relaxing and beautiful scenery, this restaurant has a smart, rustic elegance. The menu is set according to a specific theme, which changes every evening and might range from grilled fish to game dishes. A house speciality is barbecued meat. Closed Sun dinner; Mon.

ARMA DI TAGGIA La Conchiglia

€€€€€ 🖼️

Via Lungomare 33, 18011 **Tel** *0184 43169* **Road Map** *A4*

La Conchiglia is well loved by locals and tourists alike for its high-quality cuisine. The elaborate dishes echo whatever is seasonally available. Try the specials or San Remo prawns on a bed of beans, the artichoke-filled tortelli with fish sauce, or the squid with artichokes. Limited spaces, so it is best to book. Good wine list. Thu in winter.

BAIARDO Jolanda

€€ 🖼️ 🚗

Via Roma 47, 18031 **Tel** *0184 673 017* **Road Map** *A4*

This traditional and affordable little restaurant specializes in game when in season. The house speciality is wild boar (cinghiale). Jolanda has a rustic and historical feel to it, serving up hearty local cuisine that befits the decor. A delicious locally pressed olive oil accompanies most dishes. Closed Mon in winter; Nov.

BERGEGGI Claudio
😊😊😊😊😊 🗺🔒

Via XXV Aprile 37, 17028 Tel 019 859 750 **Road Map** C4

Reputed to be the best fish restaurant on the Riviera, Claudio is located in a hotel with 25 rooms. There is also a tapas bar. The house speciality is excellently prepared seafood, such as the bouquet of shellfish with citrus fruit and Mediterranean herbs. The refined setting offers a lovely summer terrace and great views. Closed Mon; Dec–mid-Mar.

BORDIGHERA La Reserve
😊😊😊 🗺🔒

Via Arziglia 20, 18012 Tel 0184 261 322 **Road Map** A5

Overlooking the sea and the beach, La Reserve has become a very popular spot, with a light, airy and modern appeal. Typical dishes include sea bass ravioli, excellent antipasti, gnocchi in a coral-coloured sauce, and fresh grilled fish. Also worth a try is the *limoncello* liqueur. Altogether, a truly beautiful setting above the sea. Closed Mon; 2 weeks in Jan.

BORDIGHERA Magiargé Vino e Cucina
😊😊😊 🗺🔒

Via della Loggia, Piazza Giacomo Viale, 18012 Tel 0184 262 946 **Road Map** A5

In the heart of the Old Town, you will find a little green door and an awning below of the Virgin Mary. This is the entrance to this pleasant and affordable restaurant which also has tables out in the square in summer. Dishes and specials include roast local lamb, salt cod, artichokes from Albenga and pesto lasagne. Closed lunch Jun–Aug; Mon.

BORDIGHERA Enoristorante degli Amici
😊😊😊 🗺🔒

Via Lunga 2, 18012 Tel 0184 260 591 **Road Map** A5

Regional Mediterranean cuisine at Enoristorante degli Amici is given a refined twist to match the fine wines. This elegant rustic restaurant also boasts a large and important wine cellar with more than 500 labels, including the best Italian wines from 17 key regions. The menu features plenty of fish and also some ethnic influences. Dinner only. Closed Mon.

BORGIO Verezzi Doc
😊😊😊😊😊

Via Vittorio Veneto 1, 17022 Tel 019 611 477 **Road Map** C4

A romantic restaurant set in a flower-filled villa from the 1930s. Fresh fish from the daily catch is combined with typically Ligurian vegetables to produce some refined regional cooking. Try one of the house specials, such as assorted fish with basil (*fantasia di mare*), artichoke soufflé, or gnocchi with beetroot and mullet.

CERVO San Giorgio
🗺🔒 😊😊😊😊😊

Via Volta 19, 18010 Tel 0183 400 175 **Road Map** B5

The owner of this charming place, nestled in a square in the historic centre, blends local flavours and fresh, seasonal food. The results are creative, simple dishes such as baby artichokes, and fish of the day with tiny olives and fresh marjoram. San Giorgio is very popular, so it is wise to book ahead. Closed Mon, Tue.

COGOLETO Taverna A Beguda
🗺🔒 😊

Lungomare Santa Maria 69, 16016 Tel 010 918 9071 **Road Map** C3

Close to the sea, this simple *trattoria* is decorated in sunny blue and yellow tones. Its light, contemporary ambience sets the tone for a menu rich in fish and seafood. Try the lobster *taglierini* pasta, or the risotto with peppers and scampi sauce. If you have room for dessert, there is a superb tiramisu or mint pannacotta. Closed Tue–Sat, lunch; Mon.

DOLCEACQUA/APRICALE Apricale da Delio
🔒 😊😊

Piazza Vittorio Veneto 9, Apricale, 18030 Tel 0184 208 008 **Road Map** A4

The previous chef of Gastone in Dolcecaqua has moved to nearby Apricale. This restaurant offers the same high-quality regional cuisine given an elegant yet rustic atmosphere. On the menu are home-made pasta and meat dishes, such as rabbit ravioli in a thyme-flavoured sauce, or goat stew with white beans from Pigna. Closed Mon, Tue.

FINALE LIGURE Ai Cuattru Canti
😊😊

Via Torcelli 22, 17024 Tel 019 680 540 **Road Map** C4

A tiny, reasonably priced restaurant tucked away in a side street off one of finale's squares. Ai Cuattru Canti serves a mixture of excellent and tasty Ligurian dishes, such as filling platters of antipasti that include little flans, great pastas and soups, and mains based on octopus or rabbit. Altogether a cosy, friendly place. Closed Sun dinner; Mon.

FINALE LIGURE Ai Torchi
🍴 😊😊😊😊😊

Via dell'Annunziata 12, Finalborgo, 17024 Tel 019 690 531 **Road Map** C4

Ai Torchi is housed in an old *frantoio* (olive-oil factory), where the current Sicilian–Neapolitan owners serve a fine and popular range of excellent fish and seafood pasta; some meat dishes find their way on to the menu too. One of the specials is *maccheroncini al sugo di polpo e zucchini* (with octopus and courgette sauce). Closed Tue (except Aug).

IMPERIA Lanterna Blu
🗺🔒 😊😊😊😊😊

Via Scarincio 32, 18100 Tel 0183 63859 **Road Map** B5

This marine-styled restaurant overlooks the port. Try the Mediterranean mix of flavours in the hot seafood antipasti, lobster and *linguettine*, or the warm seafood *carpaccio* (raw, thin slices). In addition to fish fresh from the sea, Lanterna Blu also serves great desserts. The atmosphere is classic and elegant. Closed Wed; two weeks Nov.

LAIGUEGLIA Baia del Sole
🗺🔒 😊😊😊

Piazza Cavour 8, 17053 Tel 0182 691 016 **Road Map** B4

Located above the beach in the Bay of the Sun, this is the perfect place to enjoy a relaxed alfresco lunch. The view is superb, taking in the coastline and transporting you miles away from the bustle of the beaches below. The menu offers fine local food, but the main draw is the view. Closed Tue (except Jun, Jul, Sep); Oct–Easter.

Key to Price Guide *see p188* **Key to Symbols** *see back cover flap*

NOLI La Scaletta ⓔⓔⓔ 🖼

Via Verdi 16, 17026 **Tel** *019 748 754* **Road Map C4**

At La Scaletta you can find a predominantly fish-based menu consisting of typical Ligurian dishes. Start with *trenette* or *trofiette* (the local varieties of pasta) with pesto made using fine olive oil from a local press, and continue with lobster or langoustines. The local flavours are complemented by a modest selection of local wines. Closed Tue, Nov.

NOLI Lilliput ⓔⓔⓔⓔ 🖼 🎛 🎴

Via Zuglieno 49, Voze, 17027 **Tel** *019 748 009* **Road Map C4**

Fine fish and seafood are served in this restaurant located on a hill overlooking the sea, and set in a lovely garden with shaded tables and even minigolf. Choose some grilled fish or the mixed-seafood platter. The sea bass and prawns are especially delicious, as are the pasta dishes with scampi or pesto. Cleanse your palate with a citrus and vodka sorbet.

SAN REMO Il Sommergibile ⓔⓔⓔ 🖼 🎴

Piazza Bresca 12, 18038 **Tel** *0184 501 944* **Road Map A5**

The flavour of the sea dominates the menu at Il Sommergibile ("The Submarine"). Its dark walls display the range of local wines, and the pleasant dining room has a light arched ceiling. Try some of the typically Ligurian delights, such as oven-baked fish with seasonal vegetables. The pasta with lobster is a real treat. Closed Sun, Nov.

SAN REMO Il Bagatto ⓔⓔⓔⓔ

Corso Matteotti 145, 18038 **Tel** *0184 531 925* **Road Map A5**

Il Bagatto, located in the centre of town in a small 15th-century palazzo, offers a traditional Ligurian menu following ancient recipes for fish, and also a few meat dishes. Typical fare includes *acciughe* or *verdure ripiene* (fresh anchovies or vegetables stuffed with cheese and baked in breadcrumbs). Closed Thu.

SAN REMO Da Paola e Barbara ⓔⓔⓔⓔⓔ 🎛

Via Roma 47, 18038 **Tel** *0184 531 653* **Road Map A5**

An exceptional restaurant with an international reputation, Da Paola e Barbara features a menu that mixes fine vegetables – courgettes, herbs and beans – with local fresh fish – mackerel, San Remo shrimps. Barbara's expertise in pâtisserie is revealed with her ricotta-cheese cassata. Closed Wed, Thu lunch; 1 week Jan, 2 weeks Jul, 2 weeks Dec.

SAVONA Conca Verde ⓔⓔ 🖼 🎴

Via Alla Stra 27, 17100 **Tel** *019 263 331* **Road Map C4**

Take the road up out of Savona city centre to this colourful, friendly restaurant with great views, plenty of parking and a lovely terrace. Surrounded by luxuriant gardens, Conca Verde offers grilled meat and pizzas in addition to typically Ligurian seafood and pasta dishes. The wines and seasonal desserts are also delicious. Closed Mon.

SAVONA Arco Antico ⓔⓔⓔⓔⓔ 🎴

Piazza Lavagnola 26, 17100 **Tel** *019 820 938* **Road Map C4**

Arco Antico has an intimate, sophisticated atmosphere. It offers top-class dining, but without formality. The prices match the excellent presentation and quality of food. The chef produces interesting combinations, such as the highly recommended carpaccio of porcini mushrooms, tuna and woodcock. Dinner only. Closed Sun.

SPOTORNO Pinna Rossa ⓔⓔ 🖼 🎴

Via Aurelia 39, 17028 **Tel** *019 745 161* **Road Map C4**

A bright little restaurant with a few seats outside for alfresco dining. The subtle but cheery décor revolves around small paintings of local scenes and a light maritime theme. On the menu is traditional and classic Ligurian cuisine, such as *scaloppino di ombrina* (finely sliced filets of sea perch), and octopus, potato and olive pesto tart. Closed Tue.

TAGGIA Osteria Germinal ⓔⓔⓔ 🎴

Via Gastaldi 15b, 18018 **Tel** *0184 41153* **Road Map A5**

This simple and stylish *trattoria* features bold red walls that give a bright, warm effect. Germinal is famed for its Slow Food approach and its use of traditional recipes prepared with the freshest of local produce in season. Try the wonderful antipasti, the lean meat and thyme ravioli, or the artichoke flan. Closed Mon–Wed.

VARAZZE Antico Genovese ⓔⓔⓔⓔ 🎴

Corso Colombo 70, 17019 **Tel** *019 96482* **Road Map C3**

This warm and welcoming restaurant is open daily. The menu lists regional dishes from the land and the sea. The lobster dishes with pasta are particularly fine, or you can opt for a roast lamb combined with local herbs and potato soufflé. End the meal with a choice of delicious desserts, such as the chestnut tiramisù. Good wines also on offer.

VARIGOTTI Muraglia-Conchiglia d'Oro ⓔⓔⓔⓔⓔ 🖼 🎛

Via Aurelia 133, 17029 **Tel** *019 698 015* **Road Map C4**

A light, modern and well-decorated restaurant, Muraglia-Conchiglia d'Oro is locally renowned for serving excellent fresh fish and seafood dishes. Straight from the sea, the fresh catch is displayed on ice in large wicker baskets and finds its way in good antipasti and secondi. Outdoor space is very limited in summer. Closed Tue, Wed.

VENTIMIGLIA Balzi Rossi ⓔⓔⓔⓔⓔ 🎴 🖼 🎛 🎎

Via Balzi Rossi 2, Ponte S Ludovico, 18039 **Tel** *0184 38132* **Road Map A5**

A popular and welcoming restaurant serving fine fish dishes with a creative bent. Located near the French border, Balzi Rossi boasts wonderful sea views from its terrace. Expect to find a fine blend of fresh local ingredients on the menu – from anchovies, artichokes and courgette to tuna, cod and the famous local olive oil. Closed Mon, Tue lunch.

SHOPPING

Shopping is an enjoyable experience in Liguria, as it is in the whole of Italy. If it's choice or designer clothes you're after, Genoa and San Remo are the places to go, though the big resorts have lots of boutiques, too. In terms of crafts, Liguria is a good place for buying ceramics, an ancient craft associated with Albisola and Savona. You can also find good-quality glass (Altare), lace (Rapallo and Portofino), macramé and woodcarving (Chiavari).

Characteristic sign

ANTIQUES

Before you start shopping for antiques (or modern art, in fact), you should be aware that if you want to take any such object out of the country you will need to apply to the Italian Department of Exports for an export licence (for which you will have to pay). Any reputable antiques dealer will be able to give you the details.

Antique shops proliferate in Liguria, above all in the large towns, and some are of an excellent standard. Items for sale range from objets d'art to books and prints, furniture, statues, jewellery and antique posters. Model ships and other seafaring memorabilia, such as shipboard furniture, instruments and even figureheads, are particularly sought after.

Several important antiques fairs are held in the region, including "Antiqua" and "Tuttantico" in Genoa, and the annual fair held in August in Sarzana. There is also a monthly antiques market in Genoa's Palazzo Ducale.

Wherever you shop, always ask for evidence of the authenticity of your purchase.

CERAMICS

This is one of the oldest handicrafts practised in Liguria. Evidence of ceramic production dates back to at least the 15th century. The twin-city of Albisola, the main ceramics centre in Liguria, has been a town of potters since the Renaissance. Here you can find all sorts of objects made from the local clay and typically coloured blue and white, from decorative tiles to old pharmacy jars.

In nearby Savona, pots are also traditionally painted blue and white, though you can find more modern designs and other colours, as well as figures from nativity scenes (presepi).

You can buy ceramics either in specialist shops and art galleries or, sometimes, from the potters' own workshops.

Throwing a pot, a tradition with a long history in Liguria

PLANTS AND FLOWERS

Thanks to its mild climate, Liguria is one of Italy's foremost regions in the field of horticulture: nurseries and glasshouses housing everything from camellias, to citrus trees under one roof seem to dominate the landscape in some areas, and flower shops abound. Bonsai trees (including even miniature olive trees) are popular buys, as are cacti and orchids. All kinds of tropical plants are available, too.

Plants and flowers, the pride of Liguria

As in other regions of Italy, you can find some great markets. Most towns have a market every week, while larger places such as Genoa, Ventimiglia and Rapallo, have one every day. Most visitors may not consider taking any of Liguria's famous fresh flowers home, but San Remo's flower market, the largest in Europe, is well worth a visit. Wherever you go there are shops selling local olive oil and wine, as well as Liguria's other gastronomic delights.

OLIVE OIL

A natural product that is of great importance to the region's economy is the olive, and also the oil made from it. No one knows who first planted olives along this coast

Shop selling locally made handicrafts

Dried beans sold by the sackful in a Ligurian market

but, in the Middle Ages, the monasteries played an important role in developing the art of olive-pressing.

Olives are cultivated all along the coast, but the best grow along the Riviera di Ponente, none more so than the small black olives of Taggia, which yield a golden olive oil with green tints and an almondy, lightly fruity aroma. In the area between Taggia and Albenga you can buy olive oil direct from the producers: look for signs saying *frantoio* (meaning presshouse).

Most Ligurian olive oil carries the quality mark of Denominazione d'Origine Protetta (DOP), which guarantees the provenance of the olives and the cold-pressing methods used in the manufacture.

Note that the price of a good-quality olive oil (ideally extra virgin) bought from a presshouse is higher than everyday oil from a supermarket or grocer's shop, but will definitely be worth taking home.

WINE

Liguria is not a major wine producer but still has some respected wines, both whites and reds *(see p187)*. It is fun to buy wine direct from the producers.

Sometimes you have to pay to taste the wine, which may be accompanied by cheese and salami, and you usually need to book ahead.

GASTRONOMY

The main problem with buying food in Liguria is that it's hard to know where to start, and stop. Much of what you see is best eaten on the spot. This applies to the wonderful snacks that the Ligurians love so much. Baked or fried snacks come in all shapes and sizes: from the famous *focaccia (see p186)* to *cuculli* (fritters) and *torta sardenaira*, a sort of pizza topped with tomatoes and anchovies (popular in San Remo). Bakeries and *pasticcerie* (pastry shops) sell all manner of wonderful cakes and biscuits, too.

In terms of foods to take home, you'd do better to concentrate on the local cured meats and preserved vegetables, such as sundried tomatoes, local artichoke paste and dried porcini mushrooms. Anchovies in olive oil are another good buy.

Olio Carli, a fine olive oil from Imperia

DIRECTORY

ANTIQUES

Antiqua & Tuttantico
Genoa
Fiera Internazionale
Tel 010 539 11.
www.fiera.ge.it

CERAMICS

Ceramiche Fenice
Albissola Marina
Via Repetio 22.
Tel 019 481 668.

Studio d'Arte Esedra
Dolceacqua
Via Castello 11.
Tel 0184 200 969.

Studio Ernan Desion
Albisola Superiore
Corso Mazzini 7.
Tel 019 489 916.

GLASS AND LACE

Soffieria Bormioli (glass)
Altare
Via Paleologo 16
Tel 019 58 254.

E. Gandolfi (lace)
Rapallo
Piazza Cavour 1
Tel 0185 50 234.

PLANTS

Stern & Dellerba (cacti & succulents)
San Remo
Via Privata delle Rose 7.
Tel 0184 661 290.

Vivai Olcese (plants)
Genova
Via Borghero 6.
Tel 010 380 290.

LOCAL PRODUCE

Antico Frantoio Sommariva (oil)
Albenga
Via Mameli 7.
Tel 0182 559 222.

Bottega del Formaggio (cheese & salami)
Chiavari
Via Martiri della Liberazione 208.
Tel 0185 314 225.

Bruciamonti (deli)
Genoa
Via Roma 81.
Tel 010 562 515.

Bottega della Strega (deli)
Triora
Corso Italia 48.
Tel 0184 94 278.

Cascina dei Peri (wine and oil)
Castelnuovo Magra
Via Montefrancio 71.
Tel 0187 674 085.

Enoteca Sciacchetrà (wine)
Vernazza Via Roma 50.
Tel 0187 821 210.

Panificio Canale (bakery)
Portofino
Via Roma 30.
Tel 0185 269 248.

A'Pestun'à (bakery)
Genoa
Via Boccadasse 9.
Tel 010 377 75 75.

Revello Dolce e Salato (bakery)
Camogli
Via Garibaldi 183.
Tel 0185 770 777.

OUTDOOR ACTIVITIES

More than 300 km (186 miles) of coastline provide a wonderful playground for anyone who loves sports associated with the sea, from windsurfing and diving to sailing (Liguria has more than 60 sailing clubs). Swimming is popular too, of course, though many beaches are pebbly. There is plenty to do away from the coast, too. In the hills of the interior there are numerous trails that are used by hikers, horse riders and

Exploring the countryside on horseback

mountain bikers, though the terrain makes any of these activities a relatively energetic option. The region's parks and nature reserves all have hiking trails, while the peaks of the Ligurian Alps and of the Apennines provide some scope for skiing and other winter sports. For those who take a more leisurely approach, there is always golf: there are courses in San Remo, Rapallo, Lerici, Garlenda (near Albenga) and Arenzano (near Genoa).

The breezy coastline, a boon for windsurfers

INFORMATION

For those intending to do some serious sport, the best source of information is CONI, the Ligurian sports committee. The Club Alpino Italiano (CAI) is a good source for anyone venturing into the mountains, whether it's to hike, ski or rock-climb.

SAILING

Liguria has a most beautiful coastline and is a great place to go sailing. From La Spezia to Ventimiglia, the coast has countless beaches and inlets, some accessible only by boat. While it is not difficult to navigate along this coast, it is important not to underestimate the dangers of a changing sea, even in the summer. The to-and-fro

of sea bathers can be problematic in high season.

If you do not have a boat, there are many brokerage agencies which have plenty of yachts and motor-driven boats for hire.

A good source of general information are the Pagine Azzurre (published annually in English), which includes official charts and plans of every harbour.

CANOEING

Canoes are a common sight along the coast. Inland, there are some opportunities for downhill canoeing during the winter and the spring thaw, when water is abundant in the local rivers.

WINDSURFING

Waves and year-round winds combine to make certain stretches of the Riviera di Ponente popular with windsurfers, though not everyone finds the relatively sheltered conditions exciting.

Arma di Taggia, around Porto Maurizio, Capo Mimosa (near Andora) and Levanto are among the best places to windsurf. You can hire boards in most of the big resorts along the coast, however.

DIVING

A few areas along the coast of Liguria provide some great opportunities for diving. The most popular spots

include the headland of Portofino, Ventimiglia, Alassio and the Cinque Terre marine park (with diving centres in Riomaggiore and Monterosso). The latter, created only in 1997, has some rare white and black corals, and is also home to many of the species of dolphin and whale that inhabit the Ligurian Sea. Note that diving numbers are strictly controlled here, so it is worth booking ahead.

There are around 60 dive centres in Liguria: their addresses are given on the regional tourist board websites *(see Directory)*.

ROCK CLIMBING

Stony cliffs facing the sea enable rock climbers to enjoy the sport all year round. The most popular sites are found

Exploring the fascinating sea beds along the coast

Players on one of Liguria's three 18-hole golf courses

in the area of Le Manie near Finale Ligure *(see p144)*, and nearby at Capo di Noli. Other popular sites include the cliffs at Muzzerone, near Portovenere, and Castelbianco (Albenga).

MOUNTAIN BIKING

The area around Finale Ligure is one of the most popular areas for mountain biking, with paths penetrating the Mediteranean maquis. Capo di Noli is an excellent place for exploring, for cyclists of all abilities.

HIKING

The longest signposted route in the region is the Alta Via dei Monti Liguri, which travels the full length of the Ligurian hinterland, from outside Ventimiglia to north of La Spezia. At 440 km (275 miles), it is Italy's longest continuous walk. The terrain is not difficult and the route never isolated, passing through many villages.

The Cinque Terre is another walker's paradise and has several trails. Most famous of these is the Sentiero Azzurro (Blue Path), a relatively easy route which gets very busy in summer, when it can be hard to find a room for the night without booking ahead. A quieter option is the Sentiero Crinale, which runs along the clifftop. There are also spectacular but steep trails leading to the sanctuaries scattered around this area.

Another good area to walk in is in the French part of the Val Roja, north of Ventimiglia: particularly in the Vallée des Merveilles and on the slopes of Monte Bego.

HORSE RIDING

Horse riding is popular in Liguria, and there are plenty of stables offering treks lasting a day or more. You can do some great day treks in the Cinque Terre. *Agriturismo* farms may also offer trekking opportunities.

SKIING

The Alps and the Apennines provide some opportunities for skiing, though most resorts are small. Monte Saccarello (near Móneri di Triora) and Colizzano (north of Toirano) are both good for downhill skiing. Cross-country skiing is possible from Santo Stefano Aveto, in the Apennines.

A varied and challenging landscape for mountain bikers

DIRECTORY

INFORMATION		ROCK CLIMBING	HORSE RIDING
Club Alpino Italiano (CAI) www.cai.it **CONI** www.coni.it	**Pagine Azzurre** www.pagineazzurre.com **Weather and shipping reports** www.eurometeo.com	**Information** www.thecrag.com **Rock Store** Finalborgo *Tel 019 690 208.*	**Centro Turismo Equestre 5 Terre** Campiglia *Tel 0187 758 114.* **Monte Beigua Riding** Alpicella (Varazze) *Tel 010 553 1878.*
SAILING	**DIVING**	**BIKE HIRE**	
Italian Sailing Federation (FIV) Genoa *Tel 010 513 975.* www.federvela.it **Italian Yacht Club (YCI)** www.yachtclubitalia.it	**5 Terre Diving** Riomaggiore *Tel 0187 920 011.* **Punta Mesco** Levanto www.divingcenter.net and www.puntamesco diving.com **San Fruttuoso Diving Center** Santa Margherita Ligure *Tel 0185 280 862.*	**Blu Bike** Finale Ligure *Tel 019 680 564.* **HIKING** **Information** www.parks.it **Alta Via** www.altaviadeimonti liguri.it	**SKIING** **Information** www.liguriasci.it www.fisiliguria.org **GOLF** **Information** www.federgolf.it

ENTERTAINMENT

A little bit of everything summarizes the variety of entertainment available in Liguria. There are cinemas and theatres (the Teatro Carlo Felice in Genoa is one of Italy's most famous historic theatres), casinos, discos, nightclubs, wine bars and all sorts of venues hosting live music. The vast majority of such entertainment is, inevitably, focused along the coast, and the choice is greatest during the summer. Be warned that clubs and bars in the resorts tend to be very

Night club sign in Albenga

expensive. For a cheaper night out, simply find the best bar on the seafront and watch the world go by.

Attending one of the region's numerous festivals can sometimes provide the highlight of a trip to Liguria. In addition to the many regattas and food festivals, there are various events focused around music, both modern and classical. The Festival della Canzone Italiana, held in San Remo in February *(see p31)*, is one of the most important dates in the Italian pop music calendar.

The casino in San Remo, one of Liguria's best-known nightspots

THEATRES

Every town of any size in Liguria has its own theatre, and some of the cities have several. Classical concerts, operas and ballet tend to be held in their own dedicated theatre, though San Remo's famous **Casino** hosts a whole range of entertainment, from touring ballet concerts to live music.

The main theatrical and classical music seasons tend to run in the winter, but Liguria is not a cultural desert during the summer. Outdoor performances are particularly common at this time of year. In Genoa, for example, films are shown in various parks around the city, and the ballet festival in the parks in nearby Nervi is hugely popular. The summer theatre season held in the pretty town square at Borgio Verezzi is also another permanent fixture.

DISCOS AND CLUBS

There is a trend nowadays for discos and clubs to offer far more than just a chance to dance and have a drink. Some of Liguria's major dance venues have been turned into multi-functional venues where, in addition to dance floors and bars, there are restaurants, shops, five-a-side football pitches and perhaps even a private beach. Such a description would fit **Estoril Moonlight**, one of the top clubs in Genoa.

San Remo has some of the best nightlife along the coast, and Santa Margherita is buzzing, too (it's just a short drive for revellers from Genoa): here, the **Carillon** is a gorgeous but trendy restaurant-

cum-disco, which can be very hard to get into unless you book a table.

BARS AND CAFES

Italians spend half their lives in bars and cafés, and Ligurians are no exception. The beauty of these places is that many are open in the evening, sometimes even late into the night in the resorts, and serve snacks as well as coffee and alcohol.

Typical of the riviera are the fabulous historic cafés, in business since the region's heyday in the 19th century. These usually have wonderful decor and a great atmosphere. **Caffè Klainguti** is a fine example in Genoa. Founded in 1828, it was beloved of the composer Giuseppe Verdi and serves delicious coffee and pastries. In Santa Margherita Ligure, the Art Nouveau decor is one of the big attractions of the **Caffè Colombo**. In Chiavari, **Defilla** is well worth seeking out. The latter, with mirrors, paintings and stucco galore, becomes a piano bar at night. In San Remo, try the **Bar delle Rose** at the Royal Hotel, and in Alassio the **Giacomel**, which serves fantastic ice cream.

Increasingly, Italians are in the habit of meeting up with friends at a wine bar, whether it's before

The Teatro Chiabrera at Savona

dinner or after the theatre. Wine bars offer a good choice of wines, as well light snacks. In Genoa, one name that emerges above the rest is **I Tre Merli**, attractively located in the Palazzina Millo in the Porto Antico. Also in Genoa are **Monumento**, with a bar and terrace overlooking the sea at Quarto, and **La Lepre**, a popular place in which to chill out and enjoy a drink or two; both of these open late.

Other famous names are **Winterose** in Portofino, a celebrity haunt, and **La Mandragola**, housed in an old mill in Santa Margherita.

LIVE MUSIC

There are all sorts of venues to which to go to hear live music, from the roof garden of San Remo's casino (in the summer) to the so-called disco-pubs, where you can have a drink, listen to some music, and maybe even have a dance, too.

In Genoa, **DLF**, in an old converted cinema west of

THE GENOA DERBY

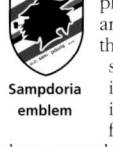

Sampdoria emblem

Local football fans love to attend matches played by the two city teams, Genova and Sampdoria, a lively meeting known as the "Derby della Lanterna". Genova, set up by a group of Englishmen in 1893, is the oldest football team in Italy, while Sampdoria was formed in 1946. The two teams share grounds at the Luigi Ferrari stadium, so on Derby Day neither team has the home turf advantage.

Genova emblem

---

the Lanterna, has live music in addition to some of the hottest international DJs. For something rather different, try the **Louisiana Jazz Club**, a relaxed venue with a bar and both local and international musicians. In summer, there is usually a programme of jazz concerts all along the coast.

Sabot in Santa Margherita Ligure stages all manner of live bands that attract a predominantly young crowd. It also holds popular live music evenings outside during the summer. In Savona, the best bands

appear at **Ju Bamboo**, a club decked out in tropical fashion, complete with palms.

WATER PARKS

Aimed of course at children, but also great fun for adults is the water park of **Le Caravelle** in Ceriale, a small resort just north of Albenga. This, the only aquapark in Liguria, has swimming pools with artificial waves, water slides, chutes, waterfalls, whirlpools and all sorts of seriously wet entertainment, as well as animated figures and shows.

DIRECTORY

SURVIVAL GUIDE

PRACTICAL INFORMATION

On the whole, you will find that Liguria has a good standard of services and infrastructure. It is easy to travel around, particularly along the coast; the people are friendly; and, in a region that has such a long and well-established tourist season, there are good sources of information, whether you go to a local tourist office or surf the Internet – many of the tourist-oriented websites have text in English as well as Italian.

Liguria regional logo

Healthcare in its all its usual forms is available throughout the region, though the best facilities are inevitably found along the coast, where you are also much more likely to find English-speaking medical staff.

In general, Ligurian museums are modern and well laid-out. Many are also accessible to people with disabilities, who are well catered for in Liguria, with good sources of information as well as other services.

The crowded beach at Camogli in the summer

WHEN TO VISIT

Of all the Italian regions, Liguria is the one with the most temperate climate. Even in winter, its climate is generally warmer than in much of Italy, with the exception of Sicily. As a result, there is only a relatively short period when tourists don't visit. Furthermore, such are the cultural attractions of the region, that there is plenty to do even when the climate isn't hot enough for long stints by the seaside.

But while Liguria is virtually a year-round attraction, there is still an identifiable high season, which extends from May to the end of September. Tourists from Britain, France, Germany and Holland, as well as Italy, pour into the region during this period,

Sign for a local tourist office

when the entire coast can become extremely crowded.

Visitors more interested in cultural pursuits should consider visiting in March and April or September and October, when the weather is cooler and the hotels quieter.

TOURIST INFORMATION

There are four Ligurian provinces – Genoa, Imperia, La Spezia and Savona – but five tourist boards or Informazione e Accoglienza Turistica (IAT): Riviera dei Fiori for Imperia; Riviera delle Palme for Savona; Genoa for the city and its environs; Tigullio, with responsibility for the rest of the province of Genoa; and lastly Cinque Terre e Golfo dei Poeti, which covers the La Spezia area. In every good-

sized town you will find a tourist office (or, in the smaller towns, a "Pro loco" office), which will have information about the local sights as well as the hotels and restaurants. Local tourist offices usually open from 8am–12:30pm and 3–7pm Monday to Friday, with some larger offices opening for longer during the summer. Some offices open on Saturday mornings.

The tourist information kiosks found at major transport terminals are generally fairly basic.

COMMUNICATIONS

Post offices are found in all Ligurian towns and there is often more than one branch. They are usually open in the morning only, from 8:30am to

Sailing along the coast, a very popular sport in Liguria

◁ **The unmistakably picturesque seafront of Portofino**

1:30pm (noon on Saturdays and the last day of the month), although in the large towns there are usually post offices that stay open until 5pm. You can also buy stamps (for postcards and normal letters) from any tobacconist shop, called a *tabaccaio*. Public telephones are not as common as they once were, owing to the growth in use of mobile phones. Those that remain are almost all operated by phone card, which you can buy from tobacconists, certain kiosks and in post offices.

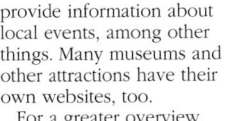

**Sign for an
Internet café**

There are plenty of Internet cafés along the coast for surfing the Internet or sending e-mails, and more are opening up all the time.

HOSPITALS AND PHARMACIES

Pharmacies observe the hours of 9am–1pm and 4–8pm, closing on Saturday afternoons and all day Sunday. These hours may be extended in the larger tourist resorts on the coast, where some pharmacies stay open continuously until 8pm and sometimes later. Every city in Liguria has a hospital. EU citizens with form EIII are entitled to emergency medical assistance free of charge, but you may have to pay for other treatments. It is therefore vital that you take out proper travel insurance.

LIGURIA ON THE INTERNET

Although websites can vary considerably in terms of the information provided – in particular whether this is precise and up-to-date – the range of information available on the Internet about Liguria is of a much better standard than that provided in most other Italian regions.

All the five regional tourist offices, as well as each local tourist office, have their own specific website, which can provide information about local events, among other things. Many museums and other attractions have their own websites, too.

For a greater overview, particularly if you haven't decided where in Liguria you wish to go, you should visit the Ligurian regional website *(see Directory)*, which is a hugely useful resource and includes links to many other local websites.

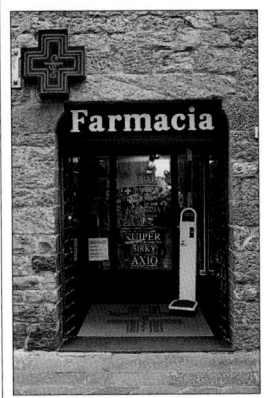

Entrance to a pharmacy in the old centre of Albenga

DIRECTORY

Other Useful Information

In common with the other regions of Italy, Liguria does not present any particular problems as far as crime is concerned, even in the most popular tourist resorts. You should, however, always observe the usual rules of common sense when travelling around. Every town possesses, besides a traffic police station, a police (*carabinieri*) station, which is open 24 hours a day and to which visitors should turn in an emergency. All towns have banks with cash machines where visitors can withdraw euros.

A team of *carabinieri* in their distinctive uniform

LAW AND ORDER

In Italy the forces of law and order are organized into two divisions: the *carabinieri* and the *polizia*. The former are responsible for public order, with communal, provincial or regional jurisdiction, and are commonly seen on patrol in the streets. The duties of the *polizia* are more wide-ranging, being generally more concerned with criminal investigations. At local level, you also find the municipal police, including the traffic police (*vigili urbani*), who can deal with minor or emergency situations that do not involve traffic.

In the event of a theft, you should report the crime at the nearest police station in order to validate any insurance claim.

Municipal Policeman

FIREFIGHTERS

In Liguria, forest fires, often encouraged by the constant wind that blows throughout the year, are suprisingly frequent. Therefore, if you are exploring the countryside it is essential to observe all the standard countryside code practices, especially with regard to not lighting a fire outside designated areas and making sure that cigarettes are completely extinguished.

The region is well equipped with fire stations, even in rural areas, and fire engines respond rapidly to alarm calls. Firefighters also attend other kinds of emergency.

PERSONAL SAFETY

Use common sense when it comes to personal safety. Do not carry large sums of cash with you when you are out, and leave any valuables, at your hotel, in a safe if possible. You may wish to keep a separate photocopy of personal documents, so that you can request duplicates in the event of theft. Of course, you should never leave home without taking out full insurance cover.

Places where you are most likely to encounter pickpockets include railway stations and ferry terminals, or any crowded place, such as a bus, market or a street festival. If you are travelling by car, make sure that you always leave the vehicle locked, and don't leave any items in full view.

Genoa is a large bustling port city with, inevitably, some districts that it is best to steer clear of. (On arrival at your hotel, it is a good idea to ask the reception staff about areas that are best avoided.) In the countryside, however, and in the resorts, you need have few concerns about your personal safety, though it pays to be alert if you are out late at night.

If you wish to hire a taxi, make sure that you choose an official one. Your hotel should be able to recommend a reputable taxi firm. Make sure that the meter is switched on or that the fee is agreed in advance.

DISABLED VISITORS

Liguria provides relatively good information for people with disabilities. Genoa has a helpful service called Terre di Mare (www.terredimare), which is designed specifically for tourists. The national hotel site (www.italiapertutti) is also a useful resource.

It is always wise to phone a hotel or attraction in advance to check their facilities.

A firefighting plane in action during a summer fire in the hinterland

Entrance to one of the larger banks in Liguria

BANKS AND EXCHANGE

Currency can be changed in various ways. You will find bureaux de change in the larger airports and towns, and it is also possible to change money in hotels and travel agencies. As a general rule, however, the banks offer the best exchange rates. Banks in Italy normally open from 8:30am to 1:30pm, and from 3pm to 4pm, Monday to Friday; note that the banks often close early the day before a public holiday. Opening hours of bureaux de change are more variable.

Every town in Liguria has cashpoint/ATM machines (known as bancomat), where it is possible to withdraw money using a debit or credit card. These can normally be used 24 hours a day.

Despite these options, you are still advised to arrive in Liguria with at least a few euros for immediate use, particularly if you are due to arrive late in the day or at a weekend. Remember that for all kinds of transaction you will need to show some form of identification.

Credit cards are widely accepted for purchases and can also be used to withdraw cash (though the latter transaction is not normally good value for money). VISA, American Express, MasterCard and Diners Club are the most commonly used cards.

THE EURO

Since January 2002 the euro has been the sole official currency in all participating states of the European Union. This means that euro notes and coins are valid throughout the so-called "eurozone", including Italy.

DIRECTORY

General emergencies
Tel 113
Carabinieri (police)
Tel 112
Fire Service
Tel 115
Breakdown service
Tel 116
Ambulance
Tel 118
Coastguard
Tel 15 30

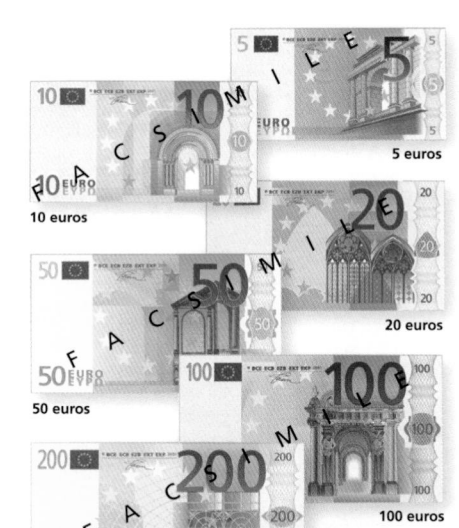

Banknotes and Coins

Banknotes come in seven denominations. The 5-euro note is grey, the 10-euro is pink, the 20 is blue, the 50 orange, the 100 green, the 200 yellow and the 500 purple. There are eight different coins. The 1- and 2-euro coins are silver and gold; those worth 50, 20 and 10 cents are gold, while those worth 5, 2 and 1 cent are bronze.

TRAVEL INFORMATION

Liguria is a narrow and relatively small region, so moving from place to place is usually easy. This is particularly true of the coast, which has good train and bus services as well as a decent road network (though traffic can be a problem in high season). While there are buses to the main inland towns, you need a car to explore inland areas properly. A car can be a hindrance on the coast in summer, however, when parking is virtually impossible in some places, including the Cinque Terre, to which you are advised to travel by foot, train or boat. In terms of reaching Liguria, Genoa has one of Italy's major airports. There are also long-distance train and coach services, with good links from France and from other parts of Italy. There are various ferry services, too, though most of these operate from within Italy. Of more use to visitors are the ferries which ply between the main Ligurian resorts in summer. For those with a private yacht, there are plenty of marinas; most of these can offer good facilities and moorings for all sizes of craft.

Typical coach, used by tourists to reach the coastal resorts of Liguria

ARRIVING BY AIR

The main airport in Liguria is the Cristoforo Colombo at Genova-Sestri, west of the city. Ryanair and BA flights arrive here direct from the United Kingdom. Alternative entry points are Nice (with easyJet, British Midland and BA), an easy train ride from the Riviera di Ponente, and Pisa (with Ryanair and BA), just 85 km (53 miles) from La Spezia. The closest airports receiving flights from North America are Milan and Rome. Regular buses link Cristoforo Colombo airport with the ferry terminal and Principe and Brignole train stations in Genoa, running from 5:30am to 11:45pm. There is also a small airport at Villanova d'Albenga, on the Riviera di Ponente, but at present this receives only domestic flights.

TRAVELLING BY CAR

Since driving to Liguria from the UK (either via the Swiss Alps or the French riviera) takes the best part of 24 hours, you would do better to fly and hire a car on arrival. The main rental companies have desks in the airport, but car hire in Italy often can be expensive; you'll often get a better rate if you arrange the car before leaving home. A motorway (autostrada) – the A10 and its continuation the A12 – provides fast access along the Ligurian coast, though this route can get busy in holiday season and at weekends. Heading inland, motorways link the coast with Parma, Milan and Turin. The other principal route is state road no. 1 (SS1), the so-called Via Aurelia, first laid by the Romans. It runs the length of the coast, sometimes offering glimpses of the sea. Inland roads tend to be narrow and winding but are in good condition and pass through often stunning scenery. If you plan to drive, note that parking in the resorts can be difficult (and stressful) in high season, and also that petrol stations are scarce in the hinterland once you head

Genoa's port and airport, both busy traffic hubs

A stretch of the motorway linking Liguria's main towns

San Remo Train Station

away from the main towns, with few opening on Sundays or in the evening.

TRAVELLING BY TRAIN

It is much simpler to reach Liguria by train than if used to be, though it is a more expensive option than flying. From the UK, you can take the Eurostar to Paris, and then the TGV right down to Nice (a journey of around 12 hours), from where the coastal line runs east into Liguria. Both fast and slow trains serve the towns along the Ligurian coast. In general, trains from the north or west arrive at Genoa's Stazione Principe, while those from the south and east arrive at Stazione Brignole. Both stations have good bus connections. The historic Genoa–Casella line, which runs inland to the Apennines, is a rare example of a narrow-gauge railway (see p88).

TRAVELLING BY COACH

Eurolines runs coaches to Liguria from elsewhere in Europe, but travelling by train or air doesn't cost much more. Within Liguria, coach travel (often more expensive than train travel) is most useful for journeys into the mountains: in many inland areas coaches are the only sole of transport. Coach services from Genoa (run by different companies) leave from Piazza Acquaverde and Piazza della Vittoria, close to Stazione Principe and Stazione Brignole respectively.

FERRIES AND MARINAS

It is possible to travel to Liguria by sea, though most services are from within Italy. Genoa's splendid Stazione Marittima is the main hub for ferries, with connections to Cagliari and other ports in Sardinia, and Palermo in Sicily. Overseas links are with Corsica, Tunis and Barcelona. Ferries from Corsica also arrive at Vado, near Savona. Several companies operate these services, including Tirrenia and Grimaldi. In summer, local ferry services run along the Ligurian coast, primarily in the Golfo del Tigullio, the Golfo dei Poeti and along the coast of the Cinque Terre. For those with their own boat, there are more than 60 landing points and marinas along the coast, including the famous tiny harbour at Portofino. The marinas are generally well equipped and can accommodate a total of around 16,000 boats.

CITY TRANSPORT

Buses in Genoa, run by the Azienda Mobilità e Trasporti (AMT), are easy to use since they charge a flat rate for trips within the city limits and nearby suburbs. Tourist tickets valid for 24 or 48 hours are also available. Tickets, sold by newspaper kiosks and tobacconists, must be bought in advance and be validated in the machine once on board. Genoa also has a nascent metro, and two funiculars, which link Piazza del Portello and Largo della Zecca with Genoa's upper districts. From Piazza del Portello you can also take the lift up to the belvedere at Castelletto.

Logo of Riviera Trasporti

DIRECTORY

AIRPORTS

Genoa
Tel 010 601 54 10.
www.airport.genova.it

Nice
Tel 00 33 17 2000.
www.nice.aeroport.fr

Pisa
Tel 050 500 707.
www.pisa-airport.com

CAR HIRE

Avis
Tel 010 650 72 80.
www.avisautonoleggio.it

Hertz
Tel 010 651 24 22.
www.hertz.com

STATE RAILWAYS

Information
Tel 199 166 177.
www.trenitalia.it

COACHES

Regional companies
La Spezia *Tel* 0187 522 511.
www.atclaspezia.it
Rapallo (Tigullio)
www.tigulliotrasporti.it
San Remo *Tel* 0189 592 706.
www.rivieratrasporti.it
Savona *Tel* 019 220 12 31.
www.acts.it

CITY TRANSPORT

Genoa (AMT)
Tel 800 085 311.
www.amt.genova.it

FERRIES

Stazione Marittima
www.stazionimarittimegenova.it

Tirrenia *Tel* 899 929 206.
www.tirrenia.it

Grimaldi *Tel* 899 199 069.
www.gnv.it

Information
www.ferriesonline.com

Acknowledgments

Dorling Kindersley would like to thank the following people and institutions whose contributions and assistance have made the preparation of this book possible.

Special Thanks

Agenzia Regionale per la Promozione Turistica "In Liguria"; APT Cinque Terre e Golfo dei Poeti; APT di Genova; APT Riviera Ligure delle Palme; APT Riviera dei Fiori; APT Tigullio; Banca Carige, Genoa; Emma Brown; Giardini Botanici Hanbury, Ventimiglia; Grotte di Toirano, Toirano; Soprintendenza per i Beni Archeologici della Liguria, Genoa; the restaurant *Il Sommergibile* in San Remo.

Design and Editorial

Publishing Managers Fay Franklin, Kate Poole
Senior Art Editor Marisa Renzullo
Revisions Designer Collette Sadler
Revisions Editor Anna Freiberger
Beverley Ager, Claire Baranowski, Uma Bhattacharya, Sally Ann Bloomfield, Susi Cheshire, Rebecca Ford, Vinod Harish, Amy Harrison, Mohammad Hassan, Jasneet Kaur, Vincent Kurien, Megan McCaffrey, Sonal Modha, Rada Radojicic, Ellen Root, Sands Publishing Solutions, Azeem Siddiqui, Conrad Van Dyk.

Photography Permissions

Thanks are due to those bodies and societies who authorized the reproduction of images, in particular: Accademia Ligustica di Belle Arti, Genoa; Acquario di Genova; Banca Carige (coin collection and photographic archive, Genoa); Galleria di Palazzo Rosso (photographic archive of Genoa town council); Genoa Cricket and Football Club, Genoa; Museo Amedeo Lia, La Spezia; Museo Archeologico dei Balzi Rossi, Ventimiglia; Regione Liguria; Palazzo Ducale, Genoa; Società Editrice Buonaparte, Sarzana; UC Sampdoria, Genoa.

While every effort has been made to contact the copyright holders, we apologize for any omissions and will be happy to include them in future editions of the guide.

Picture Credits

Top part: t = top; tl = top left; tcl = top centre left; tc = top centre; tcr = top centre right; tr = top right. Centre part: ctl = centre top left; ct = centre top; ctr = centre top right; cl = centre left; c = centre; cr = centre right; cbl = centre bottom left; cb = centre below; cbr = centre bottom right. Lower part: b = bottom; bl = bottom left; bcl = bottom centre left; bc = bottom centre; bcr = bottom centre right; br = bottom right.

Commissioned Photographs

Lucio Rossi, Polis, Milan: 1, 2–3, 8–9, 16bc, 17bl, 18tr, 18ctl, 18ctr, 18cbr, 18br, 19ctl, 19cbl, 20tr, 20br, 21tl, 22, 23bl, 23br, 24ctr, 25tl, 25bl, 26, 29ctr, 30bl, 31br, 32, 33c, 35cl, 36tl, 43cr, 46cl, 46bl, 47, 48, 49, 50tr, 50ctl, 50cbr, 51, 52–3, 54, 55tr, 55br, 56, 57tr, 58tr, 58c, 59, 60, 61tr, 64, 66, 67, 68tr, 69, 70cr, 71c, 71bl, 76, 78tl, 78cr, 79c, 79b, 80, 82, 83t, 84–5, 86, 87tr, 88t, 88cl, 89b, 102–3, 104, 106cl, 107, 108tl, 109, 111t, 112–3, 114, 115t, 115bl, 116, 117br, 120, 121t, 121c, 122–3, 124tl, 124ctl, 125, 126tl, 126br, 127br, 128–9 (except 128bl), 130–31, 132–3, 134tr, 134bl, 135tr, 135bl, 136cl, 136br, 137c, 138, 139t, 140–41, 144–5, 146–7, 148–9 (except 149br), 150–51, 152–3, 154–5, 156–7, 158, 159tc, 159bl, 159bc, 159br, 160–61, 162–3, 164–5, 166–7 (except 167br), 168, 169tl, 170tl, 170tr, 170cl, 171, 173 (section), 174bl, 175, 184bl, 185tr, 186tl, 186tr, 186ctr, 186cbr, 187tl, 187ct, 187ctr, 187cbc, 187cbr, 187cbl, 187bc, 187br, 198, 199tl, 202tr, 202bc, 206cb, 207, 209tl, 210, 211b.

Photo Credits

Acquario di Genova Photo Archive: 62c, 63bc. akg-images: *The Annunciation to Mary* (1603) Lodovico Carracci 75cl. Alamy Images: Gary Cook 11cl; CuboImages srl/Adriano Bacchella 187tl; CuboImages srl/Claudio Beduschi 10cl; Michael Diggin 10tc; Adam Eastland 187c; FAN travelstock/Timm Folkmann 11br; Rupert Hansen 166cla; Robert Harding World Imagery 172–3; Peter Horree 10br; Natalie Tepper 61c. Fabrizio Ardito, Rome: 16tl, 17t, 100–1, 105, 108br, 142–3, 169c, 208br. Archivio Electa, Milan: 37cr, 38cr, 42tl.

Eugenio Bersani, Polis, Milan: 15, 21bl, 117t, 118, 119t.

Corbis: Archivo Iconografico 39cr; Owen Franken 35br; John Heseltine 167br; Gianni Dagli Orti 34bl; Royalty-free 204–5; Gustavo Tomisch 35tr.

IL DAGHERROTIPO: Giorgio Oddi 149bl; Marcio Melodia 200t; Salvatore Barba 44–5. DK IMAGES: 186cr; John Heseltine 208c; Clive Streeter 186bca, 186bra, 187tr.DK IMAGES: Ian O'Leary all 186-187 except 187tl, 187c.

MARY EVANS PICTURE LIBRARY: 41t.

FARABOLAFOTO, Milan: 9 (section), 14, 16cr, 17cr, 19tl, 19tr, 19bl, 19br, 23tr, 28ctl, 34tr, 42c, 43t, 43bc, 43br, 45 (section), 61bc, 65tr, 65cl, 101 (section), 106br, 110cl, 111cbr, 127tl, 174cr, 184t, 184cr, 185c, 200cl, 205, 206ctl.

GETTY IMAGES: AFP/Filippo Monteforte 28bc; Taxi/Maremagnum 11tr.

MARKA, Milan: Danilo Donadoni 128bl.

PETER NOBLE: 208tr.

LINO PASTORELLI, Sanremo: 30ctl. PHOTO

SCALA, Florence: Musei di Strada Nuova - Sant' Agostino, Genoa 50bl. ANDREA PISTOLESI: 68cl.

FRANCINE RECULEZ: 168cla. DANIELE ROBOTTI, Alessandria: 77tl, 88bl, 119cr, 119br. ROGER-VIOLLET, ARCHIVI ALINARI, Firenze: 37tc. GHIGO ROLI, Modena: 19ctr, 19cbr, 20ctl, 21ctr, 170bl. PHOTO SCALA, Florence: Museo Navale di Pegli 38bl.

MARCO STOPPATO, Milan: 81.

Jacket: Front – PHOTOLIBRARY: Mauritius/Frank Lukassek. Back - AWL IMAGES: Walter Bibikow tl; DORLING KINDERSLEY: John Heseltine bl, cla, clb. Spine - PHOTOLIBRARY: Mauritius/Frank Lukassek t.

All the other photos are from ARCHIVIO FABIO RATTI, ARCHIVIO MONDADORI, ARCHIVIO ARNOLDO MONDADORI EDITORE, Milan.